JOURNALS
1987–1989
Anthony Powell

JOURNALS
1987–1989

Anthony Powell

With an introduction by
VIOLET POWELL

Heinemann : London

First published in Great Britain 1996
by William Heinemann Ltd
an imprint of Reed Consumer Books Ltd
Michelin House, 81 Fulham Road, London SW3 6RB
and Auckland, Melbourne, Singapore and Toronto

The author is grateful to
John Murray (Publishers) Ltd
for permission to quote from
Summoned by Bells by John Betjeman.

The author is grateful to
Roy Fuller and HarperCollins
Publishers Limited for
permission to quote from Roy Fuller's
'Available for Dreams' from *Kitchen Sonnets*.

The photographs are all from
the Powell family albums, with the
exception of the extract from *The Times*,
© Times Newspapers Limited, 1987

A CIP catalogue record for this title
is available from the British Library

ISBN 0 434 00378 6

Typeset by Deltatype Ltd, Ellesmere Port, Cheshire
Printed and bound in Great Britain by Clays Ltd, St. Ives plc

For my niece Antonia

I wish, as before, to thank Tessa Davies
for transcribing these *Journals*,
and my wife, Violet Powell,
for her assistance.

Contents

Introduction

The scene that was set in Volume I of Anthony Powell's Journals has remained the same for the years 1987–1989, The Chantry with its lake and grottoes being the background. A flock of sheep in the fields between the house and the lake provides entertainment by its antics. Straying lambs have to be caught, and posted back through gaps in the fencing, like parcels too large for a letter-box.

As visits away from home become rarer, more friends are welcomed for meals. An annual picnic is instituted, for which Marcelle and Anthony Quinton bring a Fortnum & Mason hamper containing a pie and soufflés, while Evangeline Bruce* brings smoked salmon sandwiches and a chocolate gâteau. There is some confusion as to whether this party resembles the arrival of Scrooge at the Cratchits on Christmas Day, a feast dominated by Tiny Tim, or the dormitory meal organized by Tiger Tim at Mrs Hippo's school. On other occasions Powell himself cooks curry which guests specially request and which is composed of vegetables when Pat and Vidia Naipaul come to luncheon.

In the run of domestic life, there is a pattern of tree surgery in juxtaposition to visits to the local dental surgery. These last have replaced visits to the late and much lamented Howard Sussman. The surgery itself has a notice begging patients not to let 'Boots' into the house, a black white-footed cat who is keen to join in professionally. On the other hand, an enormous cock called Henry lives in a hutch at the back of the building, and is incensed if his meals are late.

Throughout this volume the author keeps a Shakespeare play to be read in bed every night. He naturally develops favourite plays and favourite characters, love of Falstaff, dislike of Prince Hal (*Henry IV*), threat of Prospero as a super-bore (*The Tempest*), the attractiveness of Jessica as a girl (*Merchant of Venice*). Shakespeare and Kipling remain, as it were, out in front as admired giants of literature, though there is respect and enjoyment of, among others, Robert Musil and Joseph Conrad.

* Evangeline Bruce (1914–1995)

This volume marks the first appearance of the young painter Henry Mee, who becomes a frequent visitor as a friend, as well as professionally at work on a number of portraits of the diarist.

Towards the end of 1987 a letter arrives from the Prime Minister, Margaret Thatcher, suggesting that she should propose Anthony Powell to the Queen as a Companion of Honour so the acceptance and public announcement come at the New Year.

The Chantry, over five hundred feet up on the Mendip Hills, has a bad record for isolation by snow and ice, particularly in January and February, so it is a great relief when the day for investiture with the badge of a Companion of Honour turns out to be a February day of brilliant sunshine and mild airs.

It happens that the audience might have been designed as a Powellian set piece, as it followed on that of the Ambassador of Zaire, who had arrived with his suite to present his Letters of Credence to Her Majesty. Consequently, the courtyard of Buckingham Palace is crowded with the ceremonial carriages. Zaire, formerly the Belgian Congo, has retained French phraseology, diplomatic officials being described as *Citoyen* or *Citoyenne*, which adds an exotic touch to next day's Court Circular. The audience and the whole expedition are thoroughly enjoyable.

There has, of course, been a stack of congratulations, for which the diarist selects postcards, some military, some civil, despatched in envelopes and carefully chosen to appeal to the recipients. In the meantime, Henry Mee has proceeded with his project of a collection of distinguished characters to be gathered in a book, for which the diarist eventually writes short citations.

Although the diarist keeps up, as it were, a running commentary on the books he reviews and the books he reads for pleasure or enlightenment, perhaps the most striking passage in the Journals occurs at the beginning of 1989. It is then that he rereads the whole of *A Dance to the Music of Time*, nearly fourteen years after its publication. This analysis is approached with the same critical detachment that is a characteristic of the diarist's reviews of books on whatever subject and of whatever century. The rhythm of the sequence is considered in conjunction with the events in the world at large which inevitably influence the lives of the characters as they advance in age and meet the splendours and miseries of love and war. A discussion of the technique of writing a novel concludes that, though some redrafting may be necessary, Pilate's principle (that what he had written he had written) is probably right.

Violet Powell
Chantry
1995

JOURNALS
1987–1989

1987

Friday, 2 January

I reread *Bleak House* with ruthless skipping. The title, when first decided on by Dickens, was surely intended to apply to the Dedlocks' mansion in Lincolnshire, Chesney Wold. Bleakness is the last thing associated with Mr Jarndyce's house so far as Esther Summerson, and all the rest who go there, are concerned. This was borne out by Phiz's frontispiece to the book captioned 'Bleak House', which clearly represents Chesney Wold. Dickens was fussy about illustrations to his works, so one wonders what happened in this case.

Tuesday, 6 January

Before Christmas I received a letter from George Sassoon (son of Siegfried Sassoon) saying he had read my Memoirs, with an account of visiting his father at Heytesbury House, near Warminster, and suggesting we should come over there some time. He had clearly forgotten that some years ago I brought Paul Fussell and Kingsley Amis to see him at Heytesbury on their way to lunch with us. Paul Fussell, as part of his specialized interest in the first war, was then producing an illustrated book about Siegfried Sassoon. He had previously arranged to meet George Sassoon to talk over various things briefly. When George Sassoon rang last week he sounded rather jumpy, uncertain what he wanted, so in the end I asked him and his girlfriend to lunch here. He is fifty, married twice (children by both unions), his second wife (Mrs Messer) by curious chance living with her new husband in Chantry. George Sassoon's girlfriend (also formerly married with offspring) is named Alison Pulvertaft. Some of the time they live in Scotland, a house on Mull inherited from his mother, née Hester Gatty. Hester Gatty was a contemporary deb with Dig and Mary Biddulph, who used to laugh about her saying things like 'I can't live without colour round about me', etc. The marriage eventually broke down.

George Sassoon comes down to Heytesbury from time to time, but would like to sell the big house if that could be arranged. The interior is immensely run down. He bought two bottles of wine in Warminster as a present when they arrived for luncheon. He looks slightly like his father with addition of specs, and an eager, restless manner. By profession he is an electrical engineer, computers, etc. He said he was not at all literary, tho' turned out to have produced two or three books. The girlfriend was a plump blonde, very much a painter's type.

George Sassoon's scientific connexions do not prevent interests of a fairly exotic sort, for instance in a book called *The Sacred Blood*, which, among other things, adumbrated the theory that Jesus was direct ancestor of the Merovingian kings of France, the heir to whom is said to exist at this moment. As it happened I reviewed *The Sacred Blood* (which George Sassoon may have known). In any case the moment we sat down to lunch, he launched into a discussion about all that sort of thing. He spoke of computerizing *Dance*, so I gave him a copy of Hilary Spurling's *Handbook*. He and Alison Pulvertaft visited the village in South-West France where the Sacred Blood story, so to speak, begins.

It must be agreed that some very odd things did take place there in the nineteenth century. One objection to the decidedly tall Merovingian story is that so good a genealogist as Anthony Wagner considers the Merovingian kings to have left no descendants, tho' these things are hard to verify at that date, which Wagner would be the first to agree. At luncheon George Sassoon knocked back the best part of a bottle of claret without visible effort. An unexpectedly amusing encounter.

I decided to reread *The Golden Bowl*, but broke down, tho' a novel I once liked, which I still see has good points, but gets one nowhere in long stretches of waffle. Proust's most repetitive ramblings in some sense do, even if merely rubbing in again what he has often said before. Phrases, thoughts, attributed to the Roman Prince, however anglicized, often seem hopelessly inappropriate to an Italian of any kind, owing to James's chronically inadequate understanding of sexual passion as an element in human motive. He knows it happens, he watches it from outside, is not incapable of making it dramatic, but he cannot really grasp the way it works.

My Public Lending Right statement arrived yesterday; first year £1200+; second year £1300; this year £1800+; modest (maximum £5000) but satisfactory, as everyone was warned that this year they would get less, as there were more writers to distribute the statutory amount among.

Friday, 9 January

I am rereading, fitfully, Johnson's *Lives of the Poets*. Under Cowley there seemed a foreshadowing of Auden (spelling naturally a matter of indifference at that date), written by Richard Bentley, a friend of Horace Walpole, Gray, etc., described as 'indolent and improvident':

> Who travels in religious jars,
> Truth mixed with error, clouds with rays,
> With Whiston wanting pyx and stars
> In the wide ocean sinks and strays.

Saturday, 10 January

Anthony Thwaite is requesting Philip Larkin letters, which he is editing. I sent such as I have, which go back thirty years or more, rather to my surprise. I also sent a photograph or two by Larkin, master of the interval lens, preferring to step back into the group to photograph himself. This is perhaps yet another expression of Larkin's intense egotism. I pondered some of the writers recently dcd*, their idiosyncrasies. I never knew John Braine at all well. He said some funny things occasionally. Recently back from the US, Braine encountered Lord Soper (formerly the Revd Donald Soper) in Braine's words 'Methodist divine, humanitarian, Life Peer'. Soper asked how Braine had liked America. 'Very much,' said Braine. 'All right if you're white,' commented Soper. 'But I *am* white,' replied Braine.

Sunday, 11 January

John's forty-first birthday. Pheasant for luncheon and excellent apple pudding. V† and I drank his health (John doesn't drink) in Château Rahoul '82 which Tristram gave me for Christmas. It was good. In the course of the day George Sassoon drove up to leave his book *The Manna Machine*. There appeared to be two children, a boy and a girl, in the car, whom he presumably takes out on Sundays, so he would have been coming to Chantry anyway, as his ex-wife lives here. *The Manna Machine* turned out a decidedly strange work. Briefly, the Sassoon theory is that, when the Israelites lived on manna in the Wilderness after leaving Egypt, this nourishment was manufactured from *algae*-seaweed, processed in a nuclear machine. Sassoon says that Ancient of Days is a mistranslation, and really means the Moveable Tank. His belief is that every few thousand years extraterrestrial beings visit Earth in a spaceship.

* AP's personal abbreviation for 'deceased'.
† V is the author's wife, (Lady) Violet, whom he married in 1934. Their younger son John is frequently at his parents' house during the years covered by this volume.

On one of these expeditions these endowed the Israelites with this machine. That is why the Jews consider themselves The Chosen. Nuclear rays account for individuals being killed (including one or more specifically 'just men'), who did not know how to handle the machine, by then called the Ark of the Covenant. That is why the Philistines, having captured the Ark, sent this dangerous object back to the Israelites, yoked to oxen, without human escort. Most of Sassoon's quoted material comes from the *Torah* (Hebrew chronicle), rather than the Bible. I am a pushover for this sort of fantasy, which seemed to make an excellent case for the Ancient of Days being a mechanism of some kind. When I wrote back thanking George Sassoon I suggested Prometheus might represent earlier space visitation.

Saturday, 17 January

The cold weather, up to now extremely trying, is beginning to abate a little, which is a relief. For review, I have John Malcolm Brinnin's *Memoir of Truman Capote*. Brinnin came here twenty-five years ago, I can't remember why, possibly to talk about Dylan Thomas. This book is reasonably amusing. Capote's first novel, *Other Voices, Other Rooms*, was an able novel of its kind. It was recommended to Heinemann, oddly enough, by Malcolm Muggeridge, then their literary adviser. Malcolm is a sworn enemy of queers, indeed has an almost pathological horror of homosexuality which gives this a decidedly comic side, combined with Capote's subsequent sordid career. I attended a large luncheon party of Pam Berry's at Cowley Street, probably in the 1960s, where Capote was present, all the other guests now forgotten. They were no doubt mostly political, certainly no one else from the London literary world except me. Capote was briefly introduced, then totally ignored by everyone present. He was at far end of the table, but by chance he and I left the house together. In light of the fuss Americans make of British writers being entertained in the US, I felt a little embarrassed by the way in which he had been treated, and tried to be agreeable (probably on subject of *Other Voices*), while we walked up the street together. He seemed a not very exciting little man, two foot high, with dark specs. Brinnin's *Memoir* makes plain I really needn't have bothered to be polite. There must be few persons on earth better able to look after themselves than Capote in a social way. All the same I should be interested to know what he thought of Pam's luncheon.

Pat Herdman's death in the paper, a school contemporary not seen or heard of for years. He had an Ulster linen-manufacturing background, a completely philistine personality of the coarsest possible texture, interested only in business, fox-hunting, but could be funny. In some manner we remained friends. In early 1930s I stayed one Christmas with him and his newly married wife Mary (neé Cooper, family something to do with Tilling's company which at one moment owned Heinemann) at Strabane, Co Tyrone. I went out with the local pack on Boxing Day, falling off repeatedly, to which *From a View to a Death* owes something. Heard later my somewhat Surtees-like episode had become legendary in the neighbourhood.

Pat Herdman's grandfather had been a connoisseur of claret, his father for medical reasons forbidden to touch it. We used to descend to the cellar, bottles dating back to 1890s, perhaps earlier, open them at random, some tasting like raspberry vinegar, pressing on until some superb vintage turned up, as it always did sooner or later.

Mary Herdman was a sweet girl, her younger sister Pam, speechless, also rather sweet. They had given up whatever money they had to enable their brother, Derek Cooper, to enter the Guards; a Balzacian gesture, as so far as I can remember Rastignac's sisters also sacrificed their dowries to enable him to study Law in Paris.

I was scarcely at all in touch with the Herdmans again until my battalion was sent to Northern Ireland in 1939, when I stayed in their house for one or two weekends, while on course at the Royal Irish Fusiliers' Infantry Training Centre at Ballykinler. By that time the Herdman marriage was breaking up, Pat having extracted himself from North Irish Horse (being like most of the Irish, North or South, partly anti-British), then away on business in Southern Ireland. Pat Herdman was good example of complexity of the Irish: on the one hand a fanatical Ulsterman, on the other, much closer to the South than to Great Britain; I think politically full of duplicity. I had imagined the Cooper sisters setting up their brother in the Foot Guards, but Derek Cooper (at least latterly) was in the Life Guards (Major, OBE, MC), a regiment he had to leave after marrying Grey Gowrie's mother Mrs Hore-Ruthven, as second husband after divorce; a final Balzacian, not to say Proustian, touch.

Wednesday, 21 January

Gerald Brenan, Bloomsbury figure, writer on Spain, dcd in that country age ninety-one. V and I met him several times when we were staying with Bill and Annie Davis at La Consula, near Malaga. Contrary to the received opinion, I always found Brenan a corking bore, indeed a bore in that high-class category best suggested by the regular army officer who has read *English Literature in One Volume*, subscribes to the *New Statesman*, on strength of which thinks himself qualified to pronounce on all intellectual, political, social matters. Brenan, in fact, was not a regular officer, but served honourably in First War (MC), clearly ought to have been. He was repository of every known Bloomsbury cliché, being, I'm afraid, undeniably attractive to women, immensely conceited, latter not decreased by his own books on Spain being highly praised by reviewers. He would say things like: 'I'm writing a novel – it's rather fun.' Fun it might have been, but the novel itself never got published. Brenan had rather a nice American wife [Gamel Woolsey, dcd 1968].

Monday, 26 January

Roy Fuller sent us *Consolations*, his latest vol. of poems. Roy has something personal about his poetry which makes it altogether different from those whose influences can be traced. I think it was a great pity Roy was not made Laureate when Betjeman died. He was perhaps regarded as by then too old, tho' one doesn't see why that should be any objection. I enjoy items like Roy taking his 'winter' trousers to be cleaned. As it happens his paperback publisher recently sent *Image of a Society* (1956), a studiously 'ordinary' account of personnel in the everyday life of a Building Society in the provinces.

The trouble about writing what might be called controlled ordinariness is that life puts too many jokers in the pack for that ever quite to come off in a convincing manner. Here it has rarely been better done, if the writer insists on such a convention. Human beings are too odd in it to work. One felt that very much in the army, where intense 'ordinariness' could be found side by side with grotesque, even pathological, behaviour in the same individual. The best thing in *Image of a Society* is a vivid account of a Building Society professional balls-up, involving several employees in different ways; better, for instance, than the love affair, which never really comes off.

Thursday, 29 January

I have been suffering from an inflamed gum. I rang Sussman, who said the lower plate may be pressing. He did not seem unduly put out by the suggestion that I see a local dentist about it. The thing began to be rather a nuisance, so went to Mr Charles Lister (4 Willow Vale, Frome, a pretty side turning by the Frome river) at recommendation of Lees Mayall. Lister (whose name at once makes one think of the golden boy Charles Lister in the Julian Grenfell circle) seemed a nice young man. He did job in a minute and a half. He looks like the hero in an illustration to the *Boy's Own Paper*. He comes from Yorkshire. When he noted my birthday in his documentation he said: 'My son was born 21 December.' 'How old is he?' 'Five weeks.' I said: 'The cusp of Sagittarius and Capricorn.' Lister said: 'Exactly. My wife and my mother are both Sagittarians. I'm Leo.' I was amused at a medical man taking note of these things. V and I afterwards lunched in Frome at the Tandoori Restaurant, Indian having taken the place of Italian in provincial towns. It might have been worse (Dal soup, Tandoori mixed, Carlsberg lager). At some stage the restaurant had a nautical character, so a steering wheel, a rotating telescope are inconsequentially features of the dining-room.

Sunday, 1 February

The Stockwells at The Stables*. In the evening we watched Tristram's TV film, *East of Ipswich*, the comedian Michael Palin's memories of being a boy of seventeen unwillingly taken by his parents for a holiday at Southwold, the Suffolk seaside resort, a trip nostalgic for them, but intensely boring for him. The picture was rather slow in places, with good moments. I felt interested to see Southwold, where George Orwell lived when growing up (his retired Indian Civil Service father was secretary of local golf club, I think). Like the boy in the film, George, too, was desperately bored there, his early girlfriends, etc. One could see the place must have been pretty trying for one of George's temperament. However, I believe to the end of his days he had some of his clothes made there, a Southwold tailor, who afterwards reported Mr Blair was very hard to satisfy. All intensely Orwellian.

Friday, 6 February

Patrick Mauriès, Literary Editor of *Libération*, who did an interview with me just two years ago, rang about 8.30 a.m. to ask the name of my agent, as a new French publishing firm, Quai Voltaire, is interested in the translation of *Dance*. Later in the morning *The Times* asked if I would like to contribute four lines of verse as a Valentine for page they were having on Valentine's Day. The answer in the negative.

Monday, 9 February

The sort of thing calculated to bring on seizure: on Saturday (day before yesterday) received for first time a demand for a certain sum of Income Tax; this morning I received a demand for interest on same sum, as not yet paid. On consulting my accountant, I learn that, by some Star Chamber legislation, the law was recently altered, so that although I have not before been asked for the money (dating back to 1984–5) I am 'deemed' to have incurred interest. My accountant (quickly correcting himself) coined the excellent portmanteau word 'inequamous' (iniquitous plus inequable) to describe this tyrannical oppression on the part of the taxation authorities.

* AP's elder son Tristram and his wife Virginia, who live in Stockwell, London, with their children Georgia (b. 1969) and Archie (b. 1970). The Stables is their converted house in the grounds of The Chantry.

Wednesday, 11 February

We watched a TV book programme this afternoon, which combined celebration of Roy Fuller's seventy-fifth birthday with a review of the *Consolations* poems, Roy himself appearing. Roy does these things exceedingly well. Others on the panel included Antonia [Pinter], another practised chat-show performer (I am not sure I like the tint, and set, of her current hair-do); also an old girl called Kay Dick, in former days an eyeglass, and boyish handshake, a fan of mine.

In the evening Hilary Spurling rang. She had returned from Tulsa, Oklahoma, which she loved. She had been back since before Christmas. Hilary wanted to consult me on being offered the main *Daily Telegraph* review on weeks alternate to my own. I strongly advised acceptance. This is splendid. I am impressed by whoever (presumably David Holloway) recommended Hilary to Max Hastings, as she is far the best reviewer I know (possibly Max Hastings thought it up himself). The *DT* bookpage certainly needs someone like Hilary for a certain type of book. She had been approached by an American woman (who sounded reasonably *sérieuse*) on the subject of making a blockbusting film about Ivy Compton-Burnett from Hilary's biography. That would certainly be amusing, but sounds one of those dream-fantasies, as are so many film projects. Hilary says Paul Scott's biography is proving much more interesting than expected, Scott living a notably undercover life. Coincidentally, in the light of an earlier TV book programme, Scott had an affair with Kay Dick.

Thursday, 12 February

Liz [Longford, sister-in-law] rang in the evening with a rather incoherent message from someone called Mrs Charles Goodhart (whom I do not know), saying she hoped I would put my name to recommendation of Roy Jenkins (Balliol) for Chancellor of the University at the coming election (by MAs) at Oxford; other candidates being Ted Heath (Balliol), Robert Blake (Christ Church). The Master of Balliol (Tony Kenny) sent round a letter saying, as Jenkins and Heath were both Balliol men, the College in the circumstances was suggesting no preference for support. On the whole I am in favour of Roy Jenkins, not only as a friend, as also most suitable for job. In any case I detest Wet Tories, as typified by Heath, also a consistent rocker of the Tory party boat. We met Blake many years ago in Norfolk with Wyndham Ketton-Cremer, he seemed nice.

Oxford's abominable treatment of Mrs Thatcher in refusing her an honorary degree, something engineered by a camerilla of Trotskyist academics, makes me unwilling to lend public support to anyone even moderately tainted with Leftism like Roy. I told Liz all this, not sure that she took it in. I think she is probably unaware that Roy Jenkins is a personal friend of ours. She said she hoped I would not hold it against her. I said I should not, but regarded it as slightly intrusive on the part of Mrs Charles Goodhart (apparently wife of the Chief Adviser to the Bank of England) to presume to exert pressure on a Balliol man, and Honorary Fellow of the College, regarding two other Balliol men, also Honorary Fellows, as both were in question. I also rubbed in what I thought of Mrs Thatcher's shabby treatment by Oxford. After all, I don't like Harold Wilson's policies, but as Prime Minister he certainly ought to have an Oxford honorary degree. Frank apparently is also taking no immediate steps to make his electoral sympathies known, having some leaning towards Blake as a fellow Christ Church don.

Thursday, 19 February

For some little time Evangeline Bruce has been trying to arrange a meeting between myself and a friend of hers, Mrs Sondra Gotlieb, wife of the Canadian Ambassador at Washington, Mrs Gotlieb having stated she will fly over specially if this can be fixed. I am not keen on going to London these days, so suggested Evangeline should bring Mrs Gotlieb (with or without husband) to luncheon here some time. Mrs Gotlieb is famous for having smacked her secretary's face during a TV interview (watched by millions, an incident V and I both remember, tho' did not witness). Evangeline added: 'Sondra is always very sulky, and expects to be the centre of attention everywhere.' This intriguing project is now under discussion, the plan at present that Evangeline, with Tony and Marcelle Quinton, should come here on 5 March. The Quintons insist on bringing a picnic basket. I agreed, with the proviso that we should produce the drink. It now appears that Mrs Gotlieb may be unable to get away then, as the following week the Canadian Prime Minister is making a first appearance in Washington. After the face-smacking incident Mr Gotlieb (who adores his wife) nearly lost his job, so everyone at the Canadian Embassy must be present and correct, on their best behaviour. Evangeline referred to a 'Tiny Tim-style hamper'. I thought she meant a reconstitution of Scrooge's visit to the Cratchits on Christmas Day. Then turned out she said Tiny Tim in mistake for Tiger Tim, the latter's famous dormitory feasts at Mrs Hippo's school, which the party will no doubt resemble, perhaps with touch of Cratchits' luncheon thrown in. We await developments.

Sunday, 22 February

I cooked a vegetable curry for Vidia and Pat Naipaul for luncheon. The Stockwells had Mary Mount at The Stables. All turning up in the morning for drinks, and to see the Naipauls. Having established the principle that claret goes all right with curry, we drank at lunch the last two bottles of the Château Boyd Cantenac '70, pretty good if drinking not to be delayed any longer owing to age.

Vidia much enjoyed the Chicago trip to collect the T. S. Eliot Ingersoll Prize, addressing the Foundation at dinner on the subject of the Writer not being the same in his life as in his works. This apparently went down well. Vidia seemed a shade disappointed he had not managed to bore more acutely an audience of rich businessmen, including quite a few Southerners, he discovered. An ex-Moonie shepherded him round. Vidia ascertained that the ex-Moonie's wife made furniture for dolls' houses. Vidia asked if that were profitable industry. Apparently it is, to the extent of supporting its own trade paper called *Nutshell News*. Vidia was in cracking form. He plans to spend five months exploring the old slave States, studying the history of slavery, having already written about the slave trade, as such, in *The Middle Passage*.

Monday, 23 February

What appeared to be a character from the rural soap opera called *The Archers* knocked on the door this morning. He turned out to be a youngish farmer who wants to take over some of the fields of which Kenny Norris has at present the grass-keep. He is called Adrian Andrews, name already mentioned in this connexion to V by Pat Moore at The Lodge. I had previously thought it best to let Cooper & Tanner handle this without interference, but later in the day I rang Mr Joyce, who said he had not yet had opportunity to inspect the fields (price varying according to state of grass year by year), but would get in touch with Andrews at once to stop any further complaints about delay.

Saturday, 28 February

Roland Gant rang. The Gants have been occupied with dentists, X-rays, etc., so I presume health troubles are to be cleared up here before return to France. Roland and Nadya are lunching here Wednesday. Immediately after, the telephone went again, this time Bob Conquest. He and Liddie are over for three days. Bob saw the PM, said she was looking ten years younger, prettier than ever. Bob asked my opinion about his Larkin letters, well over a hundred in number, whether or not to let Anthony Thwaite have them, as it seemed a bit early to publish. Some rude things are said about Kingley Amis,* others might be painful to Monica Jones, others again are merely sexually embarrassing. I asked if latter were undergraduate homosexual involvements. Bob said: 'Well, chiefly odds and ends of fladge, saying, "will you send *Spanker*, I can't buy copies up here in this silly town". Harmless

* Sir Kingsley Amis (1922–1995)

enough, but a taste for spanking is perhaps not quite the right image at the moment for a distinguished deceased poet.'

Kingsley is sending Thwaite all his Larkin letters which, as he knew Philip since undergraduate days, are apparently at least equally colourful. I suggested that Bob write to Thwaite to discuss the general situation: when the *Letters* are likely to appear, what other people's are like, if Thwaite is exercising any sort of censorship. Bob is going to do that. Lees Mayall rang inviting us to luncheon on 11 March.

Wednesday, 4 March

David Heidenstam rang saying he and Robert Humphreys had submitted the script to me of *From a View to a Death* some years ago, which I had approved (I must admit having no recollection of that whatever). Was I still in principle prepared to have it done? Told him yes, but to get in touch with my agent, John Rush of Higham.

Roland and Nadia Gant to luncheon, they are going back to France next week. Roland is looking well, Nadia was at her most witchlike, Russian (latter only quarter, I think, if wholly witch). They both gave loud cries when told I was dealing with Marie-Pierre Bay at Stock (French publishers of *Le Roi Pêcheur*), whom I supposed male. Apparently female, good-looking, a terror, who in some manner put both the Gants' backs up.

The Gants are staying in the Streatham house of their medical son, where they report Asians and Blacks are completely assimilated. Roland said Hilary told him it was odd to read in Tulsa a letter from Paul Scott to Roland saying he quite agreed that I [AP] must have been a fly on the wall at the Falcon Press, so like was it to the office of *Fission* in *Books Do Furnish A Room*. The Falcon Press had Scott as accountant, Roland and several notable characters on the staff. Scott also was employed there when the firm was under the sway of Peter Baker, who eventually did time for forging an offer of money from two tycoons. Both the Gants were strangely disturbed, unbelieving, at my notion of Scott having had affair with Kay Dick, exactly why I could not discover.

Thursday, 5 March

Evangeline Bruce, Tony and Marcelle Quinton came, bringing a hamper: smoked salmon sandwiches, pie, chocolate gâteau, soufflés, bottle of champagne. Mrs Gotlieb was unable to make it, but is promised in June. Tony said one of his female pupils addressed him as 'My Lord'. We supplied Château Kirwan, '71. *The Album* (of *Dance*) proofs arrived. The book seems satisfactory, so far as one can ever judge illustrations from xeroxed pictures.

Friday, 6 March

At the Coleford surgery, Liz Carter, the charming Sister who gives me Vit. B injections enquired how V was, then said: 'Isn't she a Longford?' I replied in the affirmative. It turned out that Sister Carter's grandfather (named Dart, who would be in his nineties if still alive) was 'footman to Lady Longford'. This would appear to be V's grandmother, who lived at 24 Bruton Street. The Carter family live in Yorkshire. Coincidences continue.

Wednesday, 11 March

The *Album* proofs were returned yesterday, arrangement being contract should be in my name, the proceeds handed over by me to V as basic Editor. Much of the later selection, editing captions, etc., was done by Thames & Hudson very well. In one or two places I should myself have chosen a different picture, this rightly emphasizing the fact that the compilation is, so to speak, not my own, but an exterior comment. Two points were missed in the proofs: the latter part of a longish paragraph, attached to Field Marshal Montgomery, refers, in fact, to Sir Philip Sidney, contrasted with Monty. I ought to have noticed this slip as it is all most inappropriate for the Field Marshal. Secondly, *The Omnipresent*, of which we possess a reproduction, should certainly have been included. This we both missed.

We lunched with the Mayalls. On the way to Sturford we stopped off at large Do-It-Yourself store opposite Frome station to look at bookcases as books upstairs are piling up ominously and something must be done. I think what they have there will save the situation. Then on to luncheon, where Lees said he had written quite a lot of his Memoirs, which are very discreet.

In evening Hilary Spurling rang. She was reviewing Vidia Naipaul's new book *The Enigma of Arrival* (described on the title page as novel, but mostly straight account of Naipaul's life in Wiltshire). Hilary said I figure at one brief moment very tenuously. She wanted to know who 'Alan' was, described as talented, well-born, asked about a lot, never managed to write a book, died of drink or drugs. We decided that must be a composite character, with elements of Julian Jebb. Hilary was rather disturbed at the Julian aspect being unjust. She said Vidia is like Milton, autocratic. I see what she means. She spoke of her sculptor friend William Pye (nephew of novelist Margaret Kennedy), who she is keen should sculpt me – like Pope, she said. Apparently Pye works largely from photographs, now also all the rage for painters.

Friday, 13 March

V's seventy-fifth birthday. Alice Boyd, now High Sheriff of Cornwall, where there is a by-election, will function as Returning Officer. We watched this on TV this morning, Alice having designed for herself a splendid velvet costume, rather like a somewhat military riding habit, and large hat with emerald green ostrich feather, the whole slightly Gainsborough in effect, perhaps based on an actual picture. We lunched with Joff and Tessa Davies, as it was Tessa's birthday too. I had neurotic fears beforehand that it might be a buffet affair, quite why I don't know, as no possible reason to suspect that. On the contrary, it was an excellent luncheon with just the Mayalls and ourselves. Mary Mayall's sister Liz has been in a bad motor accident. That family are incredibly unlucky with cars, in which two of Mary's brothers were killed, not to mention mishaps to cousins.

Sunday, 15 March

Tristram and Georgia came over this morning, Virginia and Archie having to go back early (Virginia for a funeral, Archie for rehearsal of Bulgakov's *The White Guard* for his school play). Tristram recently saw Grey Gowrie's mother and her husband Derek Cooper, mentioned earlier apropos of Pat Herdman's death. Apparently they both work in refugee camps, being fanatical Arabists.

The re-allotment of the grass-feed fields from Kenny Norris to Adrian Andrews has now taken place, the latter's sheep replacing Kenny's cows and bullocks. I find this change greatly preferable. When we first came here I used to express regret that there seemed no sheep at all in the neighbourhood. To this everyone replied you couldn't possibly keep sheep round here, too wet. Now sheep are all over the place. Sheep have a more active, at least more interesting, social life than cows. I often watch them. They will have mild fights with each other, all suddenly rush off in one direction, a kind of game. Strode remarked:

> When Westwall Downes I gan to tread
> Where cleanely wynds the greene did sweepe,
> Methought a landskipp there was spread
> Here a bush and there a sheepe:

Friday, 27 March

V had a check-up with Lloyd Williams. All well, I'm glad to say. I reread *Measure for Measure*, which I enjoyed more than expected. I am inclined to think that Shakespeare, so far as he may be said to have 'identified' with Prospero, did so equally here with the Duke, who shows from time to time a similar rather unpleasant, even sadistic strain together with his wit. Had Mariana inherited the Moated Grange as heiress and lived there alone? Did Angelo suppose that property more valuable than in fact it was when he first became engaged to her? It is one of the plays where one feels a certain amount of contemporary local stuff comes in.

Saturday, 28 March

About 4.30 p.m. there was a knock on the front door. A tall, bearded figure, buttoned from head to foot in motor-bike 'leathers', with bright yellow crash helmet. I think I should have recognized him as Mr Doug Jackman (The Bungalow, Redford Hill, Timsbury), who gave me the clock some years ago. Before I could do so he announced his identity, then asked: 'Did you discover what the lettering stood for?' I grasped at once that he referred to letters on the clock, which, with the numerals, mark the twelve hours. Before I could answer, he went on: 'The two names that are so important in your book – what are they? – I had a problem with them because there were thirteen letters. Then I saw I must do one anti-clockwise. What is the name . . . ?' 'Widmerpool?' 'No, *The Music of Time* man . . .' 'Poussin?' 'Yes, yes, Poussin – Poussin and Proust – what, you didn't get it, you a Balliol man? You must have another look.' 'The clock itself has stopped.' It had done that about a year ago. 'Just an ordinary torch battery. Unscrew the three screws at the back. I must go. I've got three motor bikes at the gate.' Off he went. When we examined the clock I remembered we had worked out POUSSIN going clockwise; failed understandably to decipher TSUOR(P), which completed the twelve hours. Perhaps that wasn't very bright of me, Balliol man notwithstanding. John later inserted a new battery, the clock is ticking away again. My books have odd effects on different people.

Wednesday, 1 April

About 8 a.m. this morning, sheets of rain coming down, some of the lambs in Park Field pushed their way under the fence, making for other side of the lawn. Half-dressed, I drove them back before breakfast. They know perfectly well they are doing wrong, and rush back, several of the larger ones nearly getting stuck trying to wriggle under bottom rail. When some decided to jump over that, one got between it and second rail in place at end of fence. They make high standing jumps very well.

Thursday, 2 April

Tom Wallace called up. He is leaving Norton to become a literary agent. This is sad news as he was a keen supporter. His replacement is called Katie Nelson. *The Fisher King* paperback appears in the US in September. Tom said he thought Thames & Hudson (who, as it happens, have four rooms on Norton's premises) would probably market *The Album* themselves.

Saturday, 4 April

Jim and Alvilde Lees-Milne to luncheon. Curry. I was flattered by praise from Alvilde, herself a first-rate cook. She asked for details of its making. We drank Sancerre (Hemingway's favourite wine), which had in fact been ordered by mistake (writing down the wrong number). It went well, nice luncheon wine. Jim said someone is writing the life of Robert Byron. One wonders what would have happened to R. Byron had he lived. He was a man I never found at all sympathetic. A powerful, energetic, tyrannical personality, original rather than intelligent. Alvilde, garden expert as well as superb cook, has been advising the pop star Mick Jagger about his château near Amboise. Shades of Leonardo da Vinci who died at Amboise in the château of Cloux. Jagger's residence?

Sunday, 5 April

The Stockwells at The Stables. Tristram talked of Vidia Naipaul's *The Enigma of Arrival* (title from a Chirico picture reproduced on jacket), which I have just been reading, describing Vidia's life at the Wilsford cottage. It is billed as a novel, although almost wholly autobiographical. There are a few small changes, such as a local murder, which took place after the Naipauls left, being described as if they had been still there. It contains, in Alan, clearly a projection of the late Julian Jebb, so chilly, even unfriendly, that it disturbed Hilary Spurling. If the book is to be regarded as a novel Vidia could perfectly well insist that Alan was an invented character.

I, too, appear minimally, as remarking that individuals get to resemble physically their own employees. I have no recollection of saying this, but well may have done so, as it is possibly true. In this case I had thought the figure passing on the far side of the sort of private village green behind Vidia's cottage, beyond which is the 'big house' (all part of 1905 reconstruction of bogus Elizabethan manor by the Tennants) was Stephen Tennant himself, the Naipauls' hermit landlord. In fact it was one of the servants. Did Byron begin to resemble his valet Fletcher? An interesting question.

Wednesday, 15 April

Tristram and Virginia stopped off at The Stables on their way to stay at Venn, Pembrokeshire, with the Mounts, and came to dinner. V cooked an excellent duck; Crozes Hermitage '85. With an Easter Egg, Tristram included as a present for me

My Life in Pictures by Malcolm Muggeridge. Glancing cursorily through his work, several gems, both photographic and moral, were immediately evident.

Saturday, 18 April

Further examination of the Muggeridge Picture Life reveals a slightly horrifying side, as well as an intensely funny one.

There is nothing against publishing 138 representations of oneself (Malcolm pondering on his own bust counting as two) in the interests of publicity, nor spending some hours of one's own time in prayer and meditation. What is hard on the reader is all the sanctimonious stuff about Christianity, RC conversion and Love of the Human Race, being exchanged by Malcolm for his former preoccupation with the world of Power, when a book of this self-promotional kind is purely an expression of one form of power: while should it really be necessary to be *photographed* praying and meditating, for the benefit of the public, especially if the material world has been forsworn?

I am not particularly surprised at being omitted from Malcolm's list of 'special friends' on the blurb, but that Evelyn Waugh should be included is really preposterous. Evelyn was scarcely able to tolerate Malcolm's name coming up in casual conversation, he disliked him so much. Glancing at the broader implications of 'Christian behaviour', Malcolm, quite a long time ago, perpetrated the totally unjustifiable smear that Max Beerbohm was homosexual (there was not the very smallest reason to suppose that, all evidence being to the contrary, for instance, in Max's *Letters* to Reggie Turner). This Malcolm repeats here, with the actual lie that 'Max left for Italy after the Wilde trial in 1895'. In point of fact Max Beerbohm retired to Rapallo as quieter, and above all cheaper and pleasanter, than London in 1910, fifteen years after the Wilde trial, when indeed Wilde was becoming rehabilitated in the eyes of a more tolerant public.

Having no doubt committed in Malcolm's eyes the equivalent of that sin mentioned in the Bible for which there is no forgiveness, I was astonished not to be blocked out (like portraits of Trotsky) in a group of the *Punch* staff and Malcolm in the editorial chair. All in all, a most macabre volume.

I reread *The Diary of a Disappointed Man* (1919) by W. N. P. Barbellion, real name B. F. Cummings (I think uncle of Michael Cummings, the cartoonist, whom I always liked when we used to meet at *Punch*, and later, as that imbecile Bernard Hollowood sacked Cummings when he became editor). *The Journal of a D. M.*, one of my father's books, was probably recommended to my father by Tom Balston. I never heard how my father got on with it. I dipped into it at a very early age, fourteen/fifteen, possibly younger, I suspect I did not read it all, but was impressed with what I was able to take in.

Barbellion was a biologist, well read, well up in the arts and music, employed in Natural History Museum, South Kensington, one of my childhood haunts. He was fatally ill with creeping paralysis, married, and died at age of thirty, not without enjoying a few months of published success with *The Journal*. I reread it some few years ago, but was a little put off by the intense egotism and self-pity (which to be fair Barbellion himself draws attention to). This time I felt better disposed and decided that here was indeed a most remarkable document, 'one of the great diaries'. I can't imagine what my father made of it all, except that he was himself no enemy to self-pity. One is rather irked by perpetual use of initials; an edition with good notes saying who everyone was might be worth doing, but I think they have merely reprinted the original one. I suppose like so many things of the sort to do it properly would be too much trouble for the sales involved.

Saturday, 18 April–Monday, 20 April

V and I watched the three-part TV programme on Evelyn Waugh by Nicholas Shakespeare and Adam Low. A mixed bag. V thought the whole thing pretty indifferent, especially Parts One and Two. I was less severe about Part One, both of us agreeing the Third was best. The basis of this was really John Freeman and Elizabeth Jane Howard's respective interviews with Evelyn, with occasional tolerably good remarks by persons who knew him pretty well like Harold Acton, always a competent performer; most of them were friendly, if not uncritical. An interesting feature was the woman Geraldine Sparkes who encountered Evelyn on board ship during the Pinfold episode, without knowing anything of him apart from that; Shimi Lovat, unfriendly, if eminently credible, on the subject of Evelyn in the army, Lovat's own personality coming over as not particularly agreeable; Fitzroy Maclean, looking somewhat shifty, was, not surprisingly, equally anti-Waugh; Tony Bushell, retired actor, Evelyn's contemporary at Hertford, normal himself, was regarded as a great beauty by the Oxford queers (especially Harold Acton). Bushell is now well into his eighties; Bushell's complexion rendered in startling Technicolor tints of pink.

Hugh (Lord) Molson, another Oxford contemporary (Hot Lunch Molson) is still going strong; Bill Deedes, sometime Editor of the *Daily Telegraph* was with Evelyn as a correspondent in Abyssinia (seems the only exciting thing that has ever happened to Deedes). He kept on appearing; Frankie Donaldson was rather good.

I myself appeared in First and Third Parts, saying a word about going to the Waugh parents' house in Golders Green, then about Evelyn's clothes, demeanour, wish for a knighthood. I think I had already spoken of Evelyn's grey bowler to Nicholas Shakespeare, so forgot to mention that he wore it at least once coming here. Pansy Lamb was completely omitted, tho' producers had spoken highly of the interview with her in Rome. One suspects Pansy said things that did not fit in with the accepted Waugh canon, such as Evelyn not giving at all a reliable picture of the upper-class life. It is impossible to shake inaccurate legends, because anything that does is always removed by editors, whose endemic interests are to prevent any matter not in the *idées reçues* seeping in.

I was much amused that The Travellers' should have been shot, instead of White's Club. Like all these shows everything is in the end boiled down to a kind of popular view of the subject, little or nothing to do with what Evelyn, or anyone else, was really like. Any material that seems paradoxical is omitted or smoothed down. Evelyn had so much about his own presentation of himself that was stylized already as a grotesque figure that it is difficult to get down to reality, assuming there was indeed some reality to get down to, which one at times doubts. Perhaps what appeared was the best to be hoped.

Wednesday, 22 April

The Royal Society of Literature has once more offered me its 'Companionship of Literature'. This is the third time since the invention (I think by Freddie Birkenhead some thirty years ago) of this curiously named honorific. I explained once again (this time by personal letter to its President, Angus Wilson) that I thought honorific titles, as such, appropriately conferred only by HM the Queen.

Thursday, 23 April

Drawing the curtains in the library, V caught her foot in castor of the bergere chair in the bow window, fell, cutting her head against the shutter. We got Mr Bryant, young trainee GP I once saw in the surgery, who said a stitch not necessary, just keep an eye on things.

Sunday, 26 April

I watched about three-quarters of an hour of *Scoop* on TV.

Tuesday, 28 April

Letter from Ania Corless of Higham saying the Bulgarians wish to translate *The Valley of Bones* and *The Soldier's Art*. No doubt repercussion of my visit to Sofia ten years ago. A minuscule sum offered (in any case has to be spent in Bulgaria, I think), but one feels any Western translations for Iron Curtain countries are in the final resort good propaganda. I had in fact signed some sort of contract when I was there (later forgotten) in order to get some ready money on the spot. The books are to appear in 1989. Don't imagine *The Military Philosophers* will follow, if only on account of the mention of the Katyn massacre and the various Communist governments' unmannerly behaviour at the Victory celebrations in London.

Wednesday, 29 April

I have two copies of *Henry James's Notebooks*, as one for review was lost in post, another acquired, then the original one turned up weeks later, so I passed this on to Hilary Spurling. She spoke of current life on the *Daily Telegraph*. She asked about David Holloway, saying she had met him on and off for twenty years at least, yet never plumbed what he was like. I said David was keen on Westerns (about which he produced at least one study of some sort). David injured his back during the war flying out-of-date aircraft inducing some form of occupational complaint. I think it rare for a woman (unless in love, certainly not the case here) to admit she does not entirely understand a man, most women regarding all men as an 'open book'. I am always struck talking with Hilary how she is not quite like anyone else, male or female, an exceedingly quick intelligence all her own.

Friday, 1 May

To Coleford surgery for Vit. B injection, tetanus booster. (Tetanus Booster would be a good name for a US Senator, probably a Southerner.) Thames & Hudson's PR girl, Marion Castle, came to tea to talk about publicity for *The Album* (of *Dance*). She brought a boyfriend with her, Etienne Milner, with whom she was travelling. Tall, rather gawky, attractively monkey-faced girl. She turned out to have known Adrian Daintrey since she was seventeen. Adrian is now teaching at the City of London Guilds Art School, whose premises are opposite John [Powell]'s house in Kennington Park Road. She said she had seen Adrian regularly ever since (I imagine her about twenty-five). He is at the moment painting portrait of her at the Charterhouse. Reports him as not doing too badly, if suffering dreadfully (one is not surprised) from boredom. An agent (Sally Hunter, Motcomb Street) is now selling his past work quite well, so stacks of pictures have vanished from Charterhouse room: lots of friends are sending him drink, etc. She suggested I should ring him up after meeting her. Rather a struggle finding things to talk about when Adrian lunched with me a couple of years ago, as his interests are always strictly limited to his own affairs, with which one is not up to date. However I will consider calling him up. Marion Castle agreed he was fairly incoherent.

Her young man seemed perfectly agreeable in a slightly awkward situation. He was a shade put out by my saying Maurice Lambert (after all, quite successful academic sculptor, which Milner described himself as being) told me sculptors were never out of a job, as they could always do coats of arms over banks, to be done if commissions were thin on the ground. Maurice himself had done the guns on the machine-gun War Memorial at Hyde Park Corner. Milner said he had no difficulty in finding jobs, heads of wives of company directors, etc. John said later the Kennington Art School has sculpture section, so this couple may have met there. She appears to have publicity plans for *The Album* well in hand, and keen about it.

Saturday, 2 May

Conscience, cautioning better to act now rather than delay, caused me to ring Adrian this morning, while still having the young woman from Thames & Hudson in mind. As I foresaw, this was no great success. In first instance, it took a certain amount of explaining who I was, at which, when Adrian fully understood, he did not seem particularly pleased. However, he scarcely reacted at all on subject of Marion Castle, wrongly judged to make an acceptable topic. On the contrary Adrian was prepared to admit no more than that he met her a long time ago, even that only after much explaining. Wasn't he painting her? Yes, he thought he probably had painted her some time in the past. All rather like Augustus John at his gruffest, a *persona* Adrian always at moments apt to assume. He showed no interest whatever in news that V and I had both been rather under the weather in the autumn, admittedly not a very compelling subject; nor was he interested in *The Album*, both perhaps to be expected. Daintrey agreed he was selling back numbers of his own pictures reasonably well. That was really all to be got out of him. I felt somewhat damped when I hung up, but, as V said, Adrian was probably glad to be rung. Adrian always had his grumpy side, sudden contact with someone belonging to an early period of his life probably muddling his mind.

The Stockwells are at The Stables. Tristram came over in evening. I talked to him about the Waugh programme, its determination to be banal, just the same with Orwell, all programmes in which friends/enemies are so many actors speaking his, the producer's script, which represents his own picture of the person concerned. If their dialogue does not fit in with that script their lines are cut: if necessary (as appears to have been case with Pansy Lamb) they are sacked. The case of Pansy particularly regrettable as she had been sharing a flat with Evelyn Gardner at time of the Waugh engagement, circumstances no one else dealt with. Much of my own material was trimmed down, tho' they did leave in that Evelyn expected human behaviour to fit in with his own view of what it should be; not his view of it adapted to what human behaviour might be like if that differed. In fact, just like TV producers.

Sunday, 3 May

To luncheon, Leo and Jilly Cooper, Lees and Mary Mayall. V planned to cook *boeuf en daube*, a dish prepared the day before, one of its ingredients being pigs' trotters. V was then uncertain whether the trotters were not a bit 'off'. She consulted John and me, both of us agreeing that the trotters were all right. However, one trotter by accident was omitted, which V ate (like a heroic doctor experimenting), finding herself slightly upset inside following morning, whether or not by trotter uncertain, but trotters thought better abandoned. Accordingly, John at short notice cooked an excellent risotto. When told the story, Jilly said incident was like one of her own novels, in which a one-parent mother produces an extempore meal for man who turns out to be Mr Right. Jilly was drastically thinner, very trim and elegant.

Leo is now in Heinemann (said what would be called in the army 'on detachment'). He said a very nice girl there was called Fanny Blake, on the editorial side, whom he recommended to deal with if possible. Jilly is among the eighty-three writers in Public Lending Right who have the maximum distribution (£5000), of whom at least half even a publisher like Leo has never heard. Jilly brought with her copy of *The Fisher King* to sign; I gave them *Iron Aspidistra*.

Mary Mayall spoke of Henry Bath's period with the Guru Bhagwan (some such name), now utterly discredited in the US. To practise this creed Henry had sacerdotal robes made for himself by his Savile Row tailor. The Mayalls recently attended the funeral of their Macmillan niece Rachel. They drove to Birch Grove, Sussex, and back in one day, at best four hours each way. All the same, they said, it was wonderful to be home, which one can understand in circumstances. Risotto preceded by asparagus, followed by notable Viennese patisserie possible to buy in Frome: Pomerol, Château La Croix de Gay, '78, not bad, should improve with keeping. Enjoyable party. V, John, I, dined at The Stables.

Tuesday, 12 May

I reviewed Andro Linklater's *Compton Mackenzie*, a good biography. I suppose, if Mackenzie is remembered at all, that is for *Sinister Street* (two vols). When I was taken out on Sunday from my prep school, The New Beacon, by my mother, we used to lunch at a nice Georgian hotel in Sevenoaks, the Crown (now no more), where there were a few contemporary books in a bookcase including *Sinister Street* (Vol. 1), which I used to read a bit of in the afternoon, attracted by title. I did not understand much of it, but was impressed by Meats (the monk, Brother Aloysius), who seized the hero's hand, when he was experimenting with monastic life, saying something like: 'Curse you, your eyes remind me of a girl I knew in the Seven Sisters Road.' I think I probably read the novel in due course without retaining much more than that original impact of Meats and the memorable Seven Sisters Road name.

When (introduced by John Raymond) I met Mackenzie at the Reform Club in the 1950s, he in his seventies, I told him *Sinister Street* had made an impression on me at age of twelve or thirteen, especially Meats. Mackenzie said: 'Not so very many years ago a man touched me on the shoulder when we passed in the street. I couldn't place him. "Meats," he said.' Mackenzie imitated the slimy tone in which the man spoke the name conferred on him in the novel. I had a word or two with Mackenzie again when he and his second wife (as she in due course became) were staying in the same hotel as ourselves in Rome some years later.

Copies of *Le Roi Pêcheur* arrived today (tr. Raymond Las Vergnas). It seems all right so far as I've read. The only serious howler appears to be *Little Women* rendered as *Petites Femmes* attributed as a novel to the character Beals. In fact I think there is quite a well-known French nineteenth-century novel of that title. Louisa Alcott's book in French is called *Les Quatre Filles du Docteur March*, a copy of which V once saw. I am surprised the translator missed that as on the whole notes are well done.

Saturday, 23 May

Isobel Strachey obit. Isobel came of fairly rich family called Leslie, settled in Argentina for a generation or two, five daughters, all good-looking, I believe, Isobel was far most eccentric. She married the horrible spotty John Strachey. When he went off she lived all rest of her life at 52 Oakley Street, Chelsea, where she gave parties, wrote novels, and had shows of her drawings. She let off the basement to a succession of lodgers, usually young men who were more or less friends. She possessed an almost perfect example of the Bloomsbury drawling voice, tho' natural to her. She was never particularly involved with Bloomsbury, as such, Isobel being in her own way one of the most unaffected persons imaginable. She was very kind, and sometimes very funny. We met during the war, saw each other on and off for years. Tristram and John were friends of hers too. In fact she became quite a cult among people much younger than herself. Her quiet strangled laugh faintly is suggested in Louise Beals. Isobel had many affairs, mostly casual to a degree, I think.

On one of Isobel's visits here we had Henry and Virginia Bath to dinner. Sitting next to Henry at table Isobel drawled: 'Have you been to Cruft's?', putting that question with a giggle, the famous dog-show probably having been on TV, where she had seen it. Next time we met Henry he was furious. 'Of course she thought I was too stupid to know about anything but a dog-show.' Really it was a typical piece of Isobel joke-dialogue, which she might have put to anyone, or for that matter in one of her books. She was in many ways a delightful person and is a loss.

Alison Lurie, over for three weeks, to luncheon. Alison was in excellent form. She had been in India for a couple of weeks. *Imaginary Friends*, one of Alison's early novels, perhaps the best, is to be done on TV in three episodes at the end of June, adapted by Malcolm Bradbury (author of *The History Man*, etc.), shot at the University of East Anglia where Bradbury is a don. Alison said the University buildings (modern) of untold hideosity. She likes Bradbury, and says he is much beglamorized by a dream of getting away from academic life by becoming a professional script-writer. She says she doesn't think he altogether realizes how ghastly writing movie scripts can be for someone who sets out to be a serious novelist. I should just about say so.

Alison was told by Antonia (Pinter), or another of the Pakenhams, that the ghost of Andrews, for many years butler at Pakenham (now Tullynally) is said to walk there. Andrews, a Welshman, for a time footman to the Dynevors (cousins of the Longfords), then came from Dynevor to be butler to V's eldest brother Edward Longford. Edward was somewhat dominated by Andrews, a rather bleak essentially unJeevesian figure. It appears that workmen doing some job in kitchens/scullery area of the house not long ago, asked about the butler they saw moving about from room to room. Thomas Pakenham now owns Tullynally. He does not employ a butler. This spectre of Andrews seems to have appeared on several occasions. I gave Alison (who immediately grasped the Eliot/Auden pastiches) the *Iron Aspidistra*. Melon; duck; patisserie; Maximino de Trentino (the wine drunk in *Don Giovanni*).

Sunday, 24 May

John, with great brilliance, noticed in the TV programmes the German film called *The Flag* (1977) on Channel 4, which is evidently an adaptation of Lernet-Holenia's novel *The Standard*, a book I always admired in that particular genre. This turned out not only a late-night showing, but also doubtful whether the reception would be possible here, so Archie taped film in London. We borrowed the video from the Moores at The Lodge, and watched *Battle Flag* this afternoon. It was an awful travesty of the Lernet-Holenia novel, with American dubbing, a general style clearly intended for the American market (which doesn't begin to understand European military matters, or military behaviour, especially Austrian).

The leading lady was terrible, the male lead (a British actor Simon Ward) not too bad. Also the hero's friend, the German hussar officer and several others were reasonably good, notably a mysterious major with two dogs (more or less symbolizing Death), who appears at certain moments. I was glad to see the sort of film to be made from *The Standard*, which I suggested in my Memoirs would have provided a marvellous job for Stroheim: especially the firing on the mutinous regiment, and the escape through the rat-infested sewers of the Castle at Belgrade. Also one or two other episodes. The rats in fact were omitted, a scene certainly difficult to shoot, but by no means impossible.

Wednesday, 27 May

Yesterday Georgia [Powell] to stay for a few days. She is working on Greek and Latin books for some interim exam. She accompanied us this morning to the Bath Clinic when I went for check-up with Southwood (all well), lunching after at the Red Lion, Woolverton, on outskirts of Rode. This is a nice pub, the food chiefly founded on different variations of potatoes baked in their skins, and filled with meat. Chatto's is being rather difficult about *John Aubrey and His Friends*. Not at all satisfactory.

Friday, 29 May

Georgia returned home. Sweet girl, nice having her in the house. She worked hard at Sophocles, Horace, etc. Yesterday I discussed the *Aubrey* situation with Bruce Hunter. Chatto's (in fact the Hogarth Press) say the corrections 'overrun' in manner which necessitates resetting the whole book, as they cannot find, or parallel, type of the original edition (printer Clowes, London, Beccles, Suffolk). This seems hard to believe, also unlike me to misjudge space for correction to that extent, which I am always careful about. I wonder if this is in some manner a product of recent take-over and upheavals involving Chatto. Bruce suggested getting corrections back to check them myself, at the same time sounding Cassell (who recently wrote saying they would like to consider putting *Aubrey* into some series they run) for quick look, after corrections have been re-examined.

I myself see the real reason for all this is the unlucky star under which Aubrey was born, and always blamed for his own mishaps, lawsuits, etc. In my case, where Aubrey was concerned, three years delayed publication on the part of Eyre & Spottiswoode, row with Graham Greene (who himself had row with Eyre & Spottiswoode), then spiteful remarks of Lawson Dick; difficulties of getting book into print again after it had been quite successful (two impressions), reprinted 1967, pirated in Chicago, obviously ought to be available now for scholarly reasons; finally all this balls-up on part of Chatto.

Reviewing the Compton Mackenzie biography caused me to get *Sinister Street* (now in one vol.) out of the library. About ninety per cent of novel is utter rubbish, the remainder really rather good, original. The hero the illegitimate son of an earl, living with his beautiful mother, the earl's mistress, in Hammersmith. This would have made a fascinating situation if based on relative truth. Quite absurd, the novel, as it stands, is fairly boring reportage (childhood, schooldays, Oxford), then the hero's encounter with Meats (mentioned earlier here) at the monastery, his meetings with prostitutes of various kinds in London. All this part of the novel reveals Mackenzie's potentialities. The individual tarts (Empire promenade) are given life in a remarkable way, especially in the light of the comparative discretion which still had to be observed in writing of that sort of subject. If Mackenzie had possessed less vanity, more balance, integrity as an artist, *Sinister Street* would certainly have been the most remarkable novel of its period (which to some minute extent it remains in parts, marred by reams of prolix nonsense), perhaps even a great novel.

Sunday, 31 May

Anthony and Tanya Hobson, Anne Lancaster, were to have come to luncheon today. On Friday Tanya had an accident on the three steps leading to the Hobson dining-room, and broke both her legs. She will have to lie up for six or eight weeks, a most unhappy affair. Anthony came to lunch, and was going to look in on Tanya at the nursing-home, Bodenham, near Salisbury, on the way back. This is apparently a reasonably nice place. Anne Lancaster arrived about 12.30. She looked pretty well, if naturally a bit tired with all the business consequent on Osbert's death. She spoke of the disposal of Osbert's papers, which, with his sketch-books, she presented to his Oxford college (Lincoln) rather than allow them to be dispersed, and probably go to America. The sketch-books are otherwise likely to be cut up into separate pictures for framing, obviously something to be regretted. This all sounds eminently sensible.

Anne is also much taken up with her gardening interests, the Royal Horticultural Society, etc. Anthony, something of an authority on such matters himself, agreed Lincoln [College] was the best home for the sketchbooks. I lent Anthony the two Lernet-Holenia novels I possessed in translation, *The Adventures of a Young Gentleman in Poland* and *The Standard*. Asparagus; *boeuf en daube*, new potatoes, salad; gooseberry fool with strawberries, meringues; last two bottles of Château Kirwan '71.

Saturday, 6 June

Bob and Liddie Conquest arrived about 11.30 (the only train) for luncheon, both in good form, always struck by niceness of Liddie. The question of Philip Larkin's letters continues to exercise Bob. Kingsley Amis is now uncertain about handing over all his Larkin letters to Thwaite. Bob's collection includes one from Larkin saying he hopes he will die before Kingsley, as he would obviously be expected to write or speak some obituary memoirs, if Kingsley predeceased him, would find difficulty in thinking of single point in Kingsley's favour. The essence of this kind of savage remark (with others) is probably acceptable within circle of three old friends as satire that will be understood, but rather different when offered to general public including malicious journalists out of context. That so often true about all sorts of matters. All the same fact remains that Larkin was in many ways a fairly unpleasant character.

Bob has been commissioned to write a life of Stalin. He likes the idea. Prawn and artichoke mayonnaise; chicken, new potatoes, spinach; gooseberry fool and strawberries, meringues; Bob (now committed to white wine for health reasons) drank most of a bottle of Südtiroler Chardonnay (praised highly by him); Liddie and V Maximino de Trentino. Enjoyable party. John drove them to Westbury for the 5.30 train.

Monday, 8 June

I saw Lister about a damaged lower plate, which he put right easily. He wore white gloves, as does Sussman these days says V, to guard against AIDS.

Tuesday, 9 June

V to London to see Eve Disher's show at Foyle's Gallery. This she greatly enjoyed and was impressed by the Gallery. She gave Liz [Longford], Tristram, Virginia luncheon at Lansdowne Club.

Last year William (Bill) B. Stone (Indiana State University), Secretary of the AP Society of Kalamazoo, wrote to say he and his wife would be in England in May, could they call. He rang up some days ago and received rather less than ecstatic welcome, it being a very full week here with the Election. He had invitation to tea this afternoon. Tall, bespectacled; Mrs Stone (Jane), short, grey-haired, severely dressed. They had been on a canal tour run by Anglophil American, enjoyed it. This is only their second trip to England. They have three grown-up children. Bill Stone himself is a specialist on the American Realists (Dreiser, Norris). After giving all this information he added: 'Jane is Jewish. I'm of English descent, but no trouble with either family when we got married, because a lot of American Jews took the name of Stone instead of Stein.'

Conversation was rather heavy going, as not seldom with fans, it is somewhat mysterious why he should be so keen on my books. However, keen Bill Stone certainly is, having got into touch with London AP Society (of which I knew nothing), run by an Australian called McNulty. The latter's name strikes a faint chord, possibly a fan letter from Australia some years ago. Bill Stone remarked with truth: 'It takes an Australian or an American to start a Society like that.' The Stones reminded me of American Paris expatriates of the 1920s, a community which produced many married couples of their type. They were yet another reminder that one's novels are something quite separate from oneself and have a life of their own in which one only partially partakes.

Thursday, 11 June

Election Day. V drove us to vote at the mobile voting booth, set up on these occasions in the field by Whatley church, a pretty spot. I am fond of our little architecturally perfect neo-gothick (1846) church, tho' can't repress occasional yearnings for existing in the shadow of a mediaeval edifice like Whatley, with its effigy tomb of Sir Oliver de Servington. Quite a lot of people were arriving to vote when we turned up about 11 a.m. In the afternoon Humphries (engineer who said it is not necessary to have the lake annually inspected) rang to ask if his colleague, Peter Kydd, could see the lake with a view to finding out its potential for harnessing hydraulic power. Humphries mentioned at the time he might request this, tho' I explained I was not interested. He said he would like to go into it all the same. Seems no objection so Kydd is coming on Tuesday.

Friday, 12 June

The Tories are in again with more than one hundred majority. A triumph for Mrs Thatcher. Cicely McCall (friend of E. M. Delafield) came to tea, with whom V wanted to discuss certain Delafield points. She is eighty-five, tall, white-haired, thinking nothing of driving down here from Norfolk where she lives. She was formerly in charge of a delinquent girls' home. A nice, interesting type of capable woman. She is particularly keen on trees. Wyndham Ketton-Cremer, fellow East Anglican resident, had helped her about some comparatively antique document on subject of arboriculture which she possesses.

Sunday, 14 June

Mr Travis, of The Chantry, Gentle Street, Frome, most kindly brought parcel addressed to me here, wrongly delivered at his house about a month ago. When opened turned out to be bottle of port, a present from Ian Chapman of Hodder & Stoughton, who runs that firm's paperbacks, a gift to celebrate paperback publication of *The Fisher King*. Post Office as a rule are pretty good about getting mail with our name on it delivered here, even if directed to 'Frome', rather than 'near Frome', but this went by Red Star (i.e. by rail), whose delivery man naturally didn't know there was a house in Frome, also one four miles away, of that name. On top of that Mr Travis himself had only recently bought house in Gentle Street, moving in over weekends so the port (Dow's Thirty Years Old) languished in house next door, where it was taken in, until now. Called up Chapman, profusely apologized for apparently disregarding graceful gift.

Giving name of The Chantry to a house in Gentle Street incredibly stupid act of former Rector of Chantry, Revd A. Dobbie-Bateman (ex-Treasury with CB), who had taken Orders on retirement from Civil Service. A peculiarly obtuse man, like almost everyone else I have ever come across from the Treasury (from which, to be fair, he was eventually shunted out). There may be intelligent members of the Treasury. I can only say that I have never met one who was not a bloody fool in one form or another. Dobbie-Bateman could reduce the simplest question at a parish meeting to utter confusion within a matter of minutes. Douglas Jerrold (of Eyre & Spottiswoode, but ex-Treasury) the same dealing with elementary publishing matters. Bullard, boneheaded little man, who lived on first floor of 47 Great Ormond Street where we had top flat when first married (again to be fair, Bullard too shunted out of Treasury). If pressed I could almost certainly think of yet more unconscionable Treasury dolts.

Monday, 15 June

Saw Lister. Have to see him again next week, as he must acquire small appliance he calls a 'collar' for stud of screw refixed in lower plate. His Sagittarian/Capricornian son is called Oliver.

Curious incident yesterday. David Moore, of The Lodge, working in kitchen garden across the road, saw man come out of The Lodge, none of the Moore family being in at the time. The man, hippy type, went up the road towards the church, apparently dropping something like a parcel on the way. This object turned out to be Moores' radio. David tracked this figure to the churchyard, where he was consuming ham, flan, two cans of drink, removed from Moores' refrigerator. There was some sort of altercation at end of which (how violent remains obscure) David summoned police, who took charge of man, evidently under influence of drugs. Merrie England.

Tuesday, 16 June

As agreed, young man from engineers Mander, Raikes & Marshall, Bristol, Peter Kydd, came to see lake. Explained I was not interested in making improvements there, had no money to spend now and above all wished to avoid correspondence, sales talk. Cannot bear to think what complications in way of riparian ownership any such enterprises might lead to. John tells me there is much interest these days in hydraulic methods of saving energy in various forms. Some muddle between Bruce Hunter and his secretary through which *Aubrey* proofs (for cutting down corrections previously made) were not sent. More than ever clear ill aspect of Aubrey's stars hovers over book's reprinting.

Monday, 22 June

Hoodoo continues to haunt *Aubrey* proofs, which did not arrive until Saturday. John has now taken them back to London. Hope latest corrections (prepared on my own edition before proofs came back) will settle things once for all.

Saw Lister this morning, who managed to get plate stuck to gum while setting, accordingly had to cut it out, so must see him again, which is tedious. In small yard at side of waiting-room surgery (Willow Grange attractive cul-de-sac with river running opposite house) lives a cock called Henry, great character, who taps on window where secretaries sit, sulking when his breakfast is late. He is brownish speckled colour, rather like huge bantam.

Bill Stone (secretary, AP Society, Kalamazoo) sent nice card thanking for visit, his wife (instancing by name some half a dozen notable American writers she had met) saying what a pleasant experience to meet writer who was sober. In evening V and I watched on TV first instalment of Alison Lurie's *Imaginary Friends*, shot in three programmes of one hour, to which I shall return after seeing the lot.

Thursday, 25 June

V suffering from stiff knee, diagnosed as consequence of fall two months ago or more, has been to Mrs Gould for treatment, who says knee had wrench, nothing serious (which I feared), will recover in due course, exercises prescribed.

Reread Vidia Naipaul's *The Enigma of Arrival*, this time skipping all Trinidad, early life material, treating residence at Wilsford as entity in itself. This makes a much better, more coherent, book. I read last section, but that too should be omitted to achieve effect I prefer. Bits unrelated to Wilsford, perfectly all right in their own way, interfere with exceptionally interesting account Vidia gives of individual life, relationships, experienced during Wilsford period. I can think of nothing quite like it in description of life, people, in English countryside today. Of course Vidia anxious to make point that, thinking of himself as rootless, the country people indigenous, he found the country people round about almost equally rootless. Mere fact of his origins sufficient for reader to grasp the writer's own position.

Reader's attention should be concentrated on the picture given, without disturbance of having to contemplate what existence might have been like in Trinidad. Anyway, we have heard about Trinidad from Vidia time and again already. What strikes one is the parade of rural characters observed from outside, without inherent awareness of the sort of persons they are, which someone brought up in England would possess, anyway up to a point. One sees how interesting same kind of investigation would be if concentrated on, say, inhabitants of Chantry, even then one would have all manner of inner knowledge, prejudice, which would affect clinical nature of judgements made. The vignette of Julian Jebb (Alan) certainly not very friendly, at same time could hardly be said to be wholly untrue, except in omitting Julian's considerable reputation as TV producer/book-critic.

I think Vidia, understandably, does not grasp complications of various worlds Julian touched, social, intellectual, nor circumstances (far from easy) of his RC Bellocian background, implications that can be dealt with less effectively by purely external approach used on country people round Wilsford. Perhaps, if one knew latter more intimately as individuals, account of them, too, might not be beyond criticism, even if collective impression convincing. In same way Julian's extreme liveliness as a companion does not come over. None the less Wilsford sections of *The Enigma* seem to me a good, original piece of observation.

V and I watched third instalment of *Imaginary Friends*, completing the story. On balance amusing short series, even if, for those knowing Alison's novel, a good deal is lost; chiefly grim, even sinister, atmosphere of the American scene, also far more credible in upstate New York than a few miles from Norwich. On the whole acting good, especially Verena, the girl medium, who believes herself in touch with beings from Space, and her aunt (Billie Whitelaw).

Film suffered from incurable English theatrical tendency to make everything comic, even farcical. Also began badly, perhaps inevitable difficulty of American academic life being so different from British academic institutions and personnel. The end, when the elderly don who has gone mad is visited in his place of partial confinement by younger don concerned in the original anthropological project, well done, but, by a curiously inept piece of dialogue, the two of them talk of 'walking by the pool', so that the viewer naturally expects the elder don to show he is still unhinged by pushing younger one into the water. This, which would have made excellent climax, never takes place. Musical accompaniment to the film, also of vaguely comic order, could not have been more awful.

Monday, 29 June

Saw Lister, who has now, I hope, fixed plate. He told story of Henry, the cock, a Marram (Marram eggs particularly good) who lives in surgery backyard. Henry simply arrived, no one knowing whence he came, possibly from a kind of hostel down by the Marston road, where a fox broke in, putting poultry in disarray; possibly just escaped from Frome Market, only short way away. He set himself up in the yard as a powerful personality.

Reviewed Vol. IV of D. H. Lawrence *Letters* (up to standard), also sent Collected Edition *Women in Love*, appalling volume designed to be 'evaluated' rather than read as novel; a numeral at every 5th line of text (like verses of the Bible); 200 pp. of Introduction: Appendices; Textual Apparatus. How utterly fatuous. This, I suppose logical outcome of 'teaching' English, scourge to which Lawrence particularly subject, would have absolutely infuriated him. I reread *Women in Love*. Its flaw is lack of credibility in accepting main characters presented as local group in rural Derbyshire.

The two sisters individually convincing (*The Sisters*, which novel was originally to have been called, better title). Gerald Crich all right on his own, not *vis-à-vis* Birkin, who, like all Lawrence's self-images in his novels, never judged by same standards as other characters; indeed only possible to think of as Lawrence himself, with his overweening narcissism. One accepts that Birkin was bisexual, with strong leaning towards homosexuality, but individual homosexual relationship with Crich never comes off. One feels throughout that Crich, given the man he was, would have behaved differently, either more, or less, prepared to muck in with Birkin's homosexual fantasies, antics.

Again, Hermione Roddice, in certain respects savagely lifelike representation of Lady Ottoline Morrell, merely made baronet's only child in isolated Derbyshire. Remove Ottoline's ducal background (even allowing for her half-brother, not her father, being duke), her somewhat farcical married life, her intellectual pretensions (Henry Lamb, who had an affair with her, said she never really progressed beyond the stage of editions of poetry bound in limp leather), her grotesque salon, too much goes west for true resemblance, what remains is unconvincing on its own, however photographic. In rather same way Halliday/Pussum couple have some resemblance to Philip Heseltine and his wife when together (or so I imagine, having seen wife only once, I think, after she left Heseltine), all set out in as unfriendly a manner as possible, omitting Heseltine's wit, talent as musician. Libidnikov (utterly wrongly identified here) in fact projection of Boris Christov, White Russian emigré, about whom I cannot remember much, except he was married to girl called Phil Crocker, for whom Constant Lambert had, I think, slight (unconsummated) fancy. Christov great womanizer (hence Libidnikov), used to stroll round Woolworth's marking down girls. Can't remember how he kept body and soul together. His wife (eventually did herself in) used occasionally to be left in charge of the Varda bookshop, heroine of someone asking: 'Have you a copy of *Prometheus Unbound*?' to which Phil Christov replied: 'No, but I'm almost sure I've seen a bound copy on the shelves.'

Women in Love curious, in places powerful, best in such incidents as buying second-hand chair, then trying to give it to miner and his fiancée, with embarrassing result they won't accept it. Red-hot emotions as usual much overdone, tho' I suppose could be argued people to some extent behave like that nowadays, breaking up marriages because sexual relations not for the moment absolutely ideal. That would, in fact, have greatly disturbed Lawrence himself. The reader always, so to speak, tripping over Lawrence self-image, which at once reduces conviction, much of novel being in any case ludicrously melodramatic. None of the characters appears to have any other life than their torrid relationships with each other. One recognizes Lawrence able novelist of considerable potential, but patchiness always mars his works. Some of the short stories he brings off well; good minor poet; Letters best of all. Like Virginia Woolf, so infinitely to be preferred in Diaries and Letters to novels.

Tuesday, 30 June

Reread *All's Well that Ends Well*, curiously unpleasant play, at same time has to be agreed many examples in real life of nice girls determined to marry awful men. Bertram, apart from good looks, reputation of having fought well against the Florentines, does not possess a redeeming feature. To his other unpleasantness he adds specific statement that he does not like cats. Parolles says to the King: 'I am a poor man, at your Majesty's command.' At which the old courtier Lafeu comments: 'He's a good drum, lord, but a naughty orator.' This exchange possibly gave Lewis Carroll the King of Hearts remarking to the Mad Hatter (who has just said 'I am a poor man'): 'You are certainly a very poor speaker.'

Wednesday, 1 July

Telephone rang about 2.40 a.m. V reported voice asked for me in French, to which she replied in French '*De la part de qui?*' (suspecting, no doubt rightly, the imbecile fan), telling him to ring again at 9 o'clock. No later call.

Friday, 3 July

I saw Lister about damaged plate. Have to see him today week. I read in paper that Paul Hamlyn has sold Octopus (the group to which Heinemann belongs) to Reed International, whose property I now accordingly become. In the afternoon a character announcing himself as Henry Mee rang, saying he was a painter, had painted the Queen, various other eminent figures, for a show to be put on by English Speaking Union, and wanted to include myself. I was rather unforthcoming about this, as so many crackpots get in touch with one. Mee said he had a friend, one Maria McCassetty, who knew Tristram. He would be prepared to come down, would need only four sittings, as he works largely from drawings, photographs. I told him to write about it, if possible enclose reproductions of his work, so that I could think things over. He is known to be fan of mine, so his choice reasonable for writer among his group of notabilities. He sounded comparatively young, not very good at expressing himself. He said HM suggested he should paint Lord Carrington, which one presumes to be true.

Wednesday, 8 July

Vanessa Berridge, editing *Country Homes & Interiors*, was to have done an interview linked with *The Album* this afternoon. In the event she was indisposed, so only the photographer, Alastair Morrison, with Associate Editor Jackie Cole (female) arrived. Vanessa Berridge is to appear on some later occasion. Morrison was youngish, big, red curly hair, slight beard, he had started life in Bank of England. Jackie Cole, thin, pony-tailed hair, Bermuda-type shorts. They belonged to the arranging-of-objects-to-a-millimetre school of photography, arriving about 3 p.m. began by bringing a lot of things from the house out on to the terrace, going down to the lake (where we did not accompany them), staying until about 7.45 p.m., by which time we were both feeling somewhat exhausted, especially V bearing brunt of impact, so I indicated in plainest terms it was time for them to go. Paper has alleged circulation of 90,000, which, even allowing for slight exaggeration, surprised me, as circulation figures public property.

Friday, 10 July

Signed contract for Portuguese translation of *Dance* (Globo). Dr Anthony Cole, Royal Military Academy, Sandhurst, asked for recollections of serving with Intelligence Corps, as writing Corps's history. Referred him to my Memoirs. Rather tedious session with Lister in evening. To be hoped plate has at last been put right.

Wednesday, 15 July

Virginia, down to keep an eye on The Stables garden, lunched with us at Chewton Dairies, favourite haunt of hers (which I had not seen). Dairies, about eight miles from here, look rather like stable-block, outbuildings, of large country house. One of these blocks a cheese factory, on first floor of which restaurant installed. On one side of this restaurant large windows look down on to ground floor, where cheese is being made. People, before or after eating, stand transfixed at this process taking place. Food (I had chicken pie, salad) not at all bad, glasses of white wine from local Pilton vineyard, also all right. Place very full, two coaches having just arrived, ceiling too low, therefore awful row. In evening photographer Alastair Morrison, who came for *Country Homes & Interiors*, rang to say also commissioned for the *Mail on Sunday* pictures for interview.

Thursday, 16 July

Mail on Sunday Colour Supplement *You* sent Peter Lewis to do interview. Some uncertainty whether this was same Peter Lewis who did End-of-Sequence interview for *Dance* in *Daily Mail* years ago (being mildly rude, in spite of having been given cucumber sandwiches), and/or produced goodish life in photographs of George Orwell. On arrival turned out somewhat gnome-like figure, probably in early sixties, longish white hair, had written Orwell book. I thought him quite unlike disobliging earlier interviewer, remembered as much less elderly man some dozen years ago. V, however, immediately identified him as same. As I thought him different, no difficulty in making myself agreeable, certainly would have been the case otherwise. Now wholly accept V right. Up at Wadham during Wardenship of Maurice Bowra. That had been after doing National Service. Brought with him set of *The Album* proofs (journalists always getting these things before one does oneself) which looked satisfactory. Remains to be seen if anything will appear in *Mail on Sunday*, if so, whether or not good-mannered.

Saturday, 18 July

Request arrived from the Frome Sunday Afternoon Theatre Company (R. Thomas, 1a Shepherd's Barton, Frome) to make, by the lake and in big grotto, film about 'Death and Resurrection', from book on that subject by one Rogan Taylor, whoever he may be. This seemed to deserve encouragement, so gave permission.

Wednesday, 22 July

V sent book for review by *DT* about the Hon. Kitty Pakenham, wife of 1st Duke of Wellington, written by Joan Wilson, former librarian at Stratfield Saye, where she presumably succeeded Francis Needham (Jack Spraggon to Gerry Wellington's Earl of Scamperdale). Book not well done, full of clichés, imaginary descriptions, etc., in fact worst form of biographical writing (tho' Liz Longford in Introduction inexplicably describes it as 'scholarly', than which it could not be less), in any case only going as far as Waterloo, when what happened later at least as important biographically, if subject to be judged worth writing about at all, which it is. V diagnosed author as getting tired, unable to cope with Kitty Wellington's later years. A few facts produced are, however, of some interest. Legend current that when Wellington was just Arthur Wellesley, young officer (at one moment in 41st, later The Welch Regiment), with no apparent future, the Longfords, having frozen him off, then framed him a dozen years later, after he had become famous. Seems no reason whatever to suppose that true (tho' I think I first heard version from Pakenham sources, probably Pansy).

When Wellington had been serving in India for some years, a female friend sounded him on his feelings. By that time he could easily have said he had given up hope, without least imputation of having behaved badly. On the contrary, he still expressed keenness. Wellington also alleged to have recognized he was not married-man type, thought marriage with a girl he knew from similar background, whose brothers he liked, best to be hoped for. If that were true, marriage from the start was one of well-disposed convenience. Surprising, therefore, when they were wed, he showed himself from that very moment so disagreeable. This so acute that his grandson destroyed many of the Duke's letters to his wife. That seems to suggest disappointment rather than taking things cold-bloodedly. V thinks Kitty (by then thirty-three), silly, tactless, bad manager, but kind, especially to children. In last respect certainly looks as if she might have given home to one of her husband's earlier by-blows.

Story about her being marked with smallpox appears untrue. Probably had effects suggested above when younger, unnoticed at the time for a small lively girl in her early twenties, less tolerable in a woman between thirty and forty. Why Wellington, having determined to go through with marriage, did not attempt to make a better job of it, remains unexplained, an aspect never gone into in this biography. Probably bed a disappointment after being on his own with other men's wives. This subject, not an uninteresting one, required a writer of infinitely more intelligence, subtlety, understanding of human character than the writer possesses. Poor Kitty must immediately have turned out to show all the characteristics that most irritated her husband, notably bad housekeeping.

Telephone call from one Terry Yorke, living in Dead Woman's Bottom, to ask if we could give information of any sort about the Fussells [agricultural ironmasters who built The Chantry in 1826], as his son John working on 'project' on that subject. Interesting that former landowners (e.g. recent case of A-level pupil writing about Dymokes in Lincolnshire) now being widely used for educational researches. Very sensible. V suggested the boy or his father might consult my Memoirs, where some account of the Fussells and this house is given.

Thursday, 23 July

Photographer Alastair Morrison reappeared to take pictures for the *Mail on Sunday* colour magazine *You*, bringing with him small, rather depressed, somewhat punk assistant named Byron. Billed for 2 o'clock, they arrived late, but away by 3.30, triumph of speed.

Tuesday, 28 July

Vanessa Berridge, Editress of *Country Homes & Interiors*, came for interview about *The Album*. Made good impression. V thought she might be pregnant. At dinner we drank bottle of champagne swopped for bottle of port presented by Hodders on publication of *The Fisher King* in paperback, port suiting neither of us. It was called Canard-Duchêne (did not appear in Cyril Ray's book on champagne), tasted slightly peculiar, by no means Bollinger '78. [No ill effects following day.]

Friday, 31 July

Lower plate again wrong, saw Lister (construction pedants object to; Latin, Shakespeare, justify), must see him once more in fortnight's time. Letter from Roy Jenkins saying he was disappointed to find I already possessed Oxford Hon. D. Litt., as he had wished this to be his first act as new Chancellor of University. Copy of *The Album* arrived, which I think well done.

Sunday, 2 August

We watched last instalment of four BBC TV Hemingway programmes, none particularly good. I should have thought information provided could easily have been conveyed in three, possibly two. All the same, glad to see certain individuals who gave reminiscences: Hemingway's sister Sunny; son, Bumby; Malcolm Cowley; Morley Callaghan; the White Hunter (now about sixty), Hemingway employed, Dennis Zaphiro, whose voice sounded very upper-class after the others. He also gave excellent account of Hemingway. All Spaniards who appeared, natural television personalities. Hemingway in many aspects dreadful man, writing poor stuff from *For Whom the Bell Tolls* onwards (except perhaps *Moveable Feast*, dating from earlier period, therefore less contaminated by conceit). All the same one feels he deserves his fame, Nobel Prize, etc., on strength of first impact. Extraordinary fatuity of his behaviour, self-conscious grin, etc., latterly extremely painful. A sad story.

Monday, 3 August

Mrs Futcher (who 'does' for The Stables) came up to the house about 3.30 p.m. to say that between putting dustbins out this morning, her arrival at The Stables this afternoon, she found door into Stoney Lane broken in. Three boys from Frome asked to go down to the lake about lunch-time, one of them had been here before, so hardly likely their responsibility. Also door appeared to have been pushed in from lane side. Got in touch with Mildav.

Tuesday, 4 August

Mr Millard of that firm came in afternoon to examine door by The Stables. We agreed two slotted-in bars the answer, when lower half of door repaired, then lock to prevent door being lifted off hinges (key kept in Stables hall).

David Twiston-Davies rang from *Telegraph*. He is now on obit page, wanted me to write about Igor Vinogradoff, just dcd. Did not feel up to this, knowing little or nothing about Igor's early life, except that he wanted to marry Julian Morrell (daughter of Lady Ottoline), which they only brought off after both had been married for years to other people. Igor was in BBC at one period (during war, I think), where his total nonchalance indicated he would be sacked sooner or later, probably sooner. This he continually escaped, at last sent for by Director General with that aim in mind. Igor came gasping into the DG's room: 'Give me a cigarette, please – nerves completely shattered – that lift – first took me to top floor – then to ground floor again – too high again – then too low –' At this point Igor looked at his watch. 'Good God, I have an appointment I mustn't miss. I'm afraid I can't stay another second – so sorry.' Got up, left the room before DG could utter a word. I suggested Igor's son-in-law, Anthony Hobson, might write obit.

Thursday, 6 August

Two press-cuttings, congratulatory letter from V's cousin David Rhys on account of a Mr Anthony Powell having received the Royal Victoria Medal (silver) at Sandringham, where no doubt he works. Looks as if Anthony Hobson did write Igor Vinogradoff's obit in *DT*, as it mentions Igor advised Sotheby's about Russian books.

Friday, 7 August

Letter from Bruce Hunter saying Chatto (Hogarth Press) will now publish *Aubrey* paperback in February next year. Although one always prefers to have book out sooner rather than later, something to be said for avoiding Christmas rush, especially for this particular book.

Saturday, 8 August

At behest of two characters making appeal in *TLS*, wrote to Secretary of State for Education (Kenneth Baker) urging him to safeguard Latin in 'new curriculum'.

Monday, 10 August

Dotty fan Keith Green rang yesterday about 9 a.m. Told him he ought to see psychiatrist. He said he had. I suggested he see him again, hung up. I have been going through *The Album* slowly, in fact taking three days. Impressed with amount covered, how well. The one slip, where paragraph opening with FM Montgomery's unexpectedly sensitive hands (apropos of Zutphen being on the map Monty was expounding), goes on (after three dots) to speak of Sir Philip Sidney being the sort of man Vigny had in mind who had become a soldier because he thought that right, rather than because he liked it. Sidney is not mentioned here, so that appears to refer to Monty inconceivable in any other profession than the military one. Doubt, however, whether any reviewer will notice this. V informed Jamie Camplin of oversight (for which I am to blame, missing it in proof). I think rightly he is against erratum slip.

Friday, 14 August

Saw Lister twice, hope plate finally put right. Anthony Hobson rang in evening. V talked to him. Tanya suffering from recurrence of cancer trouble in back resulting from fall, hopes to return home next week after treatment. Sounds rather worrying.

Saturday, 15 August

Long-arranged luncheon party with John (The Congressman) and Rosemary Monagan took place at the Bridge House, Nunney. Monagans arrived about midday. They are staying in London with their friend Kenneth Bradshaw, just retired (KCB) as Clerk of House of Commons, who brought them down in his car. He is known by us as The Regicide, as said to be descended from John Bradshaw, who signed death-warrant of King Charles I; in fact must at best be collateral, as that Bradshaw produced only two daughters. The John Bradshaw who formerly owned house in Presteigne now the Radnorshire Arms (where we once spent a night) different family, at least different branch from Regicide's, with whom sometimes confused.

Haligan's in Frome turned out not to do luncheons on Saturdays, so it was arranged for luncheon party to take place at the Bridge House, Nunney, overlooking the river (run by Mr and Mrs Edgeley, latter known to V through Women's Institute), said to be good. V, who was a shade off colour, not greatly impressed. John [Powell] and I thought it all right so far as 'English fare' goes: anchovy eggs (other openers); roast beef, Yorkshire pudding; damson tart (various other puddings); '79 claret not very exciting, to put it mildly. Monagans in good form, The Congressman shade aged, otherwise lively. Writing book about Judge Holmes, son of Oliver Wendell Holmes, American worthy, who lived into his

nineties, of whom one had vaguely heard. Ken Bradshaw, bachelor, RC, intelligent, much more amusing figure than expected. Only House of Commons Clerk known hitherto was Douglas Gordon, who, Ken Bradshaw said, had been on point of retiring when he himself took on the job. Douglas Gordon died more or less in Bradshaw's arms (heart failure) when both were on some parliamentary jaunt in Poland. Bradshaw obviously aware Douglas Gordon bit of a joke. He was always known by the Lloyd brothers as the Oc Conc (a friend once referred to Gordon as an 'occasional concubine'). The Monagans had a look at Nunney Castle after luncheon, then returned to the house for tea, where I presented them and Bradshaw (fan) with *Iron Aspidistra*. Enjoyable, if tiring, day.

Sunday, 16 August

Sir Charles and Lady Pickthorn, who live in the exceptionally pretty eighteenth-century Nunney Manor (which at one moment Evelyn Waugh contemplated buying, would not have been big enough for his family), just by Castle, came for pre-luncheon drinks, bringing Primrose Palmer, Felicia Lamb's daughter. When the Pickthorns arrived in Nunney they asked us to dinner, we (on Rupert Hart-Davis's principle that one knew enough people already) opting out. Helen Pickthorn (daughter of Sir James Mann, armour expert, Director of Wallace Collection) knew Felicia at some earlier stage of their lives. Charles Pickthorn, retired merchant banker, son of high-powered die-hard Tory MP, academic, who used to interest himself in the Poles during the war. I think Alick Dru knew elder Pickthorn in private life. Owing to Helen Pickthorn's obsession with Felicia she rang to say Primrose Palmer was staying with them, so we had to ask them in. Primrose nice, superlatively untidy girl, looking like her aunt Henrietta Phipps, rather than her mother. She is secretary to the well-known blind journalist, T. E. Utley, who seems to be now running obits for *The Times*. Until recently was on *DT*.

Tuesday, 18 August

Two characters, mid twenties, from Frome Sunday Afternoon Theatre Company, came about 10 a.m. to shoot film about 'Death and Resurrection' in the large grotto: R. Thomas, incipient beard; Mike Jones, fair curly hair. Warm, dull day, not ideal for photography, so agreed they should return next sunny day. I asked if we could have video of result, which they seemed to think feasible.

Thursday, 20 August

The two Resurrection Men arrived again to spend day in the grotto. Only one

appeared later to announce they had checked out. He said: 'Mike didn't want to come up to the house because his face was all covered with blue paint.' I am curious to know what form the film took, hope if any trespassers were about they were terrified out of their lives by apparitions at the grotto. In afternoon Marion Brace came for interview about *The Album* for *Observer Weekend*. One could have preferred *Colour Supplement* or *Review*, but better than nothing. Nice, pretty, reasonably intelligent, married, twenty-eight, keen on cats, her own 'two South London cats'.

Friday, 21 August

V's sister Pansy, staying with Helen Asquith at Mells, came to tea. Pansy over from Rome, where she gives help to English-speaking visitors at the entrance of St Peter's. She looked better than when last seen, indeed in excellent form, more unable than ever to understand that anyone but herself could conceivably be instructed in any known subject.

We talked of Cynthia Asquith (J. M. Barrie's secretary), a life of whom I recently reviewed. I never met her, seen once only at party of Augustus John's, where Hope-Johnstone blew smoke rings for one of her children, whichever child it was saying: 'Now blow square ones.' Pansy and Henry Lamb had known Cynthia Asquith quite well, both liking her. I was interested in this, particularly that Henry (eclectic in his likings) approved, as book did not give wholly pleasant picture of her.

Cynthia Asquith's story became very macabre when Barrie entered, who was indeed a most macabre man. Pansy (now RC for some years) had been to summer quarters of English seminary in Rome, up by Lake Albano, nice, where she met the two Goodman granddaughters of Julian Vinogradoff (née Morrell). They were thrilled to come across someone who had known their great-grandmother, Lady Ottoline, in the flesh (if Lady Ottoline's integument could be so called). Pansy going to Whitfield where her sister Mary's eightieth birthday is being celebrated (which it is hoped will not take the form of Mary washing up for a hundred guests), then on to Tullynally, energetic for eighty-three.

Wednesday, 26 August

Virginia down for The Stables garden, lunched with us at the Bridge House, food good (V and I onion soup, Virginia anchovy eggs: V and I navarin of lamb, Virginia sole; all coffee ices). Stockwells had enjoyable time in Italy. Virginia and Georgia, in a church in Florence, thought several people were looking at a relic, so joined them, turned out to be actual corpse, presumably some relation. Georgia went away at first, rather horrified, then returned to have good look. Georgia did well in A levels,

which she reported to us, also said she was hooked on *Dance*, of which she has now read first three or four vols. Family on their way separately to stay with Mounts in Pembrokeshire.

Sunday, 30 August

Read Conrad Russell's *Letters* (ed. Giana Blakiston, his niece), borrowed from Frome library. Conrad Russell (1873–1942) lived at Little Claveys, Mells, about a mile from here, where he farmed. Survivor from Raymond Asquith generation, proposed to Katharine Asquith when Raymond Asquith killed (as had been most of Conrad Russell's contemporaries). Made enough money in the City to exist on, never married, kept going on sentimental passions for Katharine Asquith nearby, Diana Cooper, latterly Daphne Weymouth (Bath, Fielding). His name still something of a legend when we first came down here. At the onset the *Letters* (reasonably well edited by Giana, if rather meagre so far as notes are concerned) got one down by the enormous self-satisfaction characteristic of Russell family, to some extent also of his whole generation, class, combined with a good many protestations on his own part of extreme humility, etc. thrown in.

By the end of the book, however, one did come to think he was a nice man, extremely well up in Shakespeare, the Classics, funny about a lot of things, especially Evelyn Waugh's pretensions (Evelyn always asked if he should 'bring his man', when he went to stay at Mells, where he went quite often). Greatly disliking *Brideshead*, Conrad Russell made point (which never occurred to me) that, in the (unlikely) event of the Flytes having been 'barons since Agincourt', the barony transmitted to 'heirs general', it would not have gone automatically to the eldest daughter, but fallen into abeyance between the two daughters. Conrad Russell might have added that, if not absolutely impossible, extreme improbability of barony being transmitted father-to-son in direct line in same family without male heir being nephew or cousin, or daughter existing through whom by marriage barony would potentially pass to another family at an earlier stage. For instance, earldom of Derby, cf. several similar titles, baronies remaining in abeyance, or being called out of abeyance, so far as one can see without making close study of the matter. Somebody living here locally, I can't remember who, said Evelyn annoyed Conrad Russell by remarking: 'What a pretty gardener you have.' Russell afterwards commenting: 'No, not really quite a gentleman.' He always referred to Evelyn as Mr Wu, play about a sinister Chinaman in London, which I can just remember being talked about *c.* 1912. Mr Wu was also what the Prime Minister Asquith called Edward Montagu when writing to his girlfriend Venetia Stanley (who subsequently married Montagu).

Monday, 31 August

Stockwells looked in for luncheon on way back from Pembrokeshire. I made curry for seven. Ferdie Mount appears to be giving up the *Spectator*. Georgia and Archie driving together in one car, taking turns at the wheel. Reread *The Tempest*. Prospero makes prototypical bore's threat at close of play:

> Sir, I invite your highness and your train
> To my poor cell, where you shall take your rest
> For this one night, which, part of it, I'll waste
> With such discourse as, I do not doubt, shall make it
> Go quick away; the story of my life . . .

Mr Warrington could not improve on that.

Wednesday, 2 September

Reviewed Barbara Skelton's *Tears Before Bedtime*, Memoirs/Diary of her career until 1953, that is before she left Cyril Connolly as husband to marry George (Lord) Weidenfeld. Early life rather vague, cliché-ridden. After becoming a model (having apparently at age of seventeen been seduced by rich friend of her father's), set up in flat in Crawford Street, off Baker Street. She puts down what happens with a good deal of ability, complete disregard for what anyone might think of her. Result extremely lively. Makes no bones about causing trouble for its own sake, indeed resemblance to Pamela Flitton could hardly be more emphasized. Cyril's similar taste for conflict met its match when they lived together, in due course married. Her account of Cyril lying in bed chewing the sheets vivid to a degree. At the same time, one believes her in a way, when she insists she is shy, anxious to learn, etc. Her father regular soldier (apparently Gunner, from 1939 Army List), mother from the chorus, Danish blood, which would account for her own style of blonde looks. I think only some curious intellectual twist in herself prevented her from becoming a straight tart of slightly superior sort (if, indeed, it can be said she did rise above that), something that is always at the back of her own mind, giving Cyril dominance over her by (for instance) correcting her speech. I shall be interested to see how book is received. She is fairly rude about Peter Quennell* (who passed her on to Cyril, after apparently sharing her with several others at the same time during the war). Cyril's encouragement of his wife's affair with King Farouk of Egypt puts him within hail of the ponce area; material eminently suitable for Elizabethan, Caroline, comedy. There will probably be a chorus of shocked horror on the part of reviewers (always

* Sir Peter Quennell (1903–1993)

essence of sanctimoniousness), amongst whom Quennell might easily figure.

Sunday, 6 September

Driven by John, we lunched with the Hobsons at The Glebe House, Whitsbury, V brilliantly remembering it was Anthony Hobson's birthday. Best we could do was to take first two vols of *Dance* in Finnish, as rather long-range bibliographical offering, the Finnish jacket of *Upbringing* (Eton boy?) being indeed notable. Tanya, having had tiring previous day, retired to bed in room on ground floor next to drawing-room. We saw her there, not looking too bad, I thought, tho' perhaps being rather flushed made her seem better than she really felt, as V thought. Emma Hobson, in some publishing firm, present, rather *distraite*, probably in love. Frances Partridge staying, now eighty-seven, still in extremely good form, last survivor of genuine Bloomsburies (even if somewhat younger than inner élite, bullied by them), through marriage to Ralph Partridge, love of Lytton Strachey ('Lytton's pathic', as Hope-Johnstone used to call him). Probably great relief for Frances to be now on her own, out of reach of the old Bloomsbury ruling gang, she herself now famous personality who took to writing at the age of eighty. Talk about Barbara Skelton's book, which only V and I had read. Large chunk of Frances Partridge's published *Diary* had been quoted as one of Babs's chapter-heads, described her own hair-raising behaviour at the Campbells (Robin Campbell's wife, of course, Lady Mary St Clair Erskine, as opposed to Honble Mary Ormsby-Gore, now Mayall) at Stokke, occasion when Babs made them all rise at 7 a.m., then said she was too sleepy to get out of bed, having taken sleeping pill night before. When they took her in to catch 11 o'clock train, forgot her basket, for which she had to return to the house; finally got away after 1 o'clock. Babs's own description of all this on the whole more damaging than anyone else's so far as she herself concerned. Excellent claret (something Barton, '76).

Enjoyable day, but both very tired after our return. None the less watched *The Happy Valley*, TV film about Lord Erroll's murder in Kenya seen through eyes of sixteen-year-old girl Juanita Carberry, daughter of horrible John Carberry (disclaimed Lord Carbery). Really not too bad, giving good idea of the Kenya that has been called 'Ealing-on-the-Equator', as opposed to mountains, valleys, Masai, etc., apt to make up background of most Kenya films. The actor playing John Carberry not at all unlike him, as I remember the real Lord Carbery (who changed his name) when met on plane back from Marseilles. Actual man even nastier, more sinister, with phoney American accent. As usual fair number of anachronisms in the dialogue, behaviour, for instance, more kissing than would have taken place as social greeting at that date (1940–1). Delves Broughton altogether unlike true Delves Broughton in appearance, probably difficult to portray. In circumstances actor chosen got by. I had hoped for representation of some of the many people involved in the case with whom I had some acquaintance, but cast strictly limited in number. Juanita Carberry (Holly Aird) rather good, with keen sense of timing. Lady Delamere (Delamere her fourth husband) then wife of Jock Delves Broughton, Erroll's self-proclaimed murderer, had her own death in this morning's obits. Her timing, too, showed a fine sense of drama, it must be admitted. The papers say more will come out about the murder. I cannot see why Delves Broughton should have said he killed Erroll had he not done so; true, of course, people do make the most extraordinary claims with a view to trying to appear more interesting than they really are.

Thursday, 10 September

Bob Conquest, over here very briefly for conference of some sort held at Leeds Castle, rang. Had seen Prime Minister, shade older, but in good trim, as six o'clock struck said: 'What about a drink?' both going for Scotch. Kingsley Amis, returned from Swansea, reported himself as having had 'four drinks too many'. I was aware Kingsley was in Gower Peninsula from receiving postcard reporting he had seen notice in shop-window:

CYCLES

BEICS

Lower line in slightly smaller lettering. Splendid flowering of Cymreigio. Copies of *The Album* arrived. Presented to: Tristram and Virginia, John, Georgia, Archie; Hilary and John Spurling; Roy and Kate Fuller; Rupert Hart-Davis; Roland and Nadia Gant; Nancy Cutbirth (AP Society, Kalamazoo).

Sunday, 13 September

Review in *TLS* of Mollie Butler's book about her two husbands notes that her second, Rab Butler, was temperamentally incapable of reading novels, found his wife's taste for Jane Austen, P. G. Wodehouse, etc., inexplicable. Review also mentioned that on some official occasion even the Queen noticed Butler's inability to take any interest whatsoever in some play being performed, to which he had accompanied HM. What inspired choice on part of the Royal Society of Literature to pick him for their President. Finished Peter Ackroyd's novel *Hawksmoor*, curious work involving shifts of time in relation to imaginary life of Nicholas Hawksmoor, eighteenth-century architect, with undercurrent of murders, pastiches of period-writing well done on the whole, at the same time hard to see what all these complications of characters identified in different centuries actually achieve, imaginatively speaking. Read the book with certain interest not only because Hawksmoor was such a good architect, also undoubtedly a relation of Eastland Hawksmore, whose portrait we have, who lived about the same time.

The Architect left property at West Drayton, Nottinghamshire, quite near where my direct ancestor Eastland Hawksmore lived, latter possibly having land at West Drayton too, anyway just in that neighbourhood. I suspect Architect's father may have been first cousin of Eastland Hawksmore. Family now, I think, extinct, name rare in Nottinghamshire annals. I have theory Hawksmores/Hawksmoors may originate from Hawksmore/Hugmore of Devon, whose arms they used on signet ring, possibly came North at time of the Dissolution, as we have copy of letter (1822) suggesting they were uprooted from property at Welbeck (Abbey) by the Bentincks when latter given land there by William III. I shall write to Ackroyd in case he knows name of Architect's father, not given in *DNB*.

Monday, 21 September

V saw Mr Lloyd Williams for check-up, all well, will see him again in four months. *The Album* published. *Mail on Sunday* (*Colour*) interview perfectly civil; also interview in *Observer* (*Weekend*), one of the pictures reproduced in *Telegraph*. Reread *Timon of Athens*, notable vituperation ('This yellow slave', for gold), just the one rather limited theme. Reviewed (now late) Richard Ellmann's *Oscar Wilde*. Ellmann good on giving idea what Wilde's London social life like as a pushing young man determined to make a career, sharing flat with successful young painter (painting awful pictures), latter with taste for little girls, which nearly got him into trouble, but useful contacts in Society. Ellmann thinks Wilde's syphilis, contracted as an undergraduate (of which there is in fact no definite proof), gave excuse for breaking off sexual relations with his wife (she well described), when homosexual activities became frantic. Wilde's last years in Paris even more terrible than one supposed. Striking how much Wilde himself accepted Victorian view of homosexuality as a 'purple sin', rather than physiological mutation; in fact nothing would have been less sympathetic to him than contemporary attitudes.

Wednesday, 23 September

V to London for luncheon with Jamie Camplin to celebrate publication of *The Album*, at which Jamie asked if he could meet Tristram and Virginia. This took place at the Groucho Club, Dean Street, Soho, haunt of publishers, agents; strange place, as described by V. Jamie's reason, if any, for wanting this introduction not apparent. All went well, the Club is to have some sort of exhibition of *The Album* pictures on its walls during October.

Friday, 25 September

Letter from Lady Selborne, asking if I could tell her whether Tom Balston was keen on wood-engraving, as Duckworth published several books with illustrations of that kind. Sent her what I could, suggesting she should also read my Memoirs, as Balston man difficult to describe in a nutshell, particularly aesthetic tastes, always to some extent based on his own innate contradictiousness. Received civil if slightly charmless reply from Peter Ackroyd (whose T. S. Eliot book I commended), suggesting writing to Kerry Downes about Hawksmores, authority on the Architect.

Saturday, 26 September

After reading Ellmann's *Wilde*, felt impelled to reread *Dorian Gray*, much enjoyed when read at school. While owing certain amount to *Le Peau de Chagrin, Dr Jekyll and Mr Hyde*, Wilde's idea in itself quite good one, but lacking occult explanation that seems in some manner required, however superficial, for why phenomenon of the changing portrait took place as it did. For instance, the sitting could have begun on St John's Eve; the painter, Lord Henry Wotton, engrossed in some book of magic, repeated some spell, anything of that kind to make suggested vehicle for transference. Real theme, of course, Wilde's own secret homosexual life, all Dorian Gray's 'strange sins' no more than that, tho' all oddly prophetic. Although one appreciates certain heterosexual incidents had to be worked in for propriety's sake at that period, something slightly less imbecile might have been devised than the young actress Dorian falls for, who then commits suicide. That episode does, however, illustrate with peculiar clarity the manner in which Wilde, with all his wit, flair, good nature, dramatic ability, knowledge of the world, etc., was not only not an artist (tho' always talking about that), really had no idea in what art consists. If the young actress could play the most consummate Shakespeare heroines night after night, she might, it is true, have felt a bit off colour the night Dorian took his friends to see her perform. To suggest that by falling in love she 'saw through' acting love, on account of being 'in love' herself, is as absurd as supposing the portrait of an incredibly beautiful young man would *ipso facto* be a beautiful picture. (Perhaps Wilde did believe that.) Either the girl could act or she couldn't. In fact this distinction opens an abyss of Wilde's lack of understanding of what 'being an artist' meant.

Now in Vol. 9 (last) of Pepys, to whom I still remain resistant, while admitting vividness of occasional passages: e.g., description of bore at a party (22 April 1668):

'One Swaddle, a clerk of Lord Arlington's, who dances and speaks French well but then got drunk and was troublesome.' Incidentally, for Americans and others too refined to speak of a cock when referring to a farmyard, saying cockerel, Pepys uses cockerel when referring to his own member.

Saturday, 3 October

We dined at The Stables, Virginia producing excellent dinner. Tristram knows Peter Ackroyd, gave good account of him. Tristram doing filming at Osterley. Georgia goes up to Univ on Thursday, day on which Archie takes driving test. Raining in sheets throughout dinner, so Archie drove us up to house in car, on arrival found key of front door not in my pocket. We entered by back door, could not imagine how I had lost key, which I clearly remembered putting in my trouser pocket. On ringing Stables found I must have pulled it out with my handkerchief as it was on sofa. In future will put it in coat pocket, this sort of thing driving one mad.

Tuesday, 6 October

Peter and June Luke to luncheon. She always behaves half-way between playing Gertrude in *Hamlet* and the little woman who has never been offered a drink before, in fact vast in size, putting back quite a lot when available. We talked about George Millar, who has written me fan letters from a long way back, recently sent enthusiastic one about *The Fisher King*, which gave pleasure. Millar mentioned he was friend of Peter Luke, in the Rifle Brigade together, then Millar captured, dramatic escape from Germany, glamorous career (DSO, MC) as in the *maquis*, has written quite a few books, now farms in Dorset with second wife. Peter Luke also talked of how dubious figure known as John Chandos (stage name), who once approached me about writing radio plays, nearly involved him in charge of perjury through some legal technicality of stating furniture of a flat belonged to Luke, when, in fact, liable to be seized by bailiffs for Chandos debts. Chandos also fantasist somewhat on lines of John Davenport, once gave me dinner at the Ritz, at which we each drank bottle of (goodish) wine, wine being one of his interests. Played return at The Travellers'.

Peter Luke said he heard Chandos at same party at different moments claim to have served in SAS, Highland Regiment, Brigade of Guards. I rather think Chandos obit recorded service with SOE, apparently all operational action on his part wholly imaginary. I seem to remember Roy Fuller's Memoirs chronicle equally exotic experiences of a somewhat different sort invented by John Davenport about himself, Davenport not an absolute fool as regards literary criticism. Lukes seem shade relieved to be leaving Railford Mill in the New Year, which, notwithstanding romantic situation, must indeed be grim in winter. They will probably return to Spain. Avocado; lamb (excellent); gâteau; two bottles Rioja Reserva '80. We have had over twelve dozen figs this year (150 eaten), record. I moved fig tree twice before finding present position against wall of house on south side.

Thursday, 8 October

My mother's birthday, I recalled. We lunched at the Bridge House, Nunney, rather good chicken pie. Archie passed driving test. V quoted forgotten verse I composed on Sonia Orwell twenty or thirty years past:

> She strove with all, since all were worth her strife,
> Cyril she loved, and next to Cyril, Sartre.
> She warmed both hands at Dorset county life;
> It sank; and left her with the Flore, Montmartre.

Actually her love was not Sartre but Merleau-Ponty.

David Holloway rang to arrange next book review, said Max Hastings was looking through *The Album* in the office, told him to ask when next in touch whether Barbara Skelton was model for Pamela Flitton. I replied with guarded affirmative, adding I did not wish a statement to that effect to appear in Peterborough (*DT* gossip column). At some stage after one of the *Dance* vols, Barbara wrote: 'Dear Tony, I am suing naturally, in the meantime can you advise me a good publisher for my new novel.' I sent her to Roland Gant, but negotiations did not result in anything. I think this must have been the book eventually published by Alan Ross, causing John Sutro to bring a libel action. David Holloway sent for review Richard Cobb's immense volume *The People's Armies*, written in French twenty-five years ago, now translated, deals with *sans culottes* force serving only within France during the Terror. The sadistic monster Carrier called the Section operating at Nantes the Marat Company; one of its members, who helped undertake the *noyades*, a nail-maker named Proust.

Sunday, 11 October

We watched first instalment of Olivia Manning's novel sequence *Fortunes of War* on TV, opens with Guy and Harriet Pringle (Olivia and her husband Reggie Smith) in Romania teaching at moment Germany marched into Poland in 1939: Bucharest scenes, luncheon parties, etc., convincingly done, two main characters also reasonably well cast.

Monday, 19 October

We have been lucky here where recent hurricane, which devastated much of the country, did little or no harm, gales, tho' severe, moved in kind of arc which let this neighbourhood off worst damage.

Sunday, 25 October

Virginia, down to tend The Stables garden, dined last night, luncheon today. Tristram in Northern Ireland shooting film from short story by Brian Moore. Reread *Coriolanus*, excellent play, always causes acute embarrassment to type of person apt to be producer, critic, these days, Coriolanus being first-class general not wanting cheap publicity to please the mob, persecuted by political, social envy of mob's representatives, the Tribunes. Coriolanus's Volscian enemy Aufidius also well conceived, at once hoping to make use of Coriolanus, at same time acutely jealous of him.

Thursday, 29 October

After much preparatory telephoning from Paris, London, Bernard Jeniès of *Le Nouvel Observateur* (new weekly, said to have high circulation, Left), arrived for interview, luncheon. Described by my agent as 'respected as a critic', Jeniès looked rather like George Clive, early thirties, tall, with billows of tousled fair hair, no tie, generally uncouth. V thought, probably correctly, he modelled himself on some French film star playing an attractive oaf, taciturn, masterful, who gets the girl in the end, in face of better-looking, better-mannered rivals. Complete contrast with Mauriès of *Libération*, who came here couple of years ago. Jeniès connected in some way with Stock, whose translation of *Wheel*, called *Tourne, Manège*, he brought with him for signature. It is to appear next month. He arrived about 12.05, was to have stayed until about 4 p.m., but wanting to get back to London earlier, providentially discovered train for himself, great alleviation. Seemed reasonably intelligent, took no notes, so one must be prepared for anything when the piece appears, if it ever does, if one even sees it. Jeniès said his mother Scotch, family from Toulouse neighbourhood, brought up in Brittany. I asked if he knew V. S. Naipaul, said he interviewed him, had been warned Naipaul was 'rather unpleasant', had not found him so. I was interested Vidia should have this reputation, presumably result of too much good sense on his part, contempt for current hypocrisies. Jeniès drank whisky before luncheon, Château Lacroix '81 not too bad, food rather so-so (V thought). Jeniès left without thanks of any sort, nor did he pull plug downstairs.

Saturday, 31 October

Letter from Hugh Thomas asking support for scheme to prevent main stream of British Library work being diverted from central Reading Room, and North Library, to new building in Euston. Hugh Dacre, Isaiah Berlin, and others, support this. I agreed. When I first went to the circular Reading Room the names of Great British Writers were inscribed round the dome, including a few unexpected ones like Macaulay. These have been whitewashed over, example of period opinion prevailing, when it would have been much more amusing to leave things as they were. The Reading Room scene of many comic incidents, for instance, Willie Robson-Scott, serious man, very neurotic member of The Hypocrites (about fourth year when I came up to Oxford) translating early German books about psychoanalysis in 1920s, had altercation with old man whose favourite seat Willie had taken (or vice versa). Old man snatched Freud, whoever it was, held book on high shouting at top of his voice: 'And look at the *filth* he's come here to read!'

Tuesday, 3 November

V, having cold, did not go to London as planned. I spoke with Ania Corless (Mrs), who handles foreign rights at Higham, about Polish translation of *Dance* (Panstwowy Instytut Wadawniczy), all twelve books, four vols of three, first vol. to appear four years from signature, print run of 20,000 (always sold out in Iron Curtain countries), royalties, non-transferable, available in Poland. Mrs Corless herself Polish, close relations in Resistance, General Anders Corps, etc. We discussed what she considers impossibility of mentioning Katyn massacre of officers by Russians in *Military Philosophers*. I have no objection to only certain volumes being translated, would not agree to alterations in individual vols. Of course one could not in practice prevent them from leaving out or altering mention of Katyn (and other passages Communists find politically embarrassing), for that matter pirating the whole sequence.

In fact the routine contract provides for translating the book faithfully, accurately, no addition or alteration, so there seems not much further to be done. Question of Polish translation arose in 1984, when Michael Ronikier, Visiting Professor at Trinity, Cambridge, friend of Dadie Rylands, wrote to me saying he would like to translate *Dance* and *Afternoon Men*. Ania Corless did not know if Ronikier were involved in this latest negotiation. One wonders if an ingenious Polish translator might word matters so that the Poles knew what was being discussed, while avoiding specific statements that would cause offence to Russians.

By curious chance the *Telegraph* today carried large picture of Guard of Honour mounted, for the first time, in Warsaw at Katyn Memorial there.

Wednesday, 4 November

V (in interests of *The Album*), to Bristol for quiz show on Harlech Television about identifying pictures, under editorship of Daniel Farson, George Melly, setting off at 2.15, returning 10 p.m. Others taking part included painters like Michael Wishart (formerly married to Anne Moynihan, née Dunn), Maggi Hambling, also an intellectual footballer.

Guy Fawkes Day

Lunched with Mayalls at Sturford. Lees suffered several recent operations, didn't look too bad. We talked of George and Diana Melly, met about twenty-five years ago staying with the Glenconners at Glen, in consequence of which Melly once stayed a night here on the way somewhere or other. Diana Melly now lives in a tower on the Welsh Marches (visited there by Alison Lurie from time to time, after Alison has lunched here), also occupies some of Melly's house in Notting Hill neighbourhood, tho' described as living separate existences. Gabriel Dru a bit disorientated now, Mary Mayall says, incapable of keeping up with idea of inflation prices, son Bernard Dru cashed out of Pixton, which he owned as well as Bickham. Luncheon, curry bought from Marks & Spencer by Mary, called Tikka Chicken, not too bad, sauce reasonably hot. Wonderful bright November day driving over to Sturford.

Friday, 6 November

On rising, extremely stiff in joints. V thought might be circulation trouble, insisted I saw someone at surgery in evening. Dr Thompson on duty, said indeed inadequate circulation, something amiss in left leg, foot. Produced tablets called Hexopal. While examining remarked: 'Your feet are very cold,' reminding me of something vaguely funny, remembered later Mistress Quickly speaking of Falstaff's end, her hands moving up in the bed.

Friday, 13 November

Just as we were setting off for surgery for Vit. B injection, post arrived. OHMS envelope first thought Income Tax, then saw *Prime Minister* in corner. Letter, topped and tailed by Mrs T. herself, asking if I would be agreeable to being recommended to HM the Queen for the CH. Replied I should like that very much. Question of artists receiving decorations complex one. If Government never gives artists medals, authorities and country are denounced as philistine; if artists accept them, they are censured for truckling to officialdom, 'just for a riband to stick in his coat'. Stendhal said artists required every public recognition they could get, need orders, decorations, etc., more than anyone else to keep them going; Proust delighted when he received equivalent of MBE. On the other hand, Eric Satie remarked: 'Monsieur Ravel refuses the *légion d'honneur*, but all his music accepts it.'

One admires Kipling turning down everything except honorary degrees (because he himself had never attended a university?), but of course Kipling, in one sense adherent of official ranks and rewards, in another was in the thick of political writing, as such; which certainly made acceptance of honours from a given Government matter for consideration. Kipling offered KCMG (I think) when barely thirty, which must have been temptation, as specifically Imperial decoration for services he deeply believed in, representing authority in its highest, most devoted form.

When some thirty years ago I was offered a CBE I was astonished, accepted, pleased among other things because a decoration round the neck seems to complete the turn-out when wearing a white tie with miniatures (which one rarely does nowadays). Evelyn Waugh wrote to me at the time congratulating, saying 'What one wants is a knighthood', wrote to other people saying he was surprised I accepted a CBE, a 'degrading' decoration. This was awarded when Anthony Eden was Prime Minister. Interesting to speculate whether Evelyn would, in fact, have refused a CBE, if offered at the time, especially without knowing I too was being given the decoration. I strongly suspect the answer would have been acceptance. The offer some years after mine naturally provoked satirical refusal.

Ted Heath put forward a knighthood about a dozen years ago. I was always brought up to think being a knight (especially being a knight's lady) rather an awful thing to be, even in the Services survived only by knowledge of duty done; certainly undesirable for a writer, tho' for some reason tolerated for painter (in certain circumstances), musician, architect, actor. Somerset Maugham (eventually given a CH) wrote of himself and a knighthood (one does not know if he were actually offered one) that he did not relish the idea of the butler announcing: 'Mr Thomas Hardy, Mr Rudyard Kipling, Mr Joseph Conrad, etc. – Sir William Somerset Maugham.' One would heartily agree, not to mention difficulty as things are in getting V called 'Lady Violet' rather than 'Lady Powell', without unduly complicating that issue for unsophisticated people. Betjeman, as Poet Laureate, extraneous work preserving churches, etc., seems to make his knighthood permissible: Osbert Lancaster, with widespread activities of similar sort; one could think of other instances. I expected after refusing knighthood, I should be put *hors concours* bureaucratically speaking; was as surprised as at CBE, rather cheered, as CH eminently respectable Order (65 members), which most people have never heard of, those who have know its standing.

Rereading Barbara Skelton's *Tears Before Bedtime* (which, with Vidia Naipaul's *Enigma of Arrival*, Mary Edmond's *Sir William Davenant*, I gave as my Books of the Year to *Sunday Times*), I looked up some letters of Babs (as Cyril used to call her) to find she refers more than once in an oblique manner to 'being' Pamela Flitton. The incident of the latter being sick in a huge oriental jar is based on an Oxford belle, a pretty girl, famous for having remarked: 'I think great beauty inimical to chic.' She was at a party in Wiltshire, where her nose was put out of joint by the presence of a rival beauty, and did indeed vomit into a tall vase, reported later as extremely difficult to clean. Model for the vase, at least five or six foot high, was seen in a rich Indian merchant's house in Patna, where we were taken by Mortimer Wheeler on one Indian tour. Bottle of fizz (Veuve Clicquot '80) at dinner to celebrate CH.

Saturday, *14 November*

Heard from Ania Corless that Christian Bourgois has made offer for translation of *Dance* into French. So far as I remember Julliard did first three vols soon after publication here; then Julliard himself died, various ups and downs, ending with Christian Bourgois planning to take *Dance* on, republish first three vols in one, also subsequent three vols in one. Project got well launched, fell through for no explicable reason. No reason why Bourgois should not bring it off this time, more than twenty years later. First two vols of Netherlands edition (Agathon) arrived. Almost everyone in Holland speaks English, so surprising *Dance* translated there, no doubt difference between carrying on reasonable conversation, understanding fairly complex book.

Monday, *16 November*

Laura Gatacre (née Dru. V's goddaughter) rang to say her mother, Gabriel Dru, dcd. Gabriel, as described by Mayalls, in poorish way for some time, so not altogether unexpected, seems to have passed off as well as death can. Gabriel, with whom we went through a lot of domestic trials and tribulations when she and Alick lodged with us at Chester Gate at the end of the war, housekeeping difficulties and heating troubles, I think she suited Alick (she herself proposed to him), tho' one sometimes felt a wife keener on keeping his very considerable intellectual gifts up to the mark might, for better or worse, have extracted more writing out of him; tho' Alick's curious lethargy, which went with his brilliance, element always to be reckoned with. As it was, tendency to live in a pigsty immensely increased by

Gabriel's habits, temperament. Gabriel responsible for introducing Evelyn Waugh into the Herbert family in the first instance, she and Evelyn having met on a Hellenic cruise. When he married her younger sister Laura, in consequence of this, Evelyn completely jettisoned the Drus, so far as that was possible for in-laws, Gabriel not good-looking, smart enough, for his purposes; Alick object of intense jealousy on Evelyn's part, in the first place because born RC, even more because Alick's religio-philosophic position (in many respects an extremely free and easy one) well looked on by smart priests, while being extreme reverse of Evelyn's old-fashioned bigotry, characteristic of convert.

Evelyn also loathed his brother-in-law Auberon Herbert (to whom Gabriel was utterly devoted). Gabriel attributed Evelyn's hatred of Auberon to jealousy for the manner in which Auberon got on well with Diana Cooper, with whom in a sense Evelyn was in love. With characteristic realism Alick once remarked: 'I perfectly understand Evelyn finding Gabriel a bore, but that doesn't make the way he behaves any more excusable.' Auberon Herbert nice, good-natured chap, if at times rather heavy going.

Their mother, Mary Herbert, detested Evelyn, alleged actually to have thrown a plate at him at one moment. When V and I stayed at Pixton (house of inconceivable cold, discomfort, bad management) she was far from agreeable to both of us, besides nearly freezing us to death from lack of heating, french windows permanently open in midwinter, snow on the ground, hardly anything to eat.

Sunday, 22 November

Stockwells at The Stables. They had seen Jonathan Cecil in *The Hypochondriac* (adaptation in modern dress of Molière's *Le Malade Imaginaire*), afterwards had supper with him. Tristram, recently filming at Eastbourne, went over to Lewes for Fifth of November fireworks, where they were having tremendous show in honour of 'The Lewes Martyrs' (name vaguely familiar without knowing who they were*), immense display, everyone in fancy dress, varying from Vikings to Hospital Nurses of Crimean War period, large banners proclaiming 'No Popery'.

In evening V and I watched final instalment of Olivia Manning's *Fortunes of War* on TV. This received ecstatic notices, tho' no one I talked to about it thought it much good. The leading couple, in their way, not too bad, as representing Olivia and her husband, Reggie Smith; minor characters on the whole pretty dim, film resolving itself into kind of travelogue about Romania, these scenes best. Reggie Smith's awfulness (perpetual adoption of lame ducks, in real life always letting people down, then turning up with apologies and bunches of flowers) made

* Protestants executed in reign of Mary I.

something for (good) actor to get his teeth into, but White Russian sponger (as in novel) dreadfully boring. Olivia's love affairs less convincing. I don't doubt she herself (the world's greatest grumbler) would have grumbled a good deal at what was made of her book.

Read *Julius Caesar*, enjoyable play, full of points, particularly good on friendship: 'It is the bright day that brings forth the adder.'

Wednesday, 25 November

Tristram down this morning to see Mr Grove, whom he has commissioned to prune, thin, The Stables apple trees. I am joining this operation for our own apple trees. Grove suggested branch on big copper beech opposite Stables rather dangerous, so removing that too. Told him Oliver & Lang Brown usually undertook our tree surgery, turned out he was going on to see Lang Brown later in day, so would explain. Haircut in Nunney afternoon, on to Frome to see Lister as lower plate needs filing again. Lister said: 'I saw long piece about you in one of the coloureds.' I asked if that were the *Mail on Sunday*. He said: 'Yes – glory at last.'

Friday, 27 November

Consequent on recent internal upheavals at Heinemann, new arrival, apparently main figure there, Helen Fraser, wrote to Bruce Hunter saying she had fulfilled an ambition to be my publisher. As I have no personal contact with any single member of Heinemann's staff with exception of Roger Smith (whom I met ages ago perhaps once, does some specialized job there), thinking it as well to possess an editorial connexion, suggested Helen Fraser might like to lunch here some time. Also question of V's E. M. Delafield MS, regarding which no news from Heinemann received up to date.

Accordingly arranged that both Bruce Hunter and Helen Fraser should come here (no doubt wishing to keep eye on each other), which suited us well, as one likes to see Bruce in the flesh occasionally. Helen Fraser, dark, slim, attractive, about forty or more, one understands from Bruce, looks less, married (second in his case) to Grant McIntyre, publisher with John Murray.

When she and Bruce were here, in fact half-way through luncheon, turned out Heinemann wanted to do V's E. M. Delafield. Postal delays atrocious as they are, Helen Fraser's letter on subject to Bruce not yet arrived at Higham, tho' written week ago. I mentioned question of *Dance* in one volume, on which I am not specially keen, but mooted when TV project was on. Helen Fraser said there was a scheme to try Michael Grade, who recently left BBC for Channel 4, as he might be in mood to show himself well disposed to comparatively highbrow TV proposition like *Dance*. I was interested to hear that nowadays practically no writers (or only very few) sell largely in hardback, comparable with sales in the past of, say, Michael Arlen, sales of eight/ten thousand regarded as quite good. When Bruce Hunter and Helen Fraser left one felt useful business done. Incidentally, Chatto/Hogarth Press have produced excellent cover for *Aubrey* paperback (lost Lely portrait of Aubrey, of which Canon Jackson painted water-colour from engraving). They seem to be getting out Revised Edition in February. Later in afternoon John took me into Frome where further action by Lister needed.

Monday, 30 November

On Saturday a character who announced himself as John Press rang, said he lived in Frome, our copy of *TLS* delivered mistakenly with his, should he put it in post or come over with it, which he was (very kindly) prepared to do. Thanked him profusely for suggesting latter, adding that we could easily bear to wait another day if the paper were no more exciting than usual. This facetious comment elicited no correlative response, I was conscious of having fallen somewhat short by not knowing to whom I was speaking. Today occurred to me to look up Press in *Who's Who*, to find him retired official of British Council, 'author and poet'.

Reread *Far from the Madding Crowd*, less effort in doing so than most Hardy novels. Moments of extreme improbability, as when Sjt (correct Army abbreviation rather than Sgt) Troy cuts hole in circus tent canvas, snatches from Bathsheba note reporting his own return to neighbourhood. On the whole narrative goes with more of a swing than usual, rural characters reasonably funny. Also reread Roy Fuller's *The Carnal Island*, novel I have always liked. Weakens a bit towards end, not sure wrecked ferry-boat causing old poet Daniel House's end quite right sort of termination. House's awful dog (no doubt modelled on Hardy's Wessex, which only Siegfried Sassoon seems to have been able to tolerate) called Prince Monolulu after gigantic black tipster, who used to attend all race meetings dressed in ostrich-feather head-dress, brightly coloured robes, shouting: 'I've got a horse! I've got a horse!' I was approaching post office at end of Welbeck Street, south of Wigmore Street, two postmen walking just in front, Monolulu appeared coming from opposite direction. Drawing level with postmen, he stopped them, asked: 'Heard the one about the homosexual horse?' Postmen replied in negative. 'He tossed his rider off.' Monolulu strode on towards Wigmore Street. I read some court case in which Monolulu was described as a Danish citizen, so one supposes he was born in the Virgin Islands before Denmark sold them to US in 1916. Scene of perhaps worst hangover I ever suffered, as *Canada* anchored there on passage to California night after George VI's Coronation. Saw Lister twice today about lower plate.

Tuesday, 1 December

Our Wedding Day. Bob Conquest, who always remembers this (perhaps tribute to his American side), rang with good wishes, about to set off in taxi for airport on his return journey. They were over for only about a week so unable to get down here, which was annoying. Caviar, Veuve Clicquot '80 for dinner.

Wednesday, 2 December

David Holloway has been asked to stand down from Literary Editorship of *Daily Telegraph* by Max Hastings. Unwelcome news. Apart from one having reached stage of disliking all change in any form, David always good about finding books for me to review which I want, or at least find tolerable, I am accustomed by now to his standards, can judge pretty well on telephone whether to agree or refuse. David's place being taken by Nicholas Shakespeare, whom I found agreeable doing interview, also not so long ago Waugh TV programme, so prospects might be worse. David Holloway rather put out by enforced retirement, as well he might be after twenty-seven years at job done as intelligently as might be expected on daily paper. Change-over takes effect from 1 February next year.

V and I lunched with Peter and June Luke at Railford Mill to meet George Millar and wife Isobel. Millar, as noted earlier, fan of long standing, *belle guerre*, now farms in Dorset, horned cattle, through doing some job with which he lost an eye, gives slight air of having been struck by lightning a moment before. Brought up in France when young, could indeed pass for one type of Frenchman, no doubt help during adventures with Resistance. Agreeable, easy, said he loved his time in army. Isobel Millar half Spanish, daughter of British Consul in Far East. Her husband went out of his way to say that he tired of everything in life but her, of whom he never tired. Sat between Mrs Millar and June Luke, both a trifle deaf, demanding, Mrs Millar not only determined to make conversation difficult with June, also breaking up V's conversation with the two other men, luncheon accordingly rather like trying to get served in crowded Spanish *posada*, or snatching snacks during rush hour on the Tube.

Millars described themselves as living totally unsocial life, seeing no one, getting up at 6 a.m. to do the chores on farm, no TV, keeping fierce dogs (three of which making great barking row in their car), to discourage neighbours, whom they call White Settlers, and wage perpetual war against.

Peter Luke writing play about Marie Stopes, birth-control pioneer (who also spent a lot of time sending the hat round for Lord Alfred Douglas). One might have thought Marie Stopes rather unappealing subject, especially as Peter Luke has seven children, devout RC, therefore perhaps attack on her views. Millar asked if Peter Luke had read *The Fisher King*, which he himself had much enjoyed. He had not, so sending him paperback. Good Rioja. Not uninteresting party, if very exhausting for both of us.

Friday, 4 December

When V last returned on train from London she fell in with couple called Michael and Camilla Carter, met once or twice by her at Conservative gatherings where he is some sort of functionary, turns out to be High Sheriff of Somerset this year. Much to our surprise invitation arrived for luncheon at Batcombe House, where Carters live, about eight miles from here. We thought it might be amusing to accept. Batcombe rather pretty village, Carters' house at one end, high walls all round, white eighteenth-century exterior, probably built on to much older structure. Inside rather like official residence. Michael Carter, tall, bespectacled, occupation uncertain, V thinks possibly solicitor, in general unknown quantity.

I saw little of him at luncheon party, V sitting next to him said reasonably agreeable, touch of Widmerpool. Camilla Carter, sexy, attractive. They are RCs. Party of dozen, hardly any of whom knew each other, I knew no one. Geoffrey Luttrell, Lord Lieutenant of Somerset, wife Hermione. Made no contact with him, wife agreeable. V and I had impression we had met her somewhere before, tho' not with the Drus, whom she knew, talked of with grasp of what they were like.

John Keegan, Military Correspondent of *Daily Telegraph*, his wife Suzanne; he taught history at Royal Military Academy, Sandhurst, some twenty-five years. Seemed nice, said Sandhurst job enjoyable till last few years, when Army became so intense, professionally puritanical about work, everything began to be a bit too much. That just impression one had oneself about the Army. I should be interested to hear more from him. Mrs Keegan (on my right at luncheon, fan), lot of ash-blonde hair, apparently partly German, writing book about Mahler's second wife (married Werfel, author of *The Song of Bernadette*, film which Colonel Carlisle so inimitably described).

Mrs Keegan looked young, tho' they seem to have about four more-or-less grown-up children in house in Islington, also have house at Kilmington. Keegan had not heard about David Holloway's departure, said he suspected wind blowing a bit chill in David's direction for some little time. On my left, Lady Johnstone of Rockford, attractive, revealed by *Who's Who* to have married Lord J of R in 1980 as second wife, where she is named as Mrs Yvonne Shearman. After ladies left dining-room, talked with Lord Johnstone, big Ulsterman whose father moved to North Midlands, where Lord J of R directs various businesses, also one of the treasurers of Tory Party. Seemed agreeable. Just bought house in Trowbridge area.

Man on my other side a sailor (characteristic naval type), possibly admiral, one of the directors of Westlands, helicopter firm about which great political row recently took place, still to some extent simmering. Just met his wife on return to drawing-room, seemed quite jolly, name something like Gutterbuck. Food: prawn pancake, grouse, crème brûlée: champagne as aperitif, white burgundy, superb '69 claret, sauternes (which I did not drink), etc., all said to be excellent. Service presumably hired. One likes to attend this sort of party occasionally, even if a succession of them would be wearisome.

Monday, 7 December

Saw Lister. I hope lower plate now fixed.

Wednesday, 9 December

Finished extended John Betjeman reread. There is no doubt he was an exceptionally strange figure, quite unlike anyone else one ever knew; extremely gifted poet, who seems to threaten his own gifts by not taking himself seriously enough, while at same time when Betjeman writes about, say, death of a friend, Basil Dufferin, certainly not at his best. In general, one would say, writers, poets, write as well as they can, unable themselves to choose. No doubt Betjeman aware of his own limitations, therefore trod tightrope from which he occasionally descends into futility.

Like most young men of his generation Betjeman had uncomfortable relations with parents, especially his father, tho' both seem to have been fairly trying. Situation aggravated by family firm (which he was expected to enter) producing decorative objects of astonishing hideosity. At same time perhaps Betjemanware concentrated John's attention in first instance on everyday objects of more or less monstrous nature, which play so large a part in Betjemanian verse. The poems have inevitably cast him in role of cosiness, *faux* naivety, sympathy (of distinctly condescending kind) for dwellers in Suburbia. These characteristics in truth only partly belonged to him. Very much another side too. In his immense melancholy (if not wholly, to considerable extent religious), keen social side, was element of sadism, desire to dominate, expressed, for instance, by nicknaming his wife Penelope 'Filth'. He would invent names for people, always to place them at a disadvantage *vis-à-vis* himself; e.g. calling the painter Henry Lamb (who started life as surgeon) 'The Doctor', generally distributing disobliging descriptions where he could or dared. He also had extraordinary powers to charm, especially at large gatherings, occasions like *Punch* dinners, where he would deal to perfection with some perhaps not very prepossessing middle-aged lady from Metroland, whom he found near himself at table. On the other hand he would take unreasoning dislikes: for instance, Ziman, Literary Editor of the *Daily Telegraph*, whom Betjeman could not hear mentioned without a stream of objurgation. Admittedly Z could be absolutely maddening (quite late on in my period at the *DT* I wrote Z a furious letter, which I later regretted, asked the secretary to suppress, by some extraordinary trick of fate letter never arrived), but *au fond* Z was sound, good-natured, tried to do his best about books and reviewers. Again Basil Boothroyd on *Punch*, another object of Betjeman hatred, Three-Men-in-Boat/Pooter-type figure, with quite a good idea of a joke, who ought to have represented all Betjeman supposedly stood up for in the Suburban world, even if he happened not to like Boothroyd's pieces in *Punch*.

For my own taste where Betjeman's poetry is concerned I care less for the popular ones (Miss Joan Hunter-Dunn, etc.) than those nostalgically celebrating obscure localities, or almost surrealist poems like Captain Webb, the Dawley man, swimming as a ghost along the Old Canal. *Summoned by Bells* does not really come off, especially Oxford section, latter in some passages exquisitely embarrassing. On the other hand, the desperate expressions of misery scattered among the poems are always interesting, moving:

> The peace before the dreadful daylight starts
> Of unkept promises and broken hearts

or:

> And I on my volcanic edge
> Exposed to ridicule and hate
> Still do not dare to leap the ledge
> And smash to pieces on the slate

again:

> I have no hope, I have no faith,
> I live two lives, and sometimes three,
> And life is but a living Death
> For those who share their lives with me

Does this really mean contemplated suicide? It certainly shows awareness of being himself trying to live with. On the other hand, so far from suffering ridicule and hate, one would have thought Betjeman enjoyed unrivalled popularity as contemporary poet, public personality, apart from courting as a publicist a certain amount of laughter on account of deliberate antics. He had enormous vitality of his own particular sort, from earliest days practical ability to get jobs in journalism, as adman, at all of which he was proficient, tho' admen among foremost objects of his hatred, together with young business executives. These latter, like his subalterns, apt to be a bit stylized. Betjeman is often effective in attack, if never quite at his best there as poet. His strongest enthusiasm (setting aside religious hopes, doubts) probably architecture.

In poetry he once astonished me by saying (in answer to some question of mine) that he was not in the least interested in the seventeenth-century metaphysical poets, Donne and Cowley not to mention Vaughan and Herbert. One feels that his unceasing objective was attempting to warm from his bones the chill of his own (to himself) depressing, embarrassing family background, to be exorcized by fascinating peers, 'top people' of any kind, which he did with unmatched facility, thoroughness. This might be compared – tho' performed in quite another manner – with Wilde's similar powers in the same line. Latterly Betjeman became more than a shade pompous, expecting to be treated as a Great Man when he came into a room, even at, say, a party of Osbert Lancaster's after one of Osbert's own picture shows. Osbert not at all willing to put up with that sort of nonsense from so old a friend, who shared so many of his tastes, ways of life. One looks forward to the Bevis Hillier biography while wondering whether Hillier will be up to the many subtleties required of in Betjeman's life story.

Although always on good terms with Betjeman, V and I were neither of us regarded by him as paying quite sufficient homage, in spite of Pakenham, as a house, having played (as with Evelyn Waugh) considerable part in Betjeman's early social move upwards. Edward [Longford], difficult with most people, eating out of Betjeman's hand, indeed almost worshipping him tho' (as with all Edward's friends) not equally encouraged by Christine.

Mr Millard, of Mildav, builders, asked if I could contribute £350 to putting right coping on wall down to basement entrance after it began to crumble; with which he undoubtedly had bad luck in unexpected expense of having to set this right. He used, wrongly, particular stone that must be set special side upwards, having said that he would repair it (as indeed he had to) without charge. As a mass of huge stones falling out there, breaking down the wall, was even worse luck for me. I pointed latter out, at the same time sending him *ex gratia* payment of £100, hoping that would satisfy him. [He seemed reasonably happy about this.]

Wednesday, 16 December

Lees and Mary Mayall to luncheon. They are having ten days of Christmas, with relays of children, grandchildren, their boyfriends, girlfriends, present and ex, in three waves. Robert Mayall has parted from lady all dressed in leather, looked upon as matter for relief, as at one moment marriage seemed possible. Their daughter Cordelia, now separated from husband (Summerscales), who appears to do quite well in business; children living with him. His severe views entail children being sent to a Comprehensive, and out on a paper round at 6 a.m., possibly good idea, as previous generation do not seem to have responded particularly well to accommodating treatment. Lees said they dined at Orchardleigh not long before Arthur Duckworth's demise, Arthur complaining as usual about difficulties of getting staff to run, however inadequately, a big house. Lees said: 'You seem to have a perfectly efficient butler.' Arthur Duckworth replied: 'Oh, he's not a permanent butler, he's just hired for the night. In fact he's Lord Kingsale.' This is 35th Lord Kingsale, Premier Baron of Ireland, member of Cavalry and Guards Club, etc. Both V and I thought Lord Kingsale a plumber by profession. Apparently he buttles too. Avocado, duck, patisserie, two bottles Château La Croix de Gay, Pomerol, '78, not at all bad.

Read biography of Ken Tynan by second wife Kathleen (ran away with Tynan from Oliver Gates) got from Frome Library. Never encountered Tynan beyond his giving half-smile as we passed in corridors of the Old Bailey during Chatterley Trial. Undoubtedly rather prodigy when young, flamboyant figure of post-war Oxford, where Tynan's goings-on seem to have been of most traditional undergraduate order, odd clothes, cloak, etc. At seventeen must have been unusually well read for his generation, from outset entirely immersed in the theatre. Illegitimate background odd. I had imagined Tynan's mother seduced by Midlands businessman, Knight, who just paid them occasional visit. On the contrary it was Knight's legitimate family he abandoned, Tynan experiencing completely domestic upbringing (cf. Uncle Bodger as Joe Ackerley's similar paternal situation, also, one understands, Betjeman *père*'s other family).

Tynan evidently had extraordinary capacity for charming people, famous or otherwise. Immediately after coming down, taken on as dramatic critic, accepted as authority on the theatre. Immense narcissist, absolutely sure of himself, Tynan reminded one often of Malcolm Muggeridge, like Malcolm very successful with women, like Malcolm in no sense an 'artist'. Tynan's dedication to showbiz was scarcely less to pornography, passion for shocking people; again latter like Malcolm, tho' Malcolm's nonconformist soul always finding pornography abhorrent, even to extent of hysteria.

I never read a book which conveyed clearer impression of showbiz people being concerned solely with showbiz *as such*, a world of its own, having little or no relation to what the consumer thinks, wants, enjoys; actors admired not because they can act in a manner 'like' human beings, projecting certain images of life, but because they embody certain characteristics admired by other actors. In this, showbiz people resemble journalists, apt to reach a point when only journalism, everything to do with it, of any significance. Tynan book well done, interesting not least in that

Tynan himself nowadays scarcely remembered by younger generation. Kathleen Tynan, undeniably pretty, I think we first met with Oliver Gates. She (Tynan too) Fellow Travellers, tho' his hold on politics, Communism, seems to have been essentially half-baked; hers, one would imagine, more practical, sinister. V and I once having supper at the French Embassy, when Hugh Thomas, with Kathleen Tynan in tow, joined our table. Hugh Thomas just back from Cuba. I asked him what it had been like. He drew a deep breath, was about to give a devastating account, when Kathleen Tynan (who seems to have particular affection for Castro) began to talk frenziedly of other things, thereby making it impossible to hear what Hugh Thomas had to say on subject of Cuba at that moment. At close of Tynan biography one has odd sense of emptiness, that he had made a lot of noise at the time, quite a well-known figure, yet left remarkably little behind, all his books apparently out of print.

Rereading Gronow's Memoirs. These were reprinted in selected edition not many years ago, Introduction by John Raymond. Raymond already fallen into a drunken decline by then, did no work on them at all, his Introduction hot air. A great pity. Rees Howell Gronow (1794–1865) remarkably intelligent, most unusual man to become a Regency dandy, immense social success, ending by living in Paris, two French wives, one ballet girl, other *noblesse*. One would like to know more about his Welsh background. Pedigree given in early Introduction credible in principle, then branching into sheer nonsense (my own ancestors' effigies in St David's having nothing to do with Gronows in North Wales, tho' one would like a common forebear). Coat of Arms on cover of Gronow Memoirs showing elementary heraldic solecism (metal on metal), possibly fault of binder. Well researched life of Gronow worth doing. Why, for instance, was he sent to Eton, then into Guards, on the whole unusual for his sort of minor Welsh gentry?

Monday, 21 December

My eighty-second birthday. Felt decidedly better than this time last year, for that matter year before. V gave me shirt (light blue), John (who returned to London), large coloured handkerchiefs as requested. Stockwells rang. Half-dozen Veuve Clicquot '82 from Heinemann (Helen Fraser), unexpected, nice gift. James Sandilands (who organized luncheon of City fans some years ago), bottle Veuve Clicquot '79, which we drank at dinner with V's caviar, both excellent.

Followed up Betjeman poetry reread with *Collected Verse* of Kingsley Amis, then Philip Larkin vols in chronological order. Kingsley shows distinct Larkin influences (possibly to some extent vice versa), or simply shared *Zeitgeist*, one cannot be certain. Marked burst of energy follows *Lucky Jim* period, again one is uncertain whether part of same burst, or stimulation of successful publication. Difference between them is Kingsley's acceptance (if not actual enjoyment) of life, notwithstanding colossal grumbling (up with Evelyn Waugh as one of the really great grumblers), as opposed to Philip's very real dislike of every personal involvement in living. Larkin's melancholy so enormous ('Turning over their failures / By a bed of begonias') he makes Betjeman seem scarcely melancholy at all, so great Larkin's despair of life, hatred for almost all expressions of it. What little Larkin likes (certain aspects of English countryside, etc.) disappearing before his eyes under pressure of modern conditions.

One is struck by *The Whitsun Weddings* being far the best volume, even if *High Windows* contains one or two well-known ones like 'Sexual intercourse began', etc. 'They fuck you up, your Mum and Dad', more social comment than poetry. The poem about Mr Lal once meeting Morgan Forster (seen through the eyes of a left-wing academic – important to grasp that – rather than the poet's own) remains extraordinarily funny, vivid. Both Philip and Kingsley oppressed by crushing preoccupation with Death, tho' in slightly different manner; Kingsley so to speak having another drink to forget about its imminence; Philip welcoming prospect of getting out early, if somewhat retreating on that as an aim in his poem 'Aubade'. Reread *Henry VIII*, much attributed to Fletcher, all at worst competent, some pretty good.

Wednesday, 23 December

John arrived. Virginia, advance party to The Stables, dined. Risotto, Heinemann's Clicquot '82, good. Trevor Powell sent Christmas card announcing the Heralds, at long last, have successfully hitched his branch on to main family (he and I stem from common ancestor Roger Powell, d. 1675), allowed Llywelyn Crûgeryr arms. Trevor traced connexion in first instance from Roger Powell above leaving something in his will to poor of Nonington, Herefordshire, with which his wife Fortune Hakluyt had some connexion, where Trevor's forebears lived for several generations.

Christmas Eve

My tenant Adrian Andrews recently reported theft of a black ewe (only one in his flock), saying sheep-lifting by no means uncommon in this neighbourhood. Today he arrived on doorstep (having grown beard so that I did not recognize him) with Christmas present, bottle of Mateus Rosé, something I regret to say we had not organized for him, must do so. I remarked the black ewe had reappeared. He said police found her dumped in garden over Cranmore way. Like living in Wild West.

Christmas Day

V, John and I lunched at The Stables, classical Christmas dinner laid on by Virginia. Archie still skiing in French Alps, snow said to be bad. Georgia has taken Oxford completely in her stride, enjoying the place, tho' quite calmly, no change in general demeanour, for which one had to be prepared. We listened to the Queen's speech.

Boxing Day

Drinks party at The Stables. Joff and Tessa Davies; Lees Mayall, Elizabeth (daughter by Lees's first wife), her husband (Uglow?), their daughter Georgia, Robert Mayall (now vast); Georgia Tennant with her child (age four); its father (name unknown). Lees says Mary works herself up into a frightful rage regarding Christmas at beginning of December, which continues well into January. She had remained at home with five other members of the family or its ramifications, the numbers of whom certainly seem to justify some disarray on Mary's part. The Davies's beautiful golden Burmese cat, Francis, tragically run over.

Sunday, 27 December

Tristram, Virginia, Georgia, to luncheon. Welsh pie (turkey instead of chicken, ham, leeks, etc.), Christmas pudding, magnum Cabernet di Trentino.

Monday, 28 December

Archie returned from enjoyable, if inadequately snowbound, French trip.

By chance I picked up *An Adventure* (1911, ed. 1955) in billiard room – Miss Moberly's and Miss Jourdain's experiences at Versailles – reread it, following up with Lucille Iremonger's study of subject (1957), Symposium (Gibbons, Lambert Edge, etc., 1958). Disbelievers simply assert 'the Ladies' mistook ordinary persons for ghosts, in other words invented whole story. This seems almost more improbable than their alleged experience (tho' I must admit my grandmother capable of projecting that sort of thing on a lesser scale, she was also psychic, extremely able fortune-teller). Moberly and Jourdain certainly presented their evidence in least scientific manner possible, destroying first draft, obviously collaborating, while insisting each wrote her own account, making hash of subsequent research.

Assuming (for sake of argument) such phenomena to stem from a certain kind of sensibility operating on a few individuals aroused by deep feeling for the 'apparition' in question, the Symposium mentioned above makes good case for the

Ladies being wrong to suppose Marie-Antoinette focus (whose 10 August in fact quite different from what they described). The Symposium suggests that, on the contrary, the father and son Richard, Versailles gardeners, were focus, worried by death of Louis XV, who had been their patron; the moment being 1774, year of that King's death. Moberly and Jourdain describe a younger and older man, wearing long green coats, small cocked hats, carrying staves. The Ladies could not possibly have known that instructions for that year exist saying the Richards were to change their green uniforms to Louis XVI's red and blue. A picture (reproduced in one of the books above) exists showing a gardener, presumably one of the Richards, wearing those clothes, carrying a long stick. Another picture, (apparently of slightly later date) shows a man wearing a broad-brimmed hat, cloak, like the sinister pock-marked figure in the Ladies' account. Any question of their having stumbled on one of Robert de Montesquiou's fancy-dress parties, rehearsals, fêtes, or films, is put out of court by all such occasions being officially recorded. In fact, as so often, the sceptics seem to have less probable case than those who accept possibility of some genuine hallucinatory process having taken place, unexplained as such things remain.

Thursday, 31 December

Yesterday three or four journalists, having had preview of Honours List, published today, rang about CH. One does not expect any journalist to have read a book, mine or anyone else's, but I am chronically surprised by none of them ever having heard of *Who's Who*, which none dreams of consulting before ringing up, always asking questions they ought to know the answer to as basis of interrogating anyone. There can be few professions in which ordinary common sense is indeed a handicap but it is to the 'good journalist'. Letter from Hilary Spurling, whose spies brought in news. Lees Mayall called up with congratulations in morning; Kingsley Amis (Hilly Kilmarnock intervening) in evening; Dick and Patricia Lomer sent card, with cyclamen in pot; Liz [Longford] rang while I was going to post, answered by V, who also dealt with Rosie Goldsmid at 11.20 p.m., when I was already asleep. Had bottle of Heinemann's Clicquot '82 with kedgeree for dinner. References to award in *Telegraph*, *Times*, suitable cuttings to send American friends to indicate nature of CH as decoration.

Reread three vols of Boswell's *Journals* (we are missing one, *Bowell in London*, I think). As with Pepys, tho' in quite different manner, I cannot really like Boswell, who undoubtedly had good points, capacity for taking keen interest in other people in spite of his own overweening egotism (of which he was completely aware, one of his good qualities) and ability to describe them. One really can't forgive him for behaving so odiously to the dog given him by the Corsican General Paoli. Also one gets rather sick of Boswell's perpetual doses of clap (unlike Casanova he probably never got cured by a severe regime, which Boswell was temperamentally incapable of keeping). At same time he must be given credit for not suppressing his less attractive side. This year ended on a pleasant note. I doubt if I would ever again have energy to write another novel, even a short one, trouble being largely identification of author's point of view, *vis-à-vis* other people, so hard to establish in changing world as one gets older. Such ideas as one has must go into this journal.

1988

Betty Walker (wife of Rob Walker, of Nunney Court, their son Robby school contemporary of Tristram's) rang in the evening with congrats, followed by Barbara Coombs, who inhabited a Longleat cottage, and guided round the house. We used to see something of her before she moved away. She said she has recently enjoyed my Memoirs, and was interested in the curious figure (known, I believe, as Iron-heel Jack), who frequented Gerrard Street and that neighbourhood in a long somewhat clerical black coat and broad-brimmed black hat with low crown (the general effect like the Sheriff in an old-fashioned Western). One leg shorter than the other, ended in a kind of door-scraper. Barbara Coombs said when she worked in the National Gallery this character used to go there and pick up good-looking middle-aged women. His technique was to be examining a picture, then step back on the woman, apologize for his lameness, etc., later they would leave the gallery together: the woman (said Barbara Coombs) was never seen again, adding that Iron-heel Jack had rather a nice voice, which attracted the pick-ups. My impression is he had got into some pornographic trouble, possibly did time on that account. Once Constant Lambert saw him when smoke was coming out of his coat pocket. Constant drew his attention to this, but the warning was badly received.

Saturday, 2 January

Congrats arrived from Hilary Spurling and Max Hastings, both having had a preview of the Honours List. Max said he hoped I would get on with Nicholas Shakespeare, the new Literary Editor of the *DT*. Tristram rang from Scotland in evening. He had seen Fitzroy Maclean at some party, who sent congrats. Tristram said Fitzroy Maclean's ambition latterly (when at school he told Christopher

Holland-Martin, my informant, that he would be in the Cabinet) is to become sort of K. Clark of TV, History taking the place of Art, but (said Tristram) this would need nowadays considerable skill in television.

Reread (after a long time) Edgar Allan Poe's short stories. These are disappointing, tho' I find Poe an interesting man. Sherlock Holmes owes a good deal to *The Gold Bug* and *Rue Morgue*. Speaking of these detective stories, which feature Dupin, the Narrator, in the relationship of Holmes and Watson, the author talks more than once about the mistake unimaginative people make in underrating coincidence: 'Coincidences, in general, are great stumbling-blocks in the way of the class of thinkers who have been educated to know nothing of the theory of probabilities – that theory to which the most glorious objects of human research are indebted for the most glorious illustrations' (*Murders in the Rue Morgue*). In Vol. II of Gronow's Memoirs, which I have been rereading, an illustration shows several contemporary notabilities, including Brummell, at Almack's. The Beau looks remarkably like the 'TV personality' David Frost, whose role, a Brummell of this age, he might easily find himself sustaining.

Monday, 4 January

The painter Henry Mee (130 Jamaica Road, Bermondsey) rang again. It was provisionally agreed that he should come here to do a portrait on the afternoons of 9–11 February, arriving about 2.30. I dealt with congrats, I am doing answers in three forms: letters (unless otherwise stated); Moynihan picture (marked °); other postcards to those who have already received the Moynihan as contributors, all postcards in envelopes. I thought subjects of these might be recorded: Roger Smith° (of Heinemann, just met); Francis Watson° (old friend, museum official, settled near here lately with Chinese son he adopted); Simon Wingfield-Digby (in the War Office (MIL) with me, MP, owns Sherborne Castle, not seen for years); Liz Longford (lesser known Wellington portrait, W. her subject); John Ferguson (academic met on Swan Hellenic Iranian trip); Bruce Hepburn (doctor fan, Crimean photograph of Highland regimental piper); Trevor Powell°; Montgomery Hyde, the last's letter chiefly concerned with a book he is producing in Holland, whether privately or not I am uncertain, about Christopher Millard, bookseller and Wilde bibliographer, whose hut at the back of house in Abercorn Place, St John's Wood, from which he did his chiefly mail order bookselling, I used to visit as a boy. Montgomery Hyde wanted permission to quote from my Memoirs. I was much amused to learn from him that Christopher Millard was actually uncle of Guy Millard (now knighted), diplomat. His first wife Anne we used to meet at Somerhill and parties. Millard is a comparatively common name in the West Country, I never guessed this close relationship. Couriergram congrats from Ian Chapman (Pan Books), coupling his name with Collins and Fontana.

Tuesday, 5 January

I dealt with congrats: Anne Lancaster (Tissot lady, painter's mistress); Martin Charteris° (Lit. Soc., Provost of Eton); Clarissa Avon (I always suspect Clarissa had a hand in my CBE, as awarded during Eden's Prime Minister period); Cyril Ray° (wine expert, edited *The Compleat Imbiber* to which I used to contribute); Brinsley Ford° (art connoisseur, the J. F. Lewis bought by V at a sale in Westbury probably represents his great-grandmother); Brian Pearce (fan); Jane Somerset° (Duchess of).

Wednesday, 6 January

My *DT* review did not arrive, so I wrote it again (Frazer of *Golden Bough*), and dictated over telephone. I dealt with congrats: Tony and Marcelle Quinton (Captain Congreve, eighteenth-century Artillery officer with son); Ken Taylor° (who was to have adapted TV *Dance*); Tony Kenny (Master of Balliol); David Holloway (retiring *DT* Lit. Ed.); Stephen Spender° (speaking of his own 'vulgar' knighthood, etc.); Penny Perrick° (Lit. Ed. *Sunday Times*); Archie (Madras Native Infantry, in which a Powell great-uncle served); Charles Pickthorn (he sent Nunney Castle, so I riposted with Chantry Church); George Millar (writer and fan recently met with the Lukes; Rifle Brigade, his regiment, in Peninsula); Alun Davies (fan); Mary Clive (eighteenth-century Grenadier, Clives' regiment); Simon Raven (53rd Foot, his former regiment as regular; later King's Shropshire Light Infantry); Arnold (Lord) Goodman; Nancy Smiley wrote to V, who answered.

Thursday, 7 January

Dealt with congrats: Freddie Young (B. A. Young) on *Punch* (York & Lancaster Regiment, nearest I could get to Lancashire Fusiliers, his regiment); Victor Ross (fan, publisher, Folio Soc.); Anthony Hobson (Rorke's Drift, couldn't find anything apposite); Richard Cobb° (don, authority on French Revolution); Steven Runciman (Lit. Soc., also CH); Georgia (Lady Lennox in group of 20th Regiment, eighteenth-century, she wearing their uniform); George Creswick° (local solicitor, parish councillor, etc.); Roy Jenkins (eighteenth-century Artilleryman, his Corps); Jim and Alvilde Lees-Milne (British soldiers playing skittles with Zouaves in the Crimea); Rodrigo Moynihan (Goya lady); Sir Rex Niven (see 14 March 1983: Balliol man met at King of Norway luncheon, said 'There's a man here who *hates* your books'. This time he said thirty years a long time to wait after CBE, objection to CH was that 'like Bishops' wives', no prefix. He will be ninety in November); Denys and Cynthia Sutton (Lautrec, man in bowler hat); Asa and Susan Briggs°; Dick Lomer (typed formal letter, congrats actually dealt with by them some days ago when they sent card and plant, riposted with Coldstream Guards, his regiment, at Hougoumont).

Friday, 8 January

Letter from Robert Fellowes, the Queen's Private Secretary, saying CH would be presented by HM 12.30, Wednesday 17 February, if that were convenient to me, otherwise easy to alter. Fellowes somewhat older than John at Eton, who remembers him well, in the XI, etc.; John says looks a little like Max Hastings. Replied I would be there about 12.30, enquired what clothes (Morning dress). Dealt with congrats: Innes Lloyd° (to have been producer of TV *Dance*); Graham Gauld° (BBC, radio producer of *Dance*); Antonia Pinter (Antonia sent academic painting of lady holding a walking-stick, commenting 'What is she contemplating with that stick?' Riposted with Lola Montez in riding habit with switch, saying 'Is she really going riding?'); Jean Ziman° (*DT* Lit. Ed., Z's widow); Jack and Frankie Donaldson°; Pamela Howe (BBC Bristol, Railway poster of Colour-Trooping); Avi Dinshaw° (late of Heinemann, Fram's sister); Joanna Lumley° (fan, actress); Bruce Hunter (Higham); Cicely McCall (E. M. Delafield friend of V's); Andrew Wells° (genealogist, interested in the Wells family); Billy Chappell (photograph of theatrical promoter Binkie Beaumont of incredible campness); Adam Lee° (Child's Bank, gave us luncheon there); Brigadier S. Grant (fan, Sapper, rising in rank, hope he will reach CIGS to rival my First Sea Lord, Heads of Civil Service fans), also an RAF fan, tho' I think no more than Group Captain.

Saturday, 9 January

Dealt with congrats: Millicent Hamilton-Bradbury (fan, think we have formerly corresponded); Janet Adam Smith (Boswell portrait); Isaiah Berlin (his card Taglioni, riposted with Géricault-like Hussar leading out kicking horse). Isaiah commented: 'Of course you didn't want a knighthood'. Does the old Fox (rather than Hedgehog) arrange *all* the Honours? We know that when he and Maurice Bowra were fixing the Oxford (perhaps all academic) Honours, Maurice said: 'What about your old chum?' meaning knighthood for himself, so perhaps Isaiah still does all 'intellectuals'. Kenneth Jackson (Professor, Celtic expert, met on Hellenic cruises); Nicko Henderson (Ambassador, kindly remarked CH behind only VC, OM, in fact after all Grand Crosses like himself); Vidia Naipaul (wrote

from France, Persian polo players from mediaeval manuscript); Michael Faraday°
(genealogist, said I had done better than our common ancestor Roger Vaughan
knighted at Agincourt (Shakespeare), descent probably illegitimate); Ali Forbes°
(Moynihan portrait, appropriate, as Ali said he was too poor to subscribe, he lives
below the official New York poverty rate); Monica Harcourt-Smith (fan, BBC,
Bristol); Mark Le Fanu (Authors' Society, son of Admiral, First Sea Lord, my fan);
Jamie Camplin (Thames & Hudson); Robert Graecen (Ulster literary journalist);
David and Jane Barran (Shell tycoon, used to live at Mells, each wrote a letter from
different addresses); Graham Greene (riposted with Lady Butler's *The Roll Call*, as
emphasizing our own survival); Hugh Casson° (late PRA, also CH); David Rhys° (I
believe we sent him a Moynihan before on reconsideration); Christopher Lush°
(fan, FO).

Sunday, 10 January

Dealt with congrats: Evelyn Nightingale (lady putting up notice To Let, by
Hughes); Robin Butler (met at Mrs Thatcher dinner-party at Number Ten, just
appointed Head of Civil Service); Lionel Bonsey (Lord Cardigan, reference to our
common grandmother being friend of Lady Cardigan); Gerard Irvine (now
Prebendary, ancient MS, Day of Atonement); Anthony Wagner; Bert Adlam
(Frome undertaker, Hon. Sec. RAF Association); W. N. B. Richardson (name
familiar, presumably fan); Jenny Rutter (Warminster journalist, wanted interview,
said too busy at moment); Paul de Serville (Australian fan in Devon).

Monday, 11 January

Dealt with congrats: Frank (Longford, letter illegible, Light Division in Peninsula,
as he served in Oxford & Bucks Light Infantry); Norman Willis (General Secretary
Trades Union Congress, never met, perhaps my most notable congratulatory
letter); David Phillips (fan); Ian (Lord) Bancroft (another Head of Civil Service;
Prince Albert in uniform 60th Rifles, Ian, Rifleman, tho' Rifle Brigade); William
Cookson (editor poetry magazine *Agenda*, wrote complaining about my review of
Ezra Pound biography, with whom Cookson seems somewhat obsessed, coupled
with congrats).

Tuesday, 12 January

Dealt with congrats: Christopher Dowling (Keeper, Imperial War Museum, sent
24th Regiment at Isandhwana, asked why 2nd Battalion described as 'later
Warwickshire Regt', when the 24th became South Wales Borderers, turned out to

have been briefly the Warwicks); Rachel and Kevin Billington (Duke of Buckingham, a Pakenham [Villiers] ancestor); L. Kingscote-Billing (fan, autograph collector); Arthur Crook°, formerly Ed. *TLS*, now Sec. Royal Literary Fund); Humphrey Brooke (former Sec. Royal Academy, now incapacitated by melancholia, fan, writes from time to time, commented on motto of CH Order 'In Action Faithful and in Honour Clear', written by Pope of Addison). This motto also alluded to by Woodrow (now Lord) Wyatt°. Incidentally, Pope also wrote of Addison that he would 'Damn with faint praise, assent with civil leer/And, without sneering, teach the rest to sneer', possible motto for another Order.

Jeanne Wilkins° (whose bungalow we used to rent at Lee overlooking the sea); Bruce Bonsey (Vermeer's *Lady at the virginals*, no particular point, just had the card on hand); Jean Marsden (described herself as niece of my mother's cousin General Pennington); Mrs Catherine Beddington (fan, with whom I think I have corresponded); Billa Harrod° (widow of Roy Harrod, now living in Norfolk); John Hayes (Director, National Portrait Gallery); Barbara Ker-Seymer (Swinburne children, by Richmond).

Wednesday, 13 January

Dealt with congrats of Richard Luce (Minister for Arts). The *Sunday Telegraph* ran a feature recently on the subject of highbrows not liking Mrs Thatcher, instancing a fairly seedy crowd of supposed 'intellectuals', at least one of whom I had literally never heard of. Kingsley Amis, Francis Bacon, and I quoted as being highly in favour of Mrs T. In consequence of this I received a letter from Gordon M. L. Smith, with copy of his letter to the *Sunday Telegraph* (which he feared probably too long for them to put in), saying what he thought of the bunch of nonentities attacking Mrs T. These included Lady Warnock (Queen of the Embryos, whom we met at the Nicko Hendersons), now Head of Girton. He said he had hoped something better from her. Lady Warnock's comments, as reported, certainly were regrettable enough, chiefly aimed at Mrs Thatcher's clothes. Apart from clothes being no very important aspect of being Prime Minister, so far as we can remember, Lady Warnock herself was by no means dressed with outstanding chic, but it was only a party in the country.

Thursday, 14 January

Congrats from Jeremy Theaker (a fan living in Zimbabwe, and a Jehovah's Witness), who also sent a Biblical illustrated pamphlet. I was able to reply that I was reading (in fact, reviewing) *The Bible as Literature*. Roland Gant rang, he and Nadia just back from Canada and lunching here next Saturday. Roland, who always likes to be first in the field with news of all kinds, naturally did not know about CH, and was somewhat put out by not having heard, in fact was almost huffy. I finished reread of *King John*. What a good play it is. The language holds up throughout. I had forgotten its excellence, for instance,

> Rash, inconsiderate, fiery voluntaries,
> With ladies' faces and fierce dragons' spleens.

A good model for the left-wing papers might be:

> All form is formless, order orderless,
> Save what is opposite to England's love.

Friday, 15 January

I dealt with congrats: A. D. Batley (Hon. Sec. the Radnorshire Society); Charles Pick (late Director of Heinemann); Richard Francis (Director of British Council); Gerry Bowden° (MP, friend of Tristram and John); Hugh Lloyd-Jones° (Regius Professor of Greek); James Sandilands (young stockbroker, once arranged City luncheon for fans) sent him Sickert of *Venice*.

Saturday, 16 January

I thanked Hugh Thomas for congrats and concurred with his scheme (with Hugh Dacre, Isaiah Berlin, etc.) for preserving the old round Reading Room at British Museum, rather than moving everything to St Pancras. Sheep broke out of the Park Field, which John and I drove back.

Sunday, 17 January

Roland and Nadia Gant to luncheon. They are staying over by Tisbury with James Leasor, Heinemann thriller writer. Roland looked well. One still feels he is a bit lost on his mountain top without daily publishing news, the Garrick bar, general gossip, in spite of both insisting how glad they are to have left England, would never consider returning, etc. Slightly heavy going, probably jet-lagged. Roland gave us his *Blue Guide to Corsica*, just completed. Roland has drunk nothing for years, Nadia, whisky, then a drop of Château Tour de l'Esperance '82 (tolerable), John made one of his chilli con carnes. V and I rather exhausted afterwards, tho' nice to see Roland again.

Monday, 18 January

Congrats from John Monagan (The Congressman); John D. Crawford (Canadian fan); Christopher Hatton (fan in Spain); dealt with last two, delayed writing to The Congressman as letter of mine crossed with his.

Tuesday, 19 January

V to London. Copies of paperback *John Aubrey and His Friends* arrived. Its republication a triumph, one I did not expect to live to see. At least it is in print again. Some notice would be nice, if improbable, no literary editor likely to make effort in promoting book of mainly scholarly interest, however entertaining. Dealt with congrats: Kenneth Bradshaw° (just retired Clerk of House of Commons, now KCB); John Rhodes (formerly married to Barbara Ker-Seymer, later tycoon, living in Paris); Desmond Fitzpatrick (fan); Donald Bruce (fan, academic London University, writing piece on *Dance* for *The Contemporary*).

Wednesday, 20 January

Dealt with congrats: Jonathan Cecil°; Judy Egerton (the Tate), who is doing iconography of Gyges and Candaules pictures, on which she has been working for some years. Donald Bruce (above) says the subject is treated by Primaticcio, which I passed on to Mrs Egerton, who thinks the picture is at Fontainebleau (Bruce saying it was shown with Wildenstein Collection, New York, 1960). Mrs Egerton also found a statue by Pradier called Nyssia (name given by Gautier to Candaules's queen), which appears to show her as pregnant. Several letters in the *Sunday Telegraph* on subject of the miscellany of supposed 'intellectuals' being rude about Mrs Thatcher. The paper apparently received the best part of 200 letters objecting to shoddy abuse, all pro-Thatcher. Sent a paperback of *Aubrey* to Hilary Spurling and Roy Fuller, gave copies to Georgia and Archie.

Thursday, 21 January

Congrats from Alan Pryce-Jones°; letter from Bruce Hepburn (above) apparently a doctor, delighted with my Highland Piper card, said his unit had been on duty at Buckingham Palace (at end or just after the war) and one of the men had peed in sentry-box, a colossal row, Hepburn packed off to Poland (presumably with the Scots Guards).

Friday, 22 January

Congrats from Georgina Ward, now sells 'exclusive jewellery', whether in Mexico or here not clear. Enjoyed *The Fisher King*, she said.

Saturday, 23 January

Dealt with congrats: Joff and Tessa Davies°; Helen Fraser (Heinemann); Dadie Rylands° (to whom publisher sent *Aubrey*, as also to Tony Quinton, Richard Cobb, Michael Howard, Steven Runciman, Hugh Lloyd-Jones, Hugh Dacre, at my suggestion, only Tony Quinton, Dadie Rylands, Steven Runciman, Hugh Lloyd-Jones, sending any acknowledgement, although all historians). Dadie Rylands said that at his CH audience the Queen asked him: 'Where did Othello come from?'

Thursday, 28 January

Congrats from Mervyn Horder° (written on Duckworth writing paper, firm of which he was formerly Director). Finished *The Woodlanders* (not previously read), which I quite enjoyed. I am inclined to think Hardy at his best when not trying to write Greek Tragedy, as *Tess*, *Jude*, etc. I was surprised to find in a novel published in 1887 the words: 'So he has had you!' spoken by one woman to another.

Friday, 29 January

Congrats from Peter Wills, of Cazenove's (Stockbrokers). Reread *The Two Gentlemen of Verona*, although admittedly lightweight, seemed better than as generally spoken of, obviously by Shakespeare. It must be agreed some is intensely silly, and the author evidently by the end was himself bored with writing the play.

Saturday, 30 January

Congrats from Euan Graham (former Clerk of the House of Lords, not seen for ages). Letter from Hilary Spurling who is setting out for India and Australia, on track of Paul Scott biography. She asked to be kept in touch.

Sunday, 31 January

Nicholas Shakespeare, new Literary Editor of the *Daily Telegraph*, lunched here at his own request to discuss taking over the job. He seems an agreeable young man (apparently under thirty), looking forward to working there. He appeared to have reasonably good ideas, one of which to have picture illustrating my fortnightly review. He had just returned from filming in a sinister South American town, run apparently by Amerindian gangsters in the upper reaches of the Amazon. He told me Fram Dinshaw's wife was the adopted daughter of George Howard (Castle Howard), tho' quite why the Howards should adopt a daughter when they had several children of their own not clear. [She was, in fact, adopted by Lord Strathcona; also a Howard, and with lots of children.] An undoubted beauty, she got a First in English at Cambridge, recently jettisoned former husband [Lord Portsmouth] by whom she had two children. Fram has probably been in love with her for some time. This explains a mysterious Christmas card from Fram containing three names in addition to his own. I suggested to Nicholas S. that if possible he might mention the paperback of *Aubrey*, appearing 22 February.

Richard Usborne, author of various books on P. G. Wodehouse, wrote asking me to approach the Dean in the interest of placing a slab to Wodehouse in Westminster Abbey. I am not really a Wodehousian, that is to say I cannot read his books, tho' I like being told the good bits, which are often, I agree, extremely funny, even brilliant. We never met, but his Cazalet step-grandchildren used to send him my works, which I inscribed (having not yet laid down the rule to inscribe only to those encountered in the flesh, in any case would have made exception with another writer of Wodehouse's standing), which he enjoyed, answered with flattering letters, gratifying because he liked so few contemporary novels. (He was laudatory about me in his *Paris Review* interview.)

On general principles, however, I do not feel prepared to back this Westminster Abbey project. The Abbey is not a kind of Book Marketing Board's contemporary 'Best Books', a place to commemorate all writers thought notable at a given moment. To have put D. H. Lawrence there seems to me wholly inappropriate, simply from Lawrence's own attitude to such things, regardless of what one thinks of his writing; Noël Coward utterly absurd on the strength of, say, 'Mad Dogs and Englishmen', a few dated comedies and lyrics, always irretrievably second-rate. In any case, although not merely unjust, but wholly preposterous, to persecute Wodehouse for his behaviour in the Second War (first one spent in the US), it must be admitted, having said that, his conduct might be thought something less than distinguished in both wars. So far as possible, he tried to disregard them totally (as, for that matter, did Lawrence the first; tho' certainly not Coward in second). It has been argued, no doubt correctly, that Wodehouse was an entirely non-political man, a childish mind in such a field. None the less, he himself describes 'going to listen to the news' when staying with a German family during the Second War, without the smallest suggestion that it was unpleasant to hear gains and losses presented from the enemy's point of view.

In short, although such insensitiveness might be perfectly forgivable in a friend, or acquaintance, it seems to me to disqualify Wodehouse for a national pantheon.

You can't have it both ways. If Death is to be pompously commemorated, Life must have produced the right credentials. The current scramble to put every bestseller in the Abbey is worse than the National Portrait Gallery's doing away with the Ten Year Rule, the latter change at least excused by saving money potentially through buying portraits before they have gone up in price, even if a few duds thereby get accumulated. After all, that was always the case and has its amusing side.

Tuesday, 2 February

Candlemas Day, on balance dark and foul with a few bright patches, one hopes the worst of winter is out. Congrats from Alice [Boyd], penned on her High Sheriff of Cornwall writing paper, soon destined, she says, for paper games. I suggested adding 'late' before 'High'. The *DT* carried a photograph of Dickens's great-great-grandson shaking hands with Squeers's great-great-grandson (Squeers's model named Shaw) at Bowes, Yorkshire, where some sort of Dotheboys Hall Festival was being held. I remarked to V on astonishing resemblance between the Squeers great-great-grandson and Squeers in the illustrations (shown her) to *Nicholas Nickleby* by Phiz, which I held in my hand. She entirely agreed, while pointing out that Squeers portrayed by Phiz was, in fact, Dickens's great-great-grandson, not the Shaw descendant.

Wednesday, 3 February

Congrats (with much else) from K. Harvey Packer, music-loving accountant of Christchurch, Dorset, who has written to me – and many others – for untold years with projects for trying to get Constant Lambert's journalism, and kindred Lambert subjects, republished. I finished rereading Gronow's Memoirs, which remained immensely enjoyable.

Thursday, 4 February

Dealt with congrats: Travellers' Club (T. F. Brenchley, Chairman, Library Committee, FO); Quintin Hogg, himself CH (now Lord Hailsham of Saint Marylebone, having disclaimed his peerage, then made Life Peer as Lord Chancellor), who recalled me playing Post in Eton Field Game for Goodhart's v. College A, in a thick sweater, which I didn't remember possessing. The letter to a wrong address, returned by Dead Letter Office, somewhat Gilbertian for the Lord Chancellor. Tony Quinton rang to say Evangeline Bruce has a bad throat, so Quinton/Bruce picnic is postponed.

I finished a reread of Roy Fuller's poetry (*Collected* vol., plus *Lessons of the Summer*), interesting conflux, after doing the same with Betjeman, Amis and Larkin. The strong influence of Auden on early Fuller seems to me wholly detrimental, apart from anything else, Roy being a totally different sort of person from Auden, on Roy what might be called the minor public school/detective story myth does not fit at all comfortably. Roy is also, of course, a very different sort of person from Yeats, but Yeats's influence is far better accommodated in Fuller's work.

Oddly enough, one occasionally seems to scent in Roy a touch of Sachie Sitwell, surprising if to be accepted. Roy's Marxism, pervasive at first, somewhat lessens under his own satirical gaze. It always seems a shade absurd, tho' certainly sincere.

Marxist themes gradually give way to suburban life (on which Roy is always good), spiders in the bath (almost an obsession), birds, cats, his own narcissistic reflections, summer/winter clothes, preoccupation with old age (beginning in his fifties), fear of death, attraction to very young girls, what seem like apologies to his wife Kate. All this may not sound particularly exciting, but projects, as a whole, an attractive, original, individual and very genuine poet (always expressing regret for not having fulfilled his own promise), deep melancholy (in its way possibly most profound, if less aggressive, of any of those mentioned above – which is saying a good deal when Betjeman, or Larkin, are in question, Amis less so), extraordinarily clear portrait presented of the man himself. In writing about the suburbs Fuller has none of Betjeman's (albeit often brilliant) romantic condescension. Fuller is there on the spot: 'Hi, dad, you've forgotten your stamps,' someone says to him, all the scene becomes at once utterly vivid.

Sunday, 7 February

Evangeline Bruce rang to say she had quite recovered, the picnic party with Quintons is now rearranged for today week. While Evangeline was on the line Jane arrived with the Sunday papers, accompanied by her boyfriend, the latter small, fair hair more or less what used to be called *en brosse*. He was overcome with embarrassment at the position in which he found himself; Jane as ebullient as ever. I felt I knew just what their relationship was like. Evangeline was holding on, so I described all this to her, which she appreciated.

Monday, 8 February

Tristram's Southern Tree Surgeon came to prune the apple trees and trim a branch of the huge copper beech opposite The Stables. Henry Mee, painter, rang to confirm the sitting tomorrow.

Tuesday, 9 February

Henry Mee, due 2.30, appeared about 4 p.m., having had trouble with the traffic in the gale, which was certainly considerable. He turned out utterly different from impression given on the telephone. He is in his early thirties, plump, shapeless painter-type, dark hair (perhaps slightly like a non-Jewish Hyam Myer, once regarded as a promising painter). Mee comes from Yorkshire, mining background, art schools at Newcastle and Leeds, where he was taught by Lawrence Gowing, who seems to have promoted him. Mee completely at ease, not without charm, has a house in Bermondsey built for a sea captain in 1736. It is broken into every two or three months owing to the excessive lawlessness of the neighbourhood.

He brought photographs of some of his paintings, touches of Graham Sutherland, the Academician Brian Organ, also Sickert, commendable vigour combined with being fairly rough and ready, which is much the way artists are painting at the moment. Mee painted the Queen in the Yellow Drawing-Room (as did Rodrigo Moynihan). He said he thought courtiers got on her nerves, as she was much easier tête-à-tête. One's impression is that he found HM less of a strain to deal with than did Rodrigo, no doubt owing to Mee's artless self-assurance. He has a girlfriend in Hackney where he lives some of the time. He appears to have a rather grand car, which is damaged intermittently by persons jealous of it. He went off to find somewhere to stay for the night, we suggesting the Bridge House, Nunney. His idea is to do twenty-four portraits of notabilities, a set to be kept together. These at present include the Lords Hailsham and Carrington, several actors, tycoons, etc. Mee himself is an interesting figure. Today we simply talked about ways and means for the portrait.

Wednesday, 10 February

Henry Mee in fact returned to London, deciding he had work he must do there. He arrived on the doorstep at 2 p.m. I was wearing a jumper. He asked me to change into a suit and tie, wanting a small degree of formality for these portraits. He worked all the afternoon, doing drawings in sketchbook, taking a lot of photographs, including several of Trelawney (Mee is a great cat fan). The latter may appear in the finished picture, which is to be more or less life size. Mee has three brothers; a doctor (computer side of medicine); a private detective; and a potter (their mother was also a potter). Also a (pretty) sister, who copies pictures, otherwise of indeterminate profession. We had a lot of talk about the sources of art, imminence of death, awful price of getting a decent suit of clothes made these days. He spent £600, I think, on one, but knows a place in the Gray's Inn Road or thereabouts, where they make it up for about £60 if you produce the cloth. He admired the suit I was wearing.

He talked of all the kind of things I haven't discussed for ages, my impression being of considerably more intelligence than might at first be guessed on the surface. Possibly he is heading for RA. Difficult to guess. Mee is amusing about some of his sitters; he surprised me by saying that the Queen seemed to know my name, as also Lord Carrington. When discussing with them whom he should paint, both HM and Carrington at once suggested Graham Greene. Mee (a rare and to me welcome example of that) does not care for Graham's books. He found neither prepared to support their position in this respect when pressed and (according to Mee) acknowledging my own claims. Mee said he thought the Queen was far brighter than people give her credit for. That is certainly my own view. One's impression is certainly that Mee went down well with her, anyway he himself enjoyed the sittings more than, say, Rodrigo his. There turned out later on an amusing confirmation that his visit to the Palace had been a success. Mee said when young he had no particular admirations among painters, but (unlike many painters), I found him not at all unwilling to praise near contemporaries (Moynihan, Gowing, for that matter Lamb).

While Mee was here Robert Fellowes (the Queen's Private Secretary), with whose office V had been in touch to ascertain certain details about the Buckingham Palace visit, telephoned. Fellowes (who mentioned in his first letter he was a fan) explained to V that unfortunately he himself was going to Australia the following week. He regretted he would not be present to launch me on my audience but was taking my works with him. V told him she had been a deb with his mother (who died two years ago), in which he showed interest. She also told him that Henry Mee was at that moment having a sitting (if Mee's extremely informal methods could be so called). Fellowes at once said: 'Oh, yes, he's rather a card, isn't he?' This seemed to describe Mee very well. When V told him at tea who had rung up he was full of praise for Fellowes, with whom he also seems to have got on very well. Mee returned to London in late afternoon. He will get in touch again after a few weeks, having completed the preliminary work on sketches and photographs. After he had left it occurred to me to send him the abridged Memoirs, of which I have a copy. Amusing afternoon.

Sunday, 14 February

Hugh Montgomery-Massingberd (*DT* obits) rang saying Arthur Mizener had died, would I contribute a short memoir. Apart from that somewhat intoxicated figure of Tom Howard (who used to say he was *not* an Interior Decorator, in fact in the soft furnishings wholesale business), whom I met with Elizabeth Bowen (elsewhere too) in quite early days, and got on well with, Arthur Mizener was my first American friend in the sense that we used to correspond, the Mizeners stay with us and we with them. For some reason Arthur never quite reached the peak one felt his intelligence, writing capabilities, distinguished appearance, all suggested ought to have been his. I cannot rationalize to myself why this should have been. With all his intelligence he was imprisoned perhaps in his intense sense of being American, which set certain limits beyond which he felt the intelligence must not stray. There was something tremendously buttoned up about Arthur, tho' not in the ordinary sense that one uses the term.

If he had ever gone off the rails, one felt he would utterly go off the rails, even tho' that was the most improbable thing imaginable.

I suppose the fact that he was enthralled by the idea of Scott Fitzgerald (he was Fitzgerald's first biographer, and dealt with him with great ability) in itself suggests the rackety side of life had some appeal, even tho' Mizener himself belonged (apparently) to the least rackety. One would say the Mizeners' marriage was happy (dating from College, I think), neither partner ever having stepped aside (so far as such things can be judged from the exterior always admitted). In rather the same way Mizener's literary judgements were sound, yet without the violent likes and dislikes that are part of having deep feelings for writing (no doubt had to combine them with teaching English as an academic).

I thought when at Cornell his fellow dons were a shade jealous of Arthur's qualities listed above, particularly his air of distinction, even if a never wholly realized distinction. We had been out of touch for some years owing to his state of health; his death, all the same, leaves a gap in my life. I wrote to the Mizeners' daughter, Bibsy Colt, relations with whom one always felt to be one of her parents' problems, for no particular reason, as she was always a model of good behaviour so far as one knows, then married a rich (and jolly) man of impeccable American background.

This was the day of the Quinton/Bruce picnic. They arrived about 1.30 with a magnum of champagne (Asda, supermarket cuvée, not at all bad), pâté, quails' eggs, smoked salmon sandwiches, game pie, Neufchâtel cheese, chocolates. We supplied various forms of French bread, two bottles of Château La Croix, Pomerol '79 (much improved after a month or two in this cellar, undoubtedly a good one for maturing, and excellent). Evangeline was quite recovered, nice new hair-do, looking splendid and seeming in great form. Marcelle said I used sometimes to address her as Michelle, a name she on the whole preferred, never caring for her own. She was conveying a distinct touch of Toulouse-Lautrec, a wonderfully slim figure, bright maroon hair, specs, black stockings, immensely effective tho' a shade startling if you didn't know her, also in great form. Conversation fairly resonant, so hard to record items discussed. Tony Quinton mentioned some of his dislikes: Luther, Milton, Rousseau, Tolstoy, for instance, which I share. Very enjoyable party.

Wednesday, 17 February

Day of the CH audience. Marvellous spring morning after weeks of worrying whether or not there would be two foot of snow as this time last year, several years before in middle of February. We set out for London about 8.50, the taxi having arrived slightly late owing to some muddle, driven by silent (unlike most taxi drivers) figure in a tropical suit, spectacles (not dark ones), tall, in general somewhat resembling Maclaren-Ross. He turned out later to be called Terence, came from Newcastle, but had lived in the Frome neighbourhood for twenty years. He drove quite well, none the less there were a few moments of anxiety in the Cromwell Road traffic blocks. We arrived at the Lansdowne Club about 12.15, where V remained, later doing some shopping.

I continued in the car to Buck House. We first tried to enter by the SE Gate, and were redirected by a policeman to the NE Gate, where I gave my name. The policeman telephoned, then signalled the car through. We crossed the front courtyard to an entrance opposite, whence a painfully spotty footman sent me on to the 'Grand Entrance under the arch across inner courtyard'. A state coach and several carriages, attended by a three-corner-hatted coachman, postillions, were parked in centre of the inner courtyard. They later turned out to have conveyed the Ambassador of Zaire (formerly the Belgian Congo) with his suite to present Letters of Credence to the Queen. Deutero-Maclaren-Ross drove under this entrance porch, and retired to park. I was ushered up the steps by footmen, then taken over by an Equerry in blue uniform, another in a dark suit. The latter led me to left-hand side of the entrance, where were sofas and chairs.

The large hall or saloon stretched across the full extent of the building. The character in the dark suit turned out to be Robert Fellowes's assistant, Kenneth Scott, former Ambassador to Jugoslavia, with whom I sat for a while talking of this and that. Scott was a quiet Foreign Office type, with whom I discussed the Jugs, etc., whether government continued to be from Belgrade (when I asked that he said: 'That's a good question'). I told him I had been there on an Oxford vac years ago, then a curious Musical Comedy town, where the army did all their work in the earliest morning, swaggered about in cafés during the rest of the day in white tunics, red breeks, clattering swords. Scott said everyone now starts work still at 6 a.m., knocks off at 3 p.m., then they all have a vast meal. It is difficult to reconstruct official life to fit in with such hours.

Meanwhile, from what was going on around, I had the growing impression I was taking part in a play, probably one of Shakespeare's History Plays, where at any moment one must be prepared to swell a progress, perhaps even start a scene or two if required. On the far side of the room, quite a long way from where we sat, the Zaire party was being assembled for its entrance by the Marshal of the Diplomatic Corps. The Marshal wears a military frock-coat, the other military courtiers blue patrols (with gold aiguillettes), their swords allowed to clank on the ground. Gentlemen of the Household merely wear dark grey business suits; one character apparently not in uniform was wandering about in a kilt, but I did not see him close. In fact I was the only man present, so far as I could see, in morning clothes (recommended as preferable by Robert Fellowes), my father's tailcoat (built in 1930, when he was forty-eight, excellent fit), my own spongebag trousers (1950s vintage, I think), tight without being agony. The Zaireans were too far off to distinguish what they were wearing, at least one of them was a woman. [The following day the Court Circular reported them as called *Citoyen* and *Citoyenne* (suggesting *The Scarlet Pimpernel* rather than *Heart of Darkness*). One of them, Citoyen Bango Yombo, was Attaché for Coffee and Cocoa Affairs.]

After the session with Scott I was taken over by a Scots Guards Lieutenant Colonel (cleanshaven, immensely long sword, row of medal ribbons), one of those who had been at the entrance on arrival. He was called Blair Stewart-Wilson. This handing over entailed a move to a sofa on the right-hand side of the entrance, a day's march nearer the audience chamber, which opened out of that side of the room. While sitting talking to Stewart-Wilson opposite, we were joined by Susan Hussey, Lady-in-Waiting on duty that day, a Somerset neighbour as being one of the Waldegraves' daughters, tall, agreeable, slightly birdlike features, married to Duke (Marmaduke) Hussey, formerly manager of *The Times*, now Chairman of BBC Governors, a job his wife says he loves. V and I met Duke Hussey at one of the Child's Bank luncheons, but did not talk to him as he had to leave early to cope with strike at *The Times* (which he said was all but settled which turned out far from the case).

Susan Hussey I had not met, knew her well by name as cousin of Virginia and Julia, their mother, Nina Lucas, née Grenfell like Lady Waldegrave. Susan Hussey had been entertained at The Stables on some occasion when V and I were not present. She talked of children's parties attended at the Lucas house in Hamilton Terrace, St John's Wood, especially for Eton v. Harrow at Lord's nearby, where their Grenfell grandfather always had a coach among those parked by the cricket ground. She was much impressed by our doing this jaunt in one day, her parents living only about eight miles away, so knows the distance. She asked if I did not think Ferdie Mount wrote very well. I replied that some of his political stuff was not sufficiently High Tory for me.

Meanwhile various courtiers, political, legal figures, extras in the play, paused to speak to Susan Hussey, or Stewart-Wilson, and were introduced, including Bill Heseltine, Deputy Secretary (I think) to the Queen, and Australian. He seemed nice. He said we had met a long time ago at the French Embassy (probably under the Courcel regime). He made polite remarks about my books. There was much coming and going round about, various elements seeing HM, including our new

Ambassador to Bahrein (in diplomatic uniform) kissing hands on appointment. ('No one actually gets kissed these days,' said Stewart-Wilson, who had slight touch of much more respectable Basil Hambrough, that end of the Brigade of Guards). Not much less than a dozen Privy Councillors, some new, were 'taking the necessary Oaths'. I regretted being no longer in the way of writing novels (anyway novels in which such scenes as this could be inserted), as the surroundings would be superb material, not too difficult to rearrange in connexion with individual characters or situations in a book.

Susan Hussey said she hoped we should have a bottle of fizz when we got home. I said we had drunk one when the letter arrived about the CH, adding my drinking was decidedly moderate these days, chiefly because it kept one awake. Stewart-Wilson said he found the same. I told him he was a mere boy still, which he certainly looks. He turns out to be fifty-seven, had commanded a battalion of his Regiment, served all over the place, a sprinkling of Court jobs in between. He said he had to arrange seating at annual luncheon of Knights of the Garter: the Knights are always grumbling about being put next to a fellow KG they disliked. After some minutes Stewart-Wilson said: 'I think it time for us to take post.' We stepped across the room towards the two large doors of the audience chamber on the right. Stewart-Wilson said: 'They will take a moment to clear away the footstools, as Privy Councillors have to kneel. You and I will stand here until the Page [apparently Palace term for certain footmen] opens the doors, and announces your name. We walk in, pause, bow from the neck, I retire. You walk forward towards the Queen at the far end of the room, stop, bow again. The Queen will shake hands. She will then give you the decoration, possibly hang it on you, indicate the chair in which you are to sit, sit down herself, have a short talk. She will indicate to you when the audience is at an end and get up. You will get up, bow, shake hands, turn your back on the Queen, walk to the doors, turn round, bow again, smile. The Queen will probably smile back as she leaves the room.' All this took place precisely as Stewart-Wilson had outlined, giving an even keener sense of taking part in a play, especially the last sequence, the great final scene between the Queen and myself, playing opposite her in a Molnar drama of Renunciation.

The audience chamber was about the size of a morning-room in a fairly large country house, though done up more or less as a drawing-room. Several big brocaded chairs with arms (Library Chairs?) were grouped together at the far end. The Queen's exit door was behind these on the right. I knew that I should be asked what the Queen was wearing, but found that hard to describe even to myself. I think a silkish dress in which blue appeared to merge with pale yellow, surface slightly shiny. She looked much better, far more at ease, than when I spoke with her for an embarrassed (on both sides) minute or two at a party given years ago for the Royal

Literary Fund at one of the City Livery Companies' halls, possibly the Guildhall. So far as I remember conversation was about bomb-damage in such buildings.

The only incident of the least note was that a tray of drinks was being handed round. The Duke of Edinburgh, who was in the immediate vicinity of the Queen, was offered this. His right arm moved very slightly forward, in fact so little as to be barely perceptible. The Queen, at once noticing this, equally, if not even more imperceptibly, made a gesture of negation with her head, so rapidly passing, it might have been a mere easing of her neck. The Duke's arm at once shrunk back, again no more than slight stiffening as to moral, rather than physical, attention. Meanwhile in the background of the RLF party, on the chairs by the wall, V was more or less sitting on the head of Leslie Hartley, who was all but incapably tight, to prevent him from approaching the Queen. These circumstances were complicated by John Lehmann, Chairman of the RLF, wandering about in the crowd looking for V, with the object of presenting her to HM.

Nowadays the Queen's face is a shade fuller with age, which suits her. She looks much better than on this earlier occasion, perfectly at ease, attractive in appearance (far more so than, say, her sister Princess Margaret). After I had bowed for the second time, shaken hands, she handed me the CH, the case open, saying: 'It's a nice light decoration to wear round the neck.' I said I was never sure how near the collar such decorations should be worn, what amount of ribbon shown; soldiers always wore them right up to the collar, scarcely any ribbon, a practice I followed [i.e. with CBE], which HM appeared to approve. The CH is an Order established in 1917 by George V, its design enormously characteristic of that period (as much as the War Memorials in Mells Church, which always seem to me the epitome of that moment in a slightly different manner). The CH might be called the last gasp of the Art Nouveau movement, circular border (comprehending the motto quoted earlier) enclosing a square plaque showing a Knight in armour, bearing a pennon, riding past a tree, on which hangs a shield displaying the Royal Arms. The ribbon is crimson with a gold edge, a narrower ribbon enclosed in the case, which members are instructed to use when wearing the decoration. Why then is it hung on the broad ribbon? I must make enquiries. Possibly Anthony Wagner, as herald, might know. [He did not.]

After we sat down the Queen asked if I were writing anything now. Thinking it best not to mention a Diary, I replied only odds and ends of memoirs, possibly to be published at the discretion of my heirs and successors, not before my own demise. She enquired what exactly I had written, saying: 'You have written so many books, Mr Powell.' I provided a rough adumbration of *Dance*, adding the sequence was becoming very generally translated into European languages, among which I was particularly amused that two of the three war volumes were going into Bulgarian [on the tapis at the time but still unachieved in print], doubted if they would attempt the third, as the Katyn massacre was mentioned. HM then spoke of the Iron Curtain, saying whenever she went to Berlin efforts were made to make her look at the Wall, but she would not go. I asked if she had ever seen it, she replied 'Once', but it gave her such horrors she never wanted to see it again. She said she thought things pretty bad in Bulgaria and Czechoslovakia, somewhat less awful in Hungary. I told her I had visited Budapest when an undergraduate. She said she understood there was much rivalry between Buda and Pesth on their different sides of the Danube.

She asked where I lived. I replied in Somerset on the Wiltshire border, invoking Longleat as reference point she at once took. The Queen enquired about our garden and said she had picked twenty-seven varieties of flower the previous day in Buckingham Palace garden (like the Queen in *Cymbeline* to distil poisons?), thereby probably making the gardener extremely cross. I am totally ignorant on all horticultural matters and said we had many stretches of snowdrops. HM asked: 'Have you aconites?' Having no idea of the answer to that, I replied guardedly: 'Only a few, Ma'am,' which V later confirmed as correct. This more or less closed the audience of perhaps a shade more than ten minutes. HM rose, saying she was very glad to have met me. The series of actions then took place as outlined by Stewart-Wilson, the Queen's own half-turn before going through the exit door, her final smile, giving the particularly stagey effect of (to quote *Ulysses*) 'But, alas, 'twas idle dreaming.'

I rejoined Susan Hussey and Stewart-Wilson in the ante-room, by this time somewhat clearer of extras. A word or two was exchanged. They came to the entrance with me. Terence, looking more like Maclaren-Ross than ever, was already drawn up at the foot of the steps, on which Susan Hussey and Stewart-Wilson stood to say goodbye. I waved from the car; they waved farewells in return. Terence drove to the Lansdowne, where I found V waiting in the large inner hall.

She had visited Heywood Hill's bookshop and taken John Saumarez Smith out to have a drink at the Lansdowne bar. He told her he knew Robert Fellowes who was just the same age as himself. He said his father, Sir William Fellowes (the Queen's agent at Sandringham), had his existence transformed by reading the *Lyttleton/Hart-Davis Letters*, when he realized for the first time that there were finer things in life. We lunched (chicken Kiev, carafe of Côtes du Rhone). The Savage Club have premises in the same building as the Lansdowne, and hold a weekly luncheon in the Lansdowne dining-room. Their table not far away from us, about half a dozen mildly exotic specimens of Savages were lunching together, tho' no doubt *quantum mutatus ab illo* compared with what one imagines to have been the great Savage days of the 1890s. At 3 o'clock we found Terence waiting at a convenient corner of the club in Curzon Street, and reached home at 6 p.m., after exhausting if successful day, blessed with good weather, no more worries as to logistics of the trip.

Tuesday, 23 February

Congrats from Bob Conquest. He and Liddie were in England a week or two ago, said they failed to get reply on ringing us. I finished reread of *Titus Andronicus*, enjoyable, in spite of the bad press the play usually gets. It contains the lines 'The woods are ruthless, dreadful, deaf, and dull', amended by Robert Frost to 'The woods are lovely, dark, and deep', which has appealed to more than one American Presidential candidate for quotation in his speeches. Further lines from *Andronicus* might also be useful for them in the right circumstances:

> Here lurks no treason, here no envy swells,
> Here grow no damned drugs, here are no storms.

Sunday, 28 February

V and I dispatched individual protests to the Mendip District Council against the proposed new road through Dead Woman's Bottom to link up one of the quarries with the main highway, a peculiarly futile scheme as only one quarry would be benefited and to the disadvantage of many neighbouring houses. I reread J. I. M. Stewart's excellent short biography of Thomas Hardy (1971). Stewart makes the point that Jude's period being what he calls the Heroic Age of working-class education, enquiries would certainly have produced all sorts of assistance in Jude's efforts to get to a university. This aspect is left wholly unexplored by both Jude and Hardy. I am also rereading Robert Gittings's equally good *Second Mrs Hardy* (1979). One of Hardy's aids to writing *The Dynasts* was to try on Wellington's cocked hat. Florence Hardy, when her husband was away from the home (which wasn't often) used to keep a loaded revolver in her bedroom.

Saturday, 5 March

In the afternoon Gerry de Winton rang with congrats. Gerry is a year older than me, encountered only once at school, because, as a joke, someone put my name down for the School Chess and I drew de Winton. The clock was striking seven when he entered Goodhart's to play the game; when leaving the house after defeating me twice, a quarter past seven struck. V knew him in deb days. I think we encountered him again through Osbert Lancaster. By that time Gerry had married his wife Pru, whom Osbert had known (possibly had some sort of romance with) as a war widow in Greece. Lady Littlehampton's physical appearance bears a distinct resemblance to Pru de Winton. Gerry was a PoW during the war. He escaped and was walking across the Appenines disguised as an Italian peasant carrying a sack, when a man shouted to him: 'Englishman, Englishman!' This turned out to be an ex-Cook's agent, who said no Italian would ever dream of carrying a sack over his shoulder, as Gerry was doing, but always under his arm.

The de Winton family was originally called Wilkins, changed their name to de Winton on finding a late mediaeval document giving both names as alternative. This seems perfectly authentic so far as I can see without going into the matter of detail. They have a neo-gothick Castle, Maesllwch, on the Radnorshire/Brecon border, built by a nabob ancestor. Some of this Gerry pulled down to good effect, making an attractive house. He possesses title deeds recording negotiations with early eighteenth-century Powells of The Travely, comparatively near Maesllwch. We had several enjoyable visits there. Gerry fairly crazy these days, tho' in great form. He said he owed me a postcard.

Monday, 7 March

Congrats from Mrs P. E. W. Williams, with whom I corresponded on the subject of Beryl Markham's book about Kenya, which I reviewed. Mrs Williams picnicked in Kenya with the horrible sadistic John Carberry and liked him. I finished a paperback of *A Very Private Eye*, the Letters and Diary of Barbara Pym, borrowed in hardback from Tristram, read rather hurriedly, missing a good deal. I prefer this documentary stuff to her novels, all rather sad, tho' (like a novel) has relatively happy ending in renewed success of her books some years before her death. She was intelligent, funny, makes all sorts of good observations, 'creating a world of her own'. In praise I would not go so far as David Cecil and Philip Larkin. Indeed their comments reveal more of themselves as critics than of Barbara Pym. Her novels don't need adultery, homosexuality, etc., to pep them up, as she began to feel latterly. They are perfectly all right as they stand, if situations could be made somewhat stronger, more conscientiously worked out. This is due, I think, to lack of vitality in herself, observable in her own life, and the somewhat awful men with whom she continually fell in love.

One feels she had not the smallest idea what being married would be like. For that reason, probably sensibly, she instinctively never took it on. Her intelligence, appearance, pleasant character, would undoubtedly have found a husband had she truly wanted one over and above romantic dreams. There was an innate egotism, overpowering, even if of an outwardly inoffensive kind. Early letters are affected, often silly. There is much of interest in the Diaries. A page is devoted to her in the elaborate catalogue of Christian Bourgois (French publisher also doing *Dance*), which arrived this morning. Bourgois seems to be translating all Pym novels. Barbara Pym had an unusual family background, discovered only after she died, one she would have appreciated. Her father, so far from being descended, as vaguely adumbrated, from the brother of Pym, the Roundhead, was the illegitimate son of maid at a Somerset country house, seduced apparently by a member of an Anglo-Irish family called Crampton. The name is used in her family and her own books. Her father was brought up to be a solicitor in Oswestry, and so far as one can gather suffered not the slightest psychological hang-ups on this account. He was a man of genial uncomplicated character. The problem of inventing names by novelists for their characters is illustrated in today's Deaths in the *Daily Telegraph*, where Louise Beals (*The Fisher King*) appears.

Tuesday, 8 March

Congrats from Peter and June Luke (riposted with Drum Major & Pioneer, Peninsular Period); from J. B. Bury (fan dating from *Venusberg* as a boy. He reviews for the *Burlington*).

Wednesday, 9 March

The *Sunday Telegraph* (Lit. Ed. Derwent May) asked various people whose statue should occupy empty plinth on NE of Trafalgar Square. I suggested Rudyard Kipling: the British writer of the most diversified art, keenest sense of responsibility and sacrifice, possibly since Shakespeare. India associations link him with Havelock and Napier, already present; naval stories and poems with Nelson himself. Kipling could also survey ironically the meetings that take place in Trafalgar Square.

Thursday, 10 March

Anne Lancaster asked for Osbert's letters for the Osbert Lancaster Archive established at his Oxford college, Lincoln. I sent these suggesting copies, rather than originals, should be sent to Lincoln. She also enclosed for my amusement two xeroxes of letters to Osbert from Freddie Birkenhead, who was much upset at Evelyn Waugh's *Diaries*. It is a mystery to me how people who knew Evelyn well could have had so little idea of his character. That the general public, reviewers, etc. were disturbed by the Waugh *Diaries* and *Letters* is more understandable; the general public supposing writers of funny books to be good-natured, carefree people, alas, far from the case. Freddie was probably upset at finding how boring Evelyn found him and Randolph Churchill, pouring out their clichés and hackneyed quotations, when they were all quartered together in Jugoslavia. We celebrated V's birthday (Sunday) at dinner with caviar and Veuve Clicquot '80.

Sunday, 13 March

V's birthday. Having no present until she goes to London I made a birthday card. V, Tristram, Virginia, John and Georgia, lunched with Joff and Tessa Davies, it being also Tessa's birthday. I gave Tessa a paperback of *Aubrey*. Also present: Lucinda Davies (who is in the City, looked a bit sad, I thought); Tim Heneage, neighbour, middle fifties, unmarried, I believe breeds carnivorous orchids; Jane Kwiatkowski, old friend of Tessa's, RC convert, married a Pole (whose father emigrated to England before the war), and works in Milan. Her maiden name was Trevilian. An apt quotation hovered in my mind, as usual remembered only later:

> And I said 'When a foreign postillion
> Has hurried me off to the Po;
> Forget not Medora Trevilian,
> My own Araminta, say "No!" '

Except that it ought to be 'has hurried *you* off to the Po'. We saw the two new Davies Burmese cats (after the unhappy death of Francis), respectively white, grey-speckled, friendly, V thought both the cats grossly conceited. Later in the afternoon we watched TV chat show *Gallery*, in which V participated, by happy chance shown today; the competition was recognizing pictures from detail of canvas shown; chaired by George Melly. This V did well, matched against a fairly seedy collection, amongst whom I was interested to see Maggi Hambling (who was very well spoken of by John [P] as an art teacher).

Saturday, 19 March

An invitation from Jocelyn Stevens, recently appointed Rector of the Royal College of Art, to be one of the Senior Fellows of the College. Their existence is probably an innovation instituted by Stevens.

Monday, 21 March

John Russell rang last night to arrange for himself, his wife, and Christopher Simon Sykes (photographer), to do a piece about me for American *House & Garden* on Tuesday 28 June. Congrats from Miranda Hayward°. I reviewed John Bayley on *The Short Story* recently, in which he draws analogies from contrasted poems and short stories, in the course of which he points out that in Wolfe's 'Burial of Sir John Moore' 'the sods with their bayonets turning' is obvious nonsense, a bayonet being quite unsuitable for digging (especially the bayonets of that period). Rereading *Cymbeline*, I find Lucius says '. . . make him with our pikes and partisans a grave', which would be at least equally difficult, but gives a certain authority to Wolfe, as I wrote to John.

Saturday, 26 March

I finished *Cymbeline*, enjoyed more than expected. 'I'll meet you in the valleys' would have made a possible title for *The Valley of Bones*.

> Sir,
> In Cambria are we born, and gentlemen:

might also give a title, possibly for a genealogical work. I also finished a reread of Thomas Hardy's letters to his smart friend the Honble Mrs Henniker (daughter of Swinburne's friend Monckton Milnes, later Lord Houghton). Hardy appears to have been mildly in love with Mrs Henniker for thirty years. The letters are not madly exciting, but have interesting bits. They are chiefly notable for Hardy's considerable taste for smart life as it was then, and deliberate assimilation to it so far as possible. One is struck how superior were his gifts as novelist and poet, compared to his general intelligence, which was not great: e.g. his comments on politics and war, with which Hardy to some extent dabbled in *The Dynasts*, and these letters. Some years ago V and I went for a jaunt to Poole, thinking it would be a pretty seaside town (which it is no longer), the place also interesting us in the light of Henry Lamb having a home there up to the time he married V's sister Pansy.

While we were proceeding down the main street, some obstruction caused pedestrians to walk one behind the other at a certain point in the pavement. A man, grey moustache, fifty/sixty, dark suit, Homburg hat with braided brim, was standing, smiling rather self-consciously, by the kerb. One had to pass quite close to him. When V and I joined up again we both turned to the other saying: 'Did you see the ghost of Thomas Hardy?' Obviously the ghost-of-Thomas-Hardy had cultivated the resemblance (possibly once remarked on by somebody to him), then paraded himself in the gutter for the benefit of Hardy fans visiting Poole. The model was the photograph of Hardy sitting with his second wife on the beach at Cromer. Incidentally, the actor playing Hardy in a documentary produced by Tristram some years ago visited the Hardy Museum without changing his Hardy costume and make-up, so Tristram tells us.

Sunday, 27 March

Antonia asked if she and Harold Pinter could lunch here today after the wedding at

Badminton of Matthew Carr (son of Raymond Carr, Hispanicist don) and Lady Anne Somerset, the Beauforts' daughter. She said lunching here was one of her baits for Harold to come. I asked if Harold would wear a tailcoat. She said that was her next objective. When they arrived for luncheon (having spent the night at Bath) I had not the courage to ask whether the tailcoat had been achieved. John cooked chilli con carne, at which he is adept. The wedding had been a great success, both Antonia and Harold in excellent form, Harold showing no sign of the portentous behaviour sometimes reported. Antonia looking better, I thought, than when last here.

Harold is doing an adaptation of Elizabeth Bowen's *The Heat of the Day*. I am not mad about Elizabeth Bowen's writing, but suggested *Mysterious Kôr* might also be worth a possible glance for adaptation as a short film. At the wedding Antonia said to Henry Bath (maternal grandfather of the bride): 'I think I must get myself a drink.' Henry, characteristically supposing she had asked: 'Can I get *you* a drink?' replied: 'No. Don't bother. I've really had too many already.'

I recommended Musil's *The Man Without Qualities* (which I am rereading) to Harold, who knew about Musil, but had never tackled him. I thought Musil a good idea for the Greek island they are bound for. They both had white wine for an aperitif (Südtiroler Weissburgunder), Antonia subsequently finishing the bottle, as red (Château Moulin-du-Cadet, St Emilion, very good) does not suit her. Enjoyable party.

Monday, 28 March

I saw Lister for two minutes to file down my upper plate this time. I finished a reread of Kipling's *Collected Poems*. These are abominably edited (anonymously, Hodders, 1954), vaguely chronological, but army and sea poems sometimes put together regardless of date, so that it is impossible to judge poetic development. One has the impression of an enormous energy when young, then a somewhat poorish journalist period during the South African war, good again on Sussex, with occasional bursts of excellence towards the end of his life. Even when at moments the verse is terrible stuff, Kipling's verbal facility never wholly vanishes, sometimes phrases that make one laugh ('The rich Allobrogenses never used amanuenses', etc.).

Tuesday, 29 March

Congrats from the Richmond bookseller Eric Barton (met, I think, at time of my father's death at Richmond, when Barton bought some of the books, possibly also a fan), who alerted me to a piece called 'Dr Trelawney' in the *London Magazine* (which

John is going to get) by Timothy d'Arch Smith. I've never met T. d'A. S., but once had an amusing telephone conversation with him about H. S. Ashbee (the Victorian collector of Erotica), confirming that Ashbee did not write *My Secret Life*, which d'Arch Smith denied vigorously. He is also a bookseller. He said he was always looking out for *Slavey* (erotic work written by Gerald Reitlinger's brother Henry), bought on the Quais in Paris by Constant Lambert. Constant immediately after ran into Lytton Strachey, who made a pass at him, Constant's worry was to fight off the pass while concealing *Slavey*, which would have been too much of a joke. Virginia, at The Stables for gardening, came to dinner. Spaghetti Arabella, the remaining bottle of Moulin-du-Cadet opened for the Pinters, after 48 hours (having used patent reclosing process), exposure just noticeable, I thought.

Thursday, 31 March

We watched a twenty-minute TV programme on Newstead Abbey by Peter Porter, Australian poet. Newstead is grander than I supposed, one suspects the place has been a good deal altered since Byron's day. All the same it was interesting to see it and Porter, who is slightly on the lines of Robert Lowell. He spoke of *Don Juan* as the second greatest epic in the language (one presumes *Paradise Lost* the first). When I was young Byron was almost totally written off as a poet, except for scraps such as 'She walks in beauty, like the night', 'We'll go no more a-roving', etc. Then there was a burst of books about Byron, how he slept with his half-sister, buggered his wife, had homosexual affairs.

From being all but forgotten, *Don Juan* was raised to the highest peak. No doubt the poem has very amusing passages and brilliant verbal facility. One's immediate feeling is that it might have been better had Byron made it more directly autobiographical, an English background, instead of just Newstead brought in as a house-party: perhaps impossible at period of Romantic Revival. All the same one would certainly say the English section is the least good. My maternal grandfather was about a fifth cousin of Byron's, through the Rossells, of Ratcliffe, Nottingham-shire, one of whom married 1st Lord Byron. V's *E. M. Delafield* proofs arrived which I am reading.

Saturday, 2 April

Several paragraphs in the papers regarding Malcolm Muggeridge's eighty-fifth birthday, combined with the publication of *Conversion*, describing why he joined the Roman Catholic Church several years ago, with much publicity at the time. He was photographed kneeling in prayer, meditating, etc. John brought down *Times* interview with Malcolm of some days ago, in which he states that he and Kitty regard themselves as belonging to no Church, merely finding RC the one most sympathetic. Odd statement, to say the least, after all the public genuflexions, so comparatively recently. Finished V's *E. M. Delafield*, much improved since the first draft, a sense of humdrumness being the point (*Provincial Lady*), except hair-raising convent, good account of life in passages as novice. We watched Boat Race, Oxford winning by five lengths. When I was up, Oxford never won, the papers saying the University was 'decadent' (including one occasion when the losing Oxford crew rowed an all-time record), as if the Oxford VIII were undergraduates like, say, Harold Acton, et al. It would indeed be preferable if they *were* real undergraduates, not middle-aged men, often American, as nowadays.

Easter Sunday, 3 April

V had my CH citation framed as Easter present. Answers to the *Sunday Telegraph* question about the empty plinth at Trafalgar Square have been published. Kingsley Amis, like myself (without collaboration) chose Kipling; Isaiah Berlin, Ted Hughes (Poet Laureate), both wanted Bacon, curious double; Iris Murdoch suggested Proust; Peter Hall (National Theatre manager) opted for Oscar Wilde. Others of no great note. We watched Tristram's Brian Moore story TV adaptation, which, although goodish, I failed to sit through, being allergic to Irish life. [*DT* review lukewarm about the story, spoke of 'skill lavished on it by Director Tristram Powell', later reactions from individuals, Roy Fuller, etc., very favourable to Tristram.]

Easter Monday, 4 April

Tristram, Virginia, Georgia and Archie, to luncheon on their way back from staying with the Mounts in Pembrokeshire: Welsh pie (made with turkey), plum pudding, both excellent, magnum of Trentino Cabernet. Georgia stayed on at The Stables to work.

Wednesday, 6 April

Georgia lunched with us at the Bridge House, Nunney. She returns home today. She has worked extremely hard. Archie sets out this morning for Toronto, Boston, on a North American tour of the Dulwich School play, by Raymond Chandler, an Old Alleynian (like P. G. Wodehouse, several other writers of lesser eminence, if quite well-known, also Stage figures). Blackthorn winter. The early morning mists make me buzz all over.

Thursday, 7 April

Roy Jenkins rang, saying he was having an 'executive morning'. He asked us to luncheon on 21 May. Roy said, as Chancellor of Oxford, he was trying to go round all the colleges, at present having done about twenty. I enquired if he had come across Hugh Lloyd-Jones, Regius Professor of Greek, and warned that Hugh was a High Tory. Roy said he had pretty well given up politics these days; he praised the literary pages of the *Daily* and *Sunday Telegraph*, for both of which he likes reviewing.

Friday, 8 April

V and I dined at The Stables. The Stockwells were rather late in arriving owing to a car breakdown, however Virginia produced an excellent dinner, seafood, salami, veal, I drank some New Zealand white wine, produced by Tristram, not too bad at all.

Sunday, 10 April

The Stockwells to drinks here in morning, the Lukes were invited, but unable to come. Tristram said David Cheshire and Melvyn Bragg are doing a TV film about Paddy Leigh Fermor. This should produce a good clash of egos. I finished Roy Fuller's *Crime Omnibus*, three novels written soon after the war. These are decidedly strange, throwing an interesting light on Roy himself. I enjoyed the first two (speaking as an ace non-detective story reader, except Holmes). The last one, told in the first person by psychopathic case, I did not care for on technical grounds. Roy contributes an Introduction in which he says the tycoon in *The Second Curtain* was drawn from Sir Robert (later Lord) Renwick, slightly older contemporary of mine at school (we were in same division at one moment), who always seemed rather nice for the sort of hearty boy he was, infinitely unsinister (as in story). The use of Bob Renwick is additionally interesting as Renwick married as his second wife Joan, widow of John Spencer, on whom Peter Templer in *Dance* is somewhat modelled. John Spencer was really quite a close friend of mine, not at all intellectual, an elegant businessman or stockbroker type.

The Spencers had been divorced, then remarried, John Spencer was killed serving with the Welsh Guards in the Middle East, a major, in his late thirties. He was a most unmilitary figure at school; in fact sacked from the OTC for getting tight in camp. Joan Spencer/Renwick, thin, elegant, somewhat rackety, friend of Rosie Goldsmid, could, I think, hardly be regarded as carrying on the *Dance* narrative in the form of Betty Taylor or Porter (who became an ambassadress on recovering from her breakdown). Even so, it shows how few people there are to go round for the use of novelists. The Stockwells' car towed to London.

Monday, 11 April

The photographer Lucinda Douglas-Menzies came (V at WI meeting), a sturdy girl in her thirties, her grandfather Australian. She did not know if Menzies, the Prime Minister was any relation, the name Menzies being common in those parts. A nice day so she took photographs outside. This warm weather rather catches my left leg.

Wednesday, 13 April

I saw Lister very briefly. *The Fisher King* is to be translated into Portuguese (publisher, Dom Quixote). I agreed to do piece for *Le Nouvel Observateur* about the French translation of Edith Sitwell's *English Eccentrics*. The French reviews of *Tourne, Manège* (*Wheel*) on the whole most favourable (better than in this country, except for about four excellent English ones), finding the book savage in tone, 'Powell le malicieux', one saying the story might just as well have been set in Paris; another that it could not possibly be French, the latter may be ironic in the light of the first, something often difficult to tell in French if one is only moderately conversant with the language. Reread two Selections of John Davidson's poems, to one of which T. S. Eliot contributes a Foreword, saying 'Thirty-bob a Week' made deep impression on him when he was young. The 'Runnable Stag' recurs in the mind, but Davidson's blank verse hard going. I would agree, adding 'Dymchurch Wall', and a few good individual lines. Davidson was an odd fish, with his occasional striking phrase, wit, megalomaniac personality, which comes across in the way that holds the attention.

Friday, 15 April

I wrote a piece on Edith Sitwell's *English Eccentrics* for *Le Nouvel Observateur*. Edith's book is an appalling muddle, full of Sitwellian quirks, if at the same time once in a way illuminating about its subject. For instance the chapter about Margaret Fuller is rather good. (Incidentally, the latter American, no doubt dragged in on account of poor Edith's similar unhappy passion for man from whom no response was possible; in Edith's case the White Russian painter Pavel Tchelitchew – awful both as painter and as a man – queer who simply wanted to get all he could out of her.) Edith's prose works, at which she did not excel in spite of gift for spotting grotesque aspects of a subject, were written to alleviate a chronic state of hard-upness.

I finished a reread of *Much Ado* with relief, a most unfavourite play of mine, in fact the only Shakespeare play I really don't like. Beatrice and Benedick tedious repetition of same gag; the framing of Hero wholly contrived. Only 'Sigh no more, Ladies' and a few other songs are seductive. My left leg is a nuisance on and off.

Monday, 18 April

A letter from Roy Fuller in answer to mine about *Crime Omnibus*, among other things saying, in spite of having used Bob Renwick as model for the tycoon in *The Second Curtain* (who murders several people to prevent an all but indestructible electric filament that would damage his business being put on the market), he had apparently 'bought a few shares' in Renwick's electronic firm (which, I believe, got off to a good start, and did fabulously well), so John [Powell] says.

Rereading Byron's *Don Juan* in consequence of watching the TV programme on Newstead. Incidentally, I have suddenly taken against anthologies, read in bed for years, constant changing of poet, mood, the reader having all at once to become sympathetic or unsympathetic. Instead have now turned to *Collected Works*. The Edwardian song, 'Oh, the girls they do go on so / In the land of King Alphonso' owes the rhyme 'Alphonso/Go on so' to Byron's epic, which is a good point.

Tuesday, 19 April

Lees and Mary Mayall came to luncheon. Mary was thinner; Lees with stick owing to trouble from fallen arches. As a former Deputy Marshal of Diplomatic Corps and Chief of Protocol, Lees wanted a blow-by-blow account of audience with the Queen. He said the large hall entered from the Grand Entrance in Inner Courtyard is known as the Forty-Four Room, as not redecorated since 1844; the apartment in which HM saw me is called the Twenty-Two Room, because not redecorated since 1922. I now realize the latter was exactly like the drawing-rooms in which one would find oneself waiting (of course without a drink) before a deb dinner-party in the 1920s, if that had recently been done up. Talking of formal meetings with the Queen, known as 'Kissing Hands', Lees said one Bulgarian Ambassador had been so moved when taking leave of HM on relinquishment of his appointment that he threw himself upon his knees and kissed her hand. I would like to have witnessed this.

Mayalls are going to Tulsa, Oklahoma (where Hilary Spurling recently read Paul Scott's letters) in late summer to see Mary's eldest son Bogey (Gerard) Campbell who is doing something like running a restaurant there. Bogey is alleged to be maintained by a high-born Oklahoman lady, rather like Cosmo Flitton in *Dance*, except the latter was married to his American. Robert Mayall is having to give up his bookshop (the size of a telephone-box) in Cecil Court because the rent has been doubled again.

Chilli con carne (cooked in first instance by John) preceded by melon, gâteau, Südtiroler Cabernet. I gave Lees a book on Erotica, reviewed by me some weeks ago. I did not want it in the least but there was absolutely nothing else. Enjoyable party.

I am rereading Anthony Birley's *The People of Roman Britain* (1979), an interesting work. The first recorded civil servant in Britain, a slave, had a Greek name meaning 'Blameless'.

Wednesday, 20 April

Archie's eighteenth birthday. He is back from the Toronto/Boston tour, which seems to have gone well. In afternoon there was a knock on door, grey-haired man with a Cromwellian haircut handed in the *Somerset Trust Magazine*. Speaking in a manner reminiscent of John Sparrow, precise, intellectual, he said: 'Do you know, a terrible thing? I was in the Midsomer Norton Library the other day, found they had not got a *single one* of your novels. I told them a distinguished novelist lives not a stone's throw away, you have none of his books. Frome is all right.' I uttered a few broken sentences of thanks. He said his name was Don Thompson and drove away in a small cherry-coloured car.

Tuesday, 26 April

I saw Dr Rawlins about my stiff left leg. He gave me some pills (Ledergeric). They made me slightly muzzy in the evening. I had a Vit. B injection from the rather attractive Liz Carter, the Sister, who has been doing District Nurse at Beckington. I asked if she were still understudying that job, she replied: 'Yes, I don't mind the extra work. It's on my way home. Keeps me out of mischief.' At dinner we listened to a radio programme on Cyril Connolly. The transmission was indifferent, the material rather good: Stephen Spender, Peter Quennell, Freddie Ayer, Kingsley Amis, extracts from my Memoirs. The general picture was surprisingly consistent and free from the usual humbug on these occasions. I tried to avoid reviewing Michael Foot's book on Byron, as I have a low opinion of his capabilities, but when a Byron book by Alan Massie was added, I had to agree to do a Byron piece.

I was told I must put Foot first as his book published first, but suspect simply because as a politician, he is 'news'. As expected, Foot's book was irritating, somewhat incoherent, and without much understanding. Happily, being in middle of rereading *Don Juan*, I was able to apply to it Byron's epithets for Southey's writings 'so quaint and mouthey'. Alan Massie was as usual good. One of Massie's illustrations shows portrait of Annabella Milbanke, Byron's wife (the painter unnamed). This makes her look distinctly like Byron's mother, whose portrait is a few pages earlier. This is a most interesting fact, so far as I know, never pointed out before. Once the picture has been seen, the resemblance noticed, other pictures of Annabella confirm her likeness to Mrs Byron. As it happens Massie makes the point that the bad terms on which Byron is alleged to be with his mother ('lame brat', etc.)

seem to have been much exaggerated. Byron wrote his mother hundreds of letters in which jokes, which she was by no means incapable of appreciating, were often shared.

Saturday, 30 April–Monday, 2 May

Tristram, Virginia, Archie are at The Stables. We heard more of Archie's transatlantic theatrical trip. At Toronto he stayed with a family, the father of which was at first rather sticky, then asked Archie, as long shot, whether by any chance he was relation of mine. He turned out to be a passionate *Dance* fan. During the Boston part of the tour, play performed at Andover school, visited twenty-five years ago by me with John Meck of Dartmouth, who had a son there. As a holiday job Archie is to act as guide to the Palace of Westminster, employment on which Dulwich College has some established line. Trelawney is still not well. He refuses food, but drank a little milk. He is dreadfully thin. V has got in touch with Mr Bargett, the vet, regarding this.

Wednesday, 4 May

Rosemary Hill, freelance and Edwina Woolstencroft, BBC radio interviewed V for an E. M. Delafield radio programme. V thought it all went quite well. John managed to secure a copy of the *London Magazine* containing the piece about Dr Trelawney (the character in *Dance* as opposed to our ailing cat) by Timothy d'Arch Smith, bookseller. D'Arch Smith (one cannot imagine what can be the origins of name) is apparently son of Pamela Frankau, grandson therefore of Gilbert Frankau. I remember reviewing a novel of the latter's for the *DT* before the war, describing its characters as interested only in keeping fit, rather than making money. One imagines not an obsession with his grandson, whose piece on Dr Trelawney turned out amusing. I wrote d'Arch Smith telling him that the bits of The Doctor not based on Crowley owed something to an earlier avatar, a certain Dr Oyler, who used to lead his mob of children in Grecian costume in runs across Grayshott Common, when we lived at Stonedene just before the First War. I have come across references to Oyler occasionally (I foolishly did not note them down). He was just as described in *The Kindly Ones*, with a touch of Crowley added. D'Arch Smith, something of an expert on oddities, might offer further information.

Friday, 6 May

I saw Mr Lister, who took X-rays to make sure the gum trouble was clearing up. Trelawney (Cornish Rex cat now) remains in a low state of health. I fear we must be prepared for the worst. I reread *Pericles*, a play put together in rather a haphazard manner, all the same some excellent bits, and essentially Shakespearian. One of my favourite passages is when the Pander says: 'If there be not a conscience to be used in every trade, we shall never prosper.' One somewhat piquant aspect of the plot, is Lysimachus, Governor of Mitylene, eventually marrying Marina, having inspected her at the brothel on hearing something specially choice was on sale there (Marina having been widely advertised as an inmate who will not give anyone the pox). On being shown her (presumably to knock the price down) he remarks: 'Faith, she would serve after a long voyage at sea.' The Bawd says: 'I beseech your honour, give me leave; a word, and I'll have done presently.' Lysimachus replies: 'I beseech you, do.' Lysimachus is finally moved by Marina's plight, gives her gold, recommends her to find another job, which, rather improbably, she is successful in doing. One cannot help feeling that Lysimachus, during their later married life, was not let off having once remarked his wife would do after a long voyage at sea.

Saturday, 7 May

The Trelawney (cat) situation has now come to the worst. He is a little bag of bones, finding difficulty in eating, lifting his head with an effort, tho' will still jump on my knee. It breaks one's heart. Only six months ago the vet commented that it was nice to see a cat of Trelawney's age looking so well. He is now within a month of his eleventh birthday. V and John took him in today to the vet to make an end of things. I felt ashamed that this unpleasant job fell on them. Dreadfully distressing. The most intelligent cat I have ever known, in some ways the most affectionate, jumping on one's back, nuzzling under one's chin in the evening after his supper. He hated the smallest alteration in his routine, such as not being picked up in the morning, said 'Good Morning' to. A very, very sad day.

Wednesday, 11 May

V drove me to the Bath Clinic for a check-up with Mr Southwood. Southwood then found his equipment faulty, therefore I have to return tomorrow. Southwood's physical resemblance to Widmerpool suddenly took positive shape in his showing no regret for not having examined his instruments earlier. I sent Anthony and Tanya Hobson a copy of *Il Re Pescatore*, as the book is dedicated to them. Anthony's reply said that Tanya was coming out of hospital, implications being that things were about as bad as they could be. V sent a line of sympathy. Tanya is a very sweet girl, tragic this should have happened, the fall possibly as much result of her condition as causing it to worsen. There was a brief radio programme on E. M.

Delafield in which V said a word or two.

Thursday, 12 May

Saw Southwood again this morning, all well. I asked if he came from these parts (one drives through an area of Radstock called Southwood on the way to Bath). Southwood replied that he came from London, but family from West Country two hundred years ago, where he had returned 'like the Prodigal Son', also a somewhat Widmerpoolian phraseology. I had a haircut in the afternoon in Nunney. I finished *Don Juan*, exceedingly funny in parts, bursts of wonderful versification, longwinded at other times, but narrative never properly organized, ends abruptly, but further verses may have been planned. I had at first thought the epic should have been set primarily in Great Britain, so to speak Byron's own story (as slightly touched on in *Beppo*). In fact the satire is apt to become heavy-handed when he deals with the home scene, tho' in earlier Continental sections contemporary British references are usually witty and well expressed. The whole poem, having been long disregarded, is now perhaps somewhat overpraised.

Tuesday, 17 May

I finished Philip Larkin's two novels *Jill* (1946), *A Girl in Winter* (1947). I did not remember much of the first; second was read for first time. The hero of *Jill*, a working-class scholarship boy (a policeman's son), goes up to Oxford in 1940. He has to share rooms with an aggressive rackety minor-public-school undergraduate, for whom he develops a certain hero-worship. The scholarship boy invents a fifteen-year-old sister, Jill, to make his stable companion jealous. This theme never properly worked out, but the hero comes across, and falls madly in love with, a young girl who in most respects resembles Jill. All that results from this is making a fool of himself when drunk at an undergraduate gathering, and getting ducked by the guests (he himself having gate-crashed the party). He finishes up at the end of the book ill with bronchitis.

Inserted into all this is an account of going home in term time to find out the fate of his parents after a particularly bad air raid, presumably modelled on Coventry (where Larkin, like Connolly, was born). Considering the novel was written when Larkin was only twenty-one/twenty-two, a severely naturalistic narrative is pretty well sustained, if at the same time totally uninspired. There seems no particular point in introducing the imaginary Jill, as this seems never adequately developed later. The rather unpleasant incident of wrecking the fellow 'poor scholar's' rooms appears as quite out of character for the hero; more like something from *Lucky Jim*.

Larkin contributes an Introduction to the comparatively recently published paperback, which shows his own Oxford life to have been considerably less limited than as represented in the novel. He had friends like Kingsley Amis, tho' that was not necessarily an objection to the story. *Jill* might be looked on as a fairly typical first novel (of a certain talent).

In its way, *A Girl in Winter* is much stranger. I cannot relate the latter (as with most serious novels) to any aspect I know of the author's 'myth'. That may simply be my own ignorance of Larkin's life. Kingsley or Bob Conquest might be able to throw some light. The book opens with the heroine working in depressed circumstances in the Public Library of a North Midland town, during the Second War (which of course Larkin himself did). She is a foreigner (probably a German Jewish refugee, tho' that is never specifically stated), waiting for the answer to a letter written by her to an English family with whom she stayed some years before the war on some sort of student exchange scheme. The English family never came to stay with hers in Germany. Some sort of understanding was implied (in England) with the son of the house. The narrative cuts back to this visit, which was not an overwhelming success, the heroine initially falling in love with the son, then deciding he was a bore. The long account of this English interlude is not always convincing and at times definitely tedious. She is, however, very excited with news that the son, now in the army, is going to visit her in the provincial town. When he arrives (after an excessively trying day experienced by the heroine) she again finds him a bore, but in the end goes to bed with him, as he is due to embark overseas, having visited her without getting leave (somewhat mistakenly). This the end of the story.

One is struck by Larkin writing from the point of view of a woman, a foreign woman at that, when he possessed an obsessive dislike of 'abroad', or anything to do with foreigners. We are told nothing about the heroine's previous sexual experiences, if any; indeed little or nothing about her background, except it seems relatively well-to-do. Even allowing for emotional feelings to go up and down, change violently at short notice, she behaves extremely oddly, often rather disagreeably; for instance, one finds difficulty in believing she would have been quite so chilly with the young man, when he had (so far as one understands) come to see her in circumstances that might have got him into serious trouble with the military authorities, especially as she had been living for nine months without seeing a soul she had ever met before.

John Bayley is quoted on the cover as giving high praise to *A Girl in Winter*, but, although again the narrative is well sustained, in its way a remarkable novel for the writer's age (about twenty-four), there are many inconsistencies, *longueurs*, nor can one quite see the general point. Larkin never wrote another novel, so he may have felt some of these things too about his own work, as he was always a severe critic of other people's books. Larkin had a great ambition to be a novelist but my own feeling is that he had little or no talent for that.

Wednesday, 18 May

Henry Mee arranged for another sitting today, then rang to say he was suffering from food poisoning, possibly a 'fish-pie take-away', which as a rule he found good. Date was made for 1 June.

I watched a TV programme for Anthony Burgess's seventieth (possibly seventy-first) birthday. He is undoubtedly talented, all his musical gifts and a mastery of languages, tremendous performer; at the same time produced a row of clichés, such as English hatred of writers (on examination it turns out British writers in certain respects do much better than, say, French ones), with good sense too, as for instance even the worst writers having something to teach one, as a writer. Where I suspect Burgess falls short is inadequate grasp of human character other than his own. He ranks Ford Madox Ford best writer in English of the century. While recognizing Ford's merits, I think this shows Burgess (like Connolly, Greene) insensitive to a kind of bogusness in Ford, particularly apparent in what is possibly his best book *The Good Soldier*. Archie rang asking to stay for some days while working for A levels. We are still missing Trelawney.

Friday, 20 May

Tanya Hobson has died. One did not expect this to have come quite so soon. She was always charming to meet, always funny, always the first to see a joke, a Turgenev heroine come to life, one of those girls in whom one can never quite believe in a book. Very sad for Anthony. We shall all miss her.

Saturday, 21 May

Marvellous day. Driven by John, we lunched with Roy and Jennifer Jenkins at St Amand's House, East Hendred: other guests Sir Claus and Lady (Mary) Moser; Nicko Henderson. Sir Claus, refugee origins, agreeable, she seemed so too, tho' not much opportunity of talking with her. Moser (put next to me at luncheon, Jennifer on my other side) is now Warden of Wadham, Chairman of one of the Rothschild firms, on the Covent Garden board and various other appointments.

As soon as we sat down he said he thought I had written the best piece on Maurice Bowra [in the commemorative volume edited by Hugh Lloyd-Jones, 1974]. He wanted to hear every detail about Maurice I could produce, as Bowra had 'turned Wadham from a bad College into a good one'. Maurice is now a deeply venerated figure, the new building at Wadham to be named after him. Such an accretion of myth has accumulated about Bowra, not only the man himself, but that whole Twenties period at Oxford, that is not easy to describe either today. Maurice himself changed a good deal, I think, in the years immediately after I went down. He became less overtly homosexual and outrageously anarchic in his talk. I did the best I could, but found it hard to put over what one now sees as the Bowra sparkling moment compared with what were really the comparatively sad years of success when he was finally referred to as 'Old Tragic'.

Nicko Henderson is always agreeable to meet. He spoke of orange-flavoured cod liver oil as sovereign remedy for stiff limbs, from which he himself suffers. He said he would send me a bottle. [He did, I riposted with *Iron Aspidistra*.] Roy was in excellent form. He is one of the few politicians interested in individuals. He gave an amusing description of Mitterrand at EEC gatherings, very monarchical, always attended by a Captain of Artillery in a kepi, to remind everyone that he is a Head of State, not a mere representative. V talked with Jennifer (Chairman of the National Trust) about the Old Castle at Dynevor, which does seem to be being put right at last. Good claret, Château Batailley, Pauillac, '75, described by Roy as 'that nice taste of wet dog'.

Roy, when a Gunner, apparently in the Somerset/Leicestershire Yeomanry (not Hertfordshire, as I thought), shared quarters at Angmering-on-Sea with Robin Wilson (mentioned earlier as at Goodhart's). Wilson brought in sacks of wheat for his horses, which caused rats to thrive in the house. Roy described a typical army subterfuge by which, to avoid PT, he used to turn up for his bath in PT kit, bath taken immediately after Robin Wilson commander of Battery, both knowing the other knew, while nothing ever said. Bets were laid (at Nicko's suggestion) of a bottle of '75 claret on the American Election: Jennifer, John, Nicko, self, guessing Bush; the rest Dukakis. Enjoyable party.

Monday, 23 May

I saw Lister as a stud of the plate came unmoored again. I have to see him in a fortnight's time. Archie came to stay for his work.

Tuesday, 24 May

Tanya Hobson's funeral at Whitsbury. V and I lunched at the Pembroke Arms, Wilton, perfectly tolerable Italian-orientated buffet meal, unexpectedly cheap. The Pembroke Arms' moment apparently being dinner, when the menu was fairly elaborate and the reverse of cheap. Whitsbury Church could be seen when one was at the Hobsons', so we assumed it was approached from a little further up the road than The Glebe House. In a sense that is so, but the path to church is before you reach the Hobsons' house, through a kind of park, in which stands the stud farm for brood mares which we used to pass on the way. The church is at least half a mile from the road when approached that way, quite a long walk even after we parked the car in a strategic position, later finding a field had been specially set out for that purpose. The church small, with many memorials, but could not see name of the predominant family; I should have liked to examine it further. Everything was very well kept, one imagines largely due to Tanya's efforts. The place was packed, pews sitting four. V went in first, then me, soon followed by Virginia Bath. In consequence of Tanya's parents' various marriages, remarriages and affairs of other relations, complicated connexions of the congregation were extremely tangled. There was also the difficulty of picking out individuals not seen for decades, some macabre faces just recognizable.

George Herbert's 'Teach me, my God and King', 'Let Saints on earth in concert sing', 'Guide me, O thou great Redeemer' (it should be Jehovah). Peter Levi, an ex-Jesuit priest, academic, poet, married for some years to Cyril Connolly's widow, Deirdre Craig (Tanya's half-sister through Joy Newton) read Larkin's 'Arundel Tomb' rather inaudibly, tho' he must have plenty of experience of that sort of thing. John Julius Norwich was in complete contrast reading 'They are all gone into the world of light', by Henry Vaughan (one of my favourite poets), who employed great drama, rather as if he were reciting 'The Private of the Buffs', or 'The Arab's farewell to his steed'. Everyone was asked back to the house for tea, which clearly would have involved much standing, inimical to my left leg, and also fairly long journey back, so we made a swift getaway. A sad occasion. V said that the flowers arranged by Tanya's daughters were a poem.

Sunday, 29 May

Virginia varnished the Moynihan portrait. This was a great improvement as the original varnish had dried in patches. I finished reread of *The Merchant of Venice*, a play I never much enjoyed, probably owing to hackneyed productions and having read it at school. I remember writing an essay in which I said Shakespeare did not realize what a moving figure he had made of Shylock; the beak, not without cause, saying: 'Well, if you realized that, it's reasonable to suppose Shakespeare grasped the idea too'; one of those remarks that gave a jolt to one's intelligence and do one lasting good. Was Antonio, apparently unmarried, in love with Bassanio? He speaks with extraordinary warmth of his friend. Jessica is oddly attractive in spite of behaving not particularly well to her father. I find the attraction of Jessica (agreed by V) hard to explain.

I finished the Wordsworth selection, a poet I can never find sympathetic in spite of obvious great moments. I feel rather the same about the *Collected Shelley*, which followed Wordsworth. I thought I felt better disposed towards Shelley, but, apart from well-known bits like outsoaring the shadow of our night, 'Ozymandias' (Rameses II), etc., I am back at scratch with Shelley's acres of boredom.

Tuesday, 31 May

A Finnish journalist, Keijo Kuttenen, came to interview me. Rather a plain young man, tall, specs, toneless voice. He knew his stuff about *Dance*, several vols of which had already appeared in Finland. He seemed unsurprised, totally uninterested, that I had been in Finland sixty or more years ago. This lack of surprise reminded me of an anecdote told by a Finnish Colonel called Xiliacus when we were there (who later threw in his lot with the Reds, I believe). Xiliacus was in Italy with his wife (possibly picnicking at Tivoli) and heard a couple sitting a short way behind talking Finnish. The man then got up, moving to where the Xiliacuses were sitting, asked in Finnish what time train went or something of that sort. Xiliacus replied in Finnish, without comment. When the man returned to his companion the Xiliacuses heard him say: 'I told you they would know the language.'

Wednesday, 1 June

Henry Mee, expected about 2.30, arrived after 4 o'clock, having encountered innavigable traffic. He had recovered from his fish pie, 'But only just,' he said. I supposed he wanted to make further sketches, take photographs, in fact he brought down photographs of my portrait, the latter to be on show next Tuesday at the John Player Exhibition at the National Portrait Gallery. It seems a reasonable likeness, lively, in general effect hard to judge in photographs, especially of a picture of that size, rather heavy dark impasto on the forehead looks a little awkward. Mee also brought a photograph of his 1730 Bermondsey house, a most elegant building. I think he really rather likes coming down here for a talk, especially about Death, a favourite subject of his, much taken with phrase in my Memoirs about a muffled figure in the corner of the room.

He is a great cat fan, beseeched us not to have an 'ordinary' to replace Trelawney, but getting on in life, we feel we do not want to leave too neurotic an animal behind to find a new home; not that any cat owned by me does not turn into a fancy type after a short time. Henry Mee wants to paint Rodrigo Moynihan in his two dozen notabilities. He asked me to write Rodrigo a letter to prepare him for approach, which I have done, tho' it is always rather delicate matter to introduce one painter to another. I warned Mee that Rodrigo may well be in France. He gave V a smacking kiss on arrival, leaving. We wondered if he had done the same to the Queen, the reason why he had been such a success apparently when painting her.

Thursday, 2 June

Archie left. Charming boy. He worked very hard. He seemed to me to talk excellent sense about the Shakespeare plays he had seen, for instance three performances of *Twelfth Night*.

Tuesday, 7 June

I saw Lister, who removed one of the few remaining roots. My impression is that it would have been better to have been done in the first instance. Rows continue about *Tumbledown*, the TV film based on the Falklands campaign, and the reminiscences of a young Scots Guards officer, Robert Lawrence, who won an MC there. He was shot in the head. The BBC film is said to have caused offence to the Scots Guards and Medical Officers concerned and to Lawrence's ex-girlfriend. When Tristram was last here he spoke of having met Lawrence at a party. Tristram asked Lawrence what he was going to do next, said he wanted to go into films, on the production side and planned to have his own company. As the army was what he knew most about, he would specialize in military films.

In consequence of Anthony Burgess's recent programme, I am rereading Burgess's long novel *Earthly Powers* (1980) which I did not much care for on the first round so decided to have another go at. In some Sunday paper recently Burgess referred to Graham Greene's Roman Catholicism (Burgess is a born RC) as 'Pickwickian', presumably meaning quaint, unorthodox. Today in the *Daily Express* he actively attacks Graham, describing him as a 'minor imitator of Conrad without his depths'. Hitherto, so far as I can remember, Burgess has been respectful to Greene, for instance in Burgess's list *99 Best Novels*. Much of the latter material was pinched, or at best leaned on heavily or borrowed, from Martin Seymour-Smith's *Guide to Modern Literature*, in order to get Burgess's book out quickly (as he was nettled at not being included in a recent much publicized list of Twelve Best Novels). Some of the opinions, therefore, may have been Seymour-Smith's. However, this looks rather like a Burgess/Greene declaration of war, possibly a bid on Burgess's part to be regarded as main RC novelist.

I finished Coleridge's *Collected Poems*, which must be admitted to include reams of boring stuff. 'The Ancient Mariner', 'Xanadu', with a few others keep their magic, especially former. What on earth is the poem about? Any explanations I have read are always totally inadequate. Perhaps one does not need to know. Hugh Kingsmill always said a description of Coleridge's married life was to be found in: 'Backward or forwards, half her length for a short uneasy motion.'

Wednesday, 8 June

Judith Kazantzis (née Pakenham, second Longford daughter) and Irving Wineman, with whom she now lives, came to tea, having rung up to announce their presence in the neighbourhood. Judith carrying two cushions about with her on account of something amiss with her back. She was married to a rather nice chap of Greek extraction (a lawyer on the Baltic Exchange, I think, two children). Wineman's family are of Romanian origins. He is Bostonian, large in size, quiet, reasonable to talk to. Apparently he shares a desk and word-processor in Key West with Alison Lurie, from whom we shall no doubt hear further details in near future when she lunches here. Judith was very much on her best behaviour. V, on an earlier occasion, recalling Judith's straw tiara and Collins's line about 'many a Nymph who wreaths her Brows with sedge'. They had attended the Bath Festival, where Judith read her poems aloud in a less than ideal mission hall or suchlike, where fearful explosions continually shook the place consequent on a faulty electricity circuit. She presented us with an inscribed copy of one of the poems called 'Guatemala' (privately printed by a press believedly owned by Harold Pinter), a somewhat anti-American diatribe. It then turned out that Judith had never visited Guatemala. As we had been there, the climax almost too farcical to be good art.

Virginia rang in the evening, having visited the Player show at the National Portrait Gallery and seen the Mee portrait which she strongly approved. She said it was very large, dominated the room at one end. Each picture in this exhibition has a photograph of the sitter or the painter beside it, in this case myself with Trelawney on my shoulder (taken by Mee), sad reminder of Trelawney's rejection of publicity in his lifetime (anyway TV) then coming to him after death.

Curious telephone call about 10 p.m., a woman saying she was speaking for James Mason's widow, Clarissa, who, so far as I could make out, had died in Australia, leaving a list of persons to be informed, my name among these. I asked if she widow of James Mason, the film star, which indeed she was. I pointed out that I had never met Mason nor any of his wives (not mentioning the Turkish Head Steward on the *Ankara*, who looked exactly like James Mason, always called James for that reason), woman very apologetic, then it occurred to me she wanted Anthony Powell, the theatrical designer, which I suggested, she at once agreeing.

Thursday, 9 June

V to London to see Sussman. She lunched with Rosie Goldsmid, who was anxious to see the Henry Mee picture, so both went to the NPG. Both liked it, apart from the rather too heavy shadow on the forehead when close, better observed from little distance. I might mention this to Mee if in touch again.

When I reviewed A. N. Wilson's *Tolstoy* I was interested by mention of Moscow being Dombey-mad, when Dickens's novel appeared there about 1848–9. I like to have a book of that sort going, so rereading *Dombey and Son*. The second half must have been for the first time, as the end turned out unfamiliar. One sees that the story might easily be even more acceptable in Russian terms than English: Emily Dombey, a little Dostoevskian saint; Edith, the second Mrs Dombey, a kind of Natasya Filippovna. The central flaw is that one never believes Mr Dombey is anything but very moderately rich (living apparently somewhere like Harley Street), nor with the slightest head for business, or making an impression as 'great', merely a pompous ass, of whom there may well have been plenty about. Even at the height of his prosperity he seemed unable to think of anyone better to ask to his dinner-parties than his Chief Clerk, Carker.

Dickens had absolutely no idea how anyone (Dombey, Scrooge, etc.) earned a living (except by writing or acting), tho' he is always good about losing money, going bankrupt, etc. He is also, usually correctly, described as unable to depict a gentleman. In fact (apart from his absurd name) Cousin Feenix, the ramshackle peer who reminisces about being in the House of Commons with Mr Pitt, is perfectly acceptable as a kind of early nineteenth-century P. G. Wodehouse figure. Why Edith Dombey should run away with Mr Carker is inexplicable, as she is specifically described as disliking him so much; then, having eloped, refuses to go to bed with him, dashes out into the night in Dijon, apparently in her evening dress, without any luggage. Throwing down her jewellery, making a pile of her clothes, and marriage settlement, before leaving Dombey, is appropriately Russian. The actual scene in the hotel at Dijon, with Dombey and his retainers battering on the door, Carker getting out of the window or whatever he did, is also good stuff. Captain Cuttle, much else, the most clotted rubbish. My father (who disliked Kipling's books) used to say the army was not like Kipling before he wrote, but did develop certain Kipling characteristics later. One wonders whether the Victorian Age was to some extent the same with Dickens, i.e. invented by him.

Friday, 10 June

Evangeline Bruce, Nicko and Mary Henderson came to tea after spending a day in Bath, intending to look in here, then put Evangeline on train for London at Westbury. They arrived well after 5 o'clock so too late to do that, leaving with no particular plans in view. Evangeline was wearing a large white turned-up hat of great attack, navy blue overcoat with large brass buttons . . . Nicko spoke of the Roy Jenkins luncheon. Nicko given an Hon. D. Litt. at Encaenia by Roy Jenkins, both of them making speeches at Balliol (Nicko was in fact up at Hertford), coldly received in spite of good jokes (said Nicko) by left-wing Balliol dons. The latter refused to have Maurice Keen (as too nice a man) for new Master, so we may nerve ourselves for some Marxist deadbeat, who will put the College back where it was with Lindsay or Christopher Hill.

Monday, 13 June

A brief visit to Lister. Mr Mosley called to inspect the outgoing car. He does indeed look like one of the Royal Equerries, all needed being a gold aiguillette, long sword, then almost identical.

Wednesday, 15 June

Letter from Jocelyn Stevens in reply to mine (written in March) accepting his nomination as Senior Fellow of the Royal College of Art, Stevens (Rector) saying that attendance at Convocation was *sine qua non* of the appointment; since I had said I might be too stiff in the joints to come to London. I can't conceive anything on earth that I care about less, but Stevens's combination of dilatoriness in answering and indifferent manners does not make a good impression.

Finished a reread of Anthony Burgess's *Earthly Powers*. My first impression of this novel (which I retain), was that it did not come off, but was a remarkable book none the less. The narrator is supposedly based on Somerset Maugham. One's immediate thought is that Maugham is a quite unsuitable mouthpiece for Burgess. On reconsideration one sees that, in fact, Burgess writes straightforward narrative in a manner not at all unlike Maugham's, with the same man-of-the-world realism, 'ordinariness', that Maugham affects. In both cases this does not always stand up to close examination. Burgess, of course, tho' possessing less technical facility of the old-fashioned kind is more intelligent, has much more grasp of the language as such.

Au fond, Earthly Powers is a novel about religion, that is to say Roman Catholicism, opening with the hero Toomey's rejection of that creed, as it does not recognize homosexuality as a condition into which a human being may be born. I should be interested to know how far Burgess identifies himself in the homosexual aspect. When I first heard of him (we have never met) he was vaguely spoken of as bisexual, never as a thoroughgoing queer. Toomey's sister marries an Italian musician, whose brother Carlo (turns out to be illegitimate) eventually becomes Pope. Carlo is not at all convincing as an individual, one of those power-figure priests, always on top of the world, like a character in a strip cartoon. His adventures give the author openings for a great deal of theological writing, which (if infinitely boring for non-RCs, perhaps for some RCs too) is undeniably well done. It is distinctly better, for example, than, say, Graham Greene in similar vein.

At the same time, little as I admire Graham's books, few of them could be censured for not 'coming off'. *Earthly Powers* is much too long, dragging descriptive passages that have nothing to do with the story, etc. There is a great deal of bringing in real people, Kipling, Norman Douglas, Joyce, Ford Madox Ford, lots more, many of them unlikely to have been friends or acquaintances simultaneously of Toomey and at an equal level of intimacy. They belonged to quite different literary circles, Toomey always a popular bestseller rather than at all highbrow. Such throwbacks in time are made additionally unconvincing by the author's evident ignorance of the period, for instance, not being aware that the lesbian novelist, Radclyffe Hall, was always known to her friends as John; referring to Green Park Tube Station in 1917, some ten years before it was built, and so on.

The best section of *Earthly Powers* deals with Malaya, of which Burgess has first-hand knowledge. It describes Toomey's platonic love for a young doctor who dies, possibly through black magic. In short, one feels Burgess's undoubted gifts are best displayed when his pretensions are less. He has perhaps not much sense of construction, or taste. The end of the novel is distinctly sentimental, Toomey settled in Sussex with his sister, ancient house, good cook, gardener, and scholarly Anglican vicar. As this represents the 1970s Burgess's ignorance of what living in the English countryside is like nowadays must be monumental.

Sunday, 19 June

Alison Lurie lunched here. She was preceded a week or so ago by her new novel *The Truth about Lorin Jones*. A woman (not Alison herself) is writing the life of a dead female painter, about whom she receives differing accounts from lovers, friends, dealers. It is all neatly put together, perhaps a shade too neatly, something good writers are apt to develop from knowing how to do the job. There is difficulty of retaining feeling as one gets older, tho' quite what one means by that is as hard to define as to keep up. Also rather too much at the beginning about New York lesbians, near lesbians, tho' feminism (no doubt just as depicted in US) is guyed splendidly. Philistinism is always active, always taking new forms, the New Philistinism vigorous under guise of feminism, racism, élitism, imaginary concepts really pledged, not to their alleged aims (in fact often precisely the reverse, especially racism), but anarchy, attack on critical values, classical forms.

The Key West scenes are better than New York, but a tendency towards sentimentality at the end. Apparently an editor (female) at Random House wanted alterations, so Alison quite rightly went to another publisher. What inconceivable cheek of a publisher. I speak with authority having been one.

Alison was just back from Paris, where *The Nowhere City* is being translated. She arrived on the doorstep with Jane (bearing the Sunday papers) about 12.15, taking me completely by surprise, thinking a new girl was helping with the paper round. Alison was in great form. Much amused to hear that Judith Kazantsis and Irving Wineman were recently here. She described Wineman as coming from the suburbs of Boston (family sold film equipment, she thought). At Harvard he was boyfriend of a sister of Dukakis, currently running as the Democrat Presidential candidate. Alison's first meeting with Wineman was unfavourable owing to farcical incident, but later she liked him.

This knockabout comedy took place at a party given in Key West by two queens. As something a little extra after most of the guests, anyway the more respectable ones, had left, the hosts had laced some 'brownies' (small chocolate cakes) with hashish. These they had placed on top of a six-foot-high refrigerator, pushing them well to the back. Irving Wineman, superlatively tall, is always hungry. He saw the brownies, out of sight of everyone but himself, and ate one. This was followed by another, half a dozen more, until one of the hosts saw what was happening, and snatched them away. By this time the snack was beginning to have disastrous effects on Irving, who was falling about yelling with laughter, giving Alison the impression that he was the most objectionable kind of drunk – at subsequent meetings she readjusting this view. Alison said she thought Irving regarded Judith as Mrs Browning. Incidentally, I read a day or two ago that Mrs Browning did not really suffer from the spinal disease that was supposed to afflict her, but her doctors agreed that they would treat her for that complaint all the same. Alison also spoke of going to see Diana Phipps, with whom she found Gary Hart, ex-Presidential candidate in the Democratic interest (contest abandoned on account of sex scandals). Alison said Hart looked like a waxwork (which public men are apt to develop into), no conversation, like an actor in a bad play.

She also described Arthur Mizener's funeral (where she spoke) as rather badly attended, Arthur by now having become a figure of the past. We talked of the manner in which, with many gifts, Arthur never quite got where he deserved. Alison put this down to early self-identification with Scott Fitzgerald (whom, to say the least, Arthur did not much resemble), devotion that prevented him from keeping up to date in the eyes of colleagues, pupils. Somehow he got left behind.

It is certainly true that fashions in the US change from year to year in a manner quite different from anything over here. For instance, Fitzgerald himself, now an American classic, was spoken of as totally forgotten in the latter years of his life. Nothing like the same damage can be done here, over, say, a decade, to a fundamentally good writer, or as with Arthur, critic. Alison said Rosemary Mizener had the money. 'The Mizeners were an ordinary American middle-class family', Rosemary's having made a pile out of some special kind of nut found in Hawaii, presumably purchased by only very rich monkeys. Alison is possibly writing a ghost story about an antique cupboard that ends in a museum. John made chilli con carne; Alison had a soft drink before luncheon, half a glass of wine. Enjoyable party.

I finished a reread of *Twelfth Night*, liked first three-quarters more than ever before, full of go. As Leslie Hotson points out (others before him with less evidence), Malvolio is undoubtedly take-off of Sir William Knollys, the Queen's comptroller. One of the strangest dispensations of providence, or good and wicked fairy godmothers at his christening, is that Hotson should be so brilliant a researcher into documents, while so perfectly awful a writer; the archness, coyness, affectations, repetitions of his style are all but unbearable, but must be endured (with much nonsense too) for the good stuff which no one else equals.

In short, is one to accept *Twelfth Night* as a comedy on its own, or the ragging of a pompous figure in an official position? If the former, the forcible incarceration of Malvolio, teasing him as mad, is rather unpleasant, tho' in the sadistic vein of which Shakespeare himself had a decided streak. If on the other hand, a tiresome notoriety is being held up to ridicule, no general principle invoked, that is perhaps another matter, lock Knollys up by all means. The curiously powerful figure of Feste is hard to explain, something quite beyond his own dialogue, tho' the combination of beauty, sadness, sex images, of the Wind and the Rain curtain, that is something all on its own.

I also reread the Gerard Manley Hopkins Selection with pleasure. Hopkins in principle is not very much up my street, but I find him a marvellous poet, fascinating innovations of language. Jesuitism all but did in his poetry entirely. If he had kept clear of it (probably impossible of Roman Catholicism entirely) he would have written much more, become immense influence on the poets of the Nineties. A letter from him quoted in Introduction refers quite openly to homosexual loves, poems more than once hinting at them, if less explicit.

Wednesday, 22 June

The new Master of Balliol is an American scientist, Nobel Prize winner, Baruch Blumberg. This might be worse, considering some of the Balliol Fellows. I reread Robert Musil's *Man Without Qualities*, a favourite novel. This time enjoyed first vol. as much as ever, found the second and third dragged badly. The intensely teutonic hero Ulrich is a dreadful self-satisfied bore. Musil is good at social picture of 1913 Vienna, becomes tedious when Musil is philosophical. All the same, there are excellent moments, as when Ulrich comments on photographs of himself as a child that give him no feelings of sentiment, only relief to have 'escaped from a desperate situation by the skin of his teeth'; or the gossip-columnist reporting a social event in which certain names are consigned to the 'mass grave' of 'other eminent persons'.

Bill and Virginia Robinson (Hellenic Cruise friends living in Kansas) called up on way back from Greek cruise with grandchildren. Bill said he sometimes sees, and much likes, Tristram's films shown in the US.

Monday, 27 June

Peter Munford, of Oliver & Lang Brown, called to arrange felling of a small beech (maliciously ringed by squirrels), and a chestnut that mysteriously died, both along the top of lawn. The chestnut is one of those from Norfolk given us by Wyndham Ketton-Cremer twenty-five or more years ago, so sad to lose it. Munford also arranged for the cutting up of various large chunks of timber from previous fellings that had been knocking about for some time. The chestnut to go to The Stables wood pile as suitable only for closed stoves. I reread *Lapsus Calami*, Collected Poems of J. K. Stephen, on the whole fairly awful. Stephen, beloved by schoolmasters, was a dreary professional Etonian of worst kind, although 'The Old School List' has passed into realm of Powell family jokes.

Tuesday, 28 June

John and Rosamond Russell came for an interview with us for an American glossy paper formerly called *House & Garden*, now simply *HG*, with photography by Christopher Simon Sykes. Sykes arrived at 10 a.m., with a café au lait assistant, Wain Vincent. They set off at once for the lake. The Russells turned up about midday. We had a drink, then went on to the Bridge House, Nunney, where they (on *HG*) were standing us luncheon. I gave the photographers drinks too. They stated preference for making their own arrangements as to lunch. Rosamond Russell was running the show as representative of paper, tho' one imagines that John Russell will write the article. Both in good form, she looking much cheered up since her previous visit here. We talked of Barbara Skelton's book.

John also spoke of David Hockney extremely favourably, saying Hockney is a direct jolly Yorkshireman, kind, open to the soft touch, but never gets stuck in own development as a painter. Hockney's brother apparently Mayor of Bradford, the home town also of the sculptor the late Henry Moore. When given freedom of City by the Mayor he, Moore, uttered a loud cry on hearing the name was Hockney, as he particularly dislikes David Hockney's works. This is interesting. John Russell turned out to have been contemporary at Oxford (New College) with Anthony

Hobson, whom he described as a fascinatingly complicated figure, with which one would agree. John had not heard of Tanya's death.

C. S. Sykes is immensely tall, perfectly agreeable if at first impact rather an awkward manner. [Turned out next day that Sykes had stayed at Whitfield to photograph the garden, also Roy Strong's neighbouring garden, presumably on account of George Clive being mixed up with the National Trust.] Sykes and his assistant brought more photographic impedimenta than ever seen even here before, which is saying something. The assistant was not particularly adept at clearing up the mess photographers always make. [However, in the event, the photographs excellent.] V, talking later about C. S. Sykes's uncle, Christopher Sykes the elder, recalled how Evelyn Waugh asked Sykes to arrange a meeting with T. S. Eliot, but Eliot refused to receive Evelyn. One wonders if this was possibly on account of Evelyn's egregiously offensive remarks about Anglo-Catholicism in his novels, tho' Eliot may well have had other reasons too, or just did not want to be bothered.

Friday, 1 July

V and John (I remained at home, thinking my presence would only complicate matters) visited the Snook family at East Forest Farm (about four miles away), Gare Hill (Celtic name?), a Thomas Hardyesque household from which they collected one tabby kitten. He has a white shirt-front, white paws, and was born about 1 May 1988, or shortly before. He is to bear the name Snook, and seems very pleased with himself.

Wednesday, 6 July

I reviewed Bevis Hillier's *Young Betjeman* for *DT*. It is well done. Hillier mentions, for instance, that Betjeman probably exaggerates his own homosexual adventures. In general he plays down material that a less level-headed biographer might have allowed to get out of proportion. Hillier is also good on the poetry. The Betjeman(n) family was German (rather than Dutch) sugar-bakers, established in England about 1800. They then set up Betjemanware, furniture, in which John would have been fourth generation had he entered the firm. Nothing much is said of his father Ernie Betjeman's second (illegitimate) family, probably to be dealt with in the next volume. Hillier gives proper attention to John Bowle, a comic figure, but one who played a considerable part in John Betjeman's life as a contemporary at Marlborough and Oxford. Bowle was a competitor as secretary to Sir Horace Plunkett, an hilariously funny rivalry from which (in that particular aspect only) Quiggin/Members/St John Clark slightly derives.

Lord Quinton, with Evangeline Bruce, VP and Marcelle Quinton.

PRIVY COUNSELLORS

Brooke, Peter Leonard, Minister of State, HM Treasury. Member of Parliament, the City of London and Westminster South.

Newton, Antony Harold,, Minister for Health. Member of Parliament, Braintree.

Onslow, Cranley Gordon Douglas, Member of Parliament, Woking.

COMPANION OF HONOUR

Powell, Anthony Dymoke, author.

KNIGHTS BACHELOR

Barratt, Richard Stanley, HM Chief Inspector of Constabulary.

Beck, Edgar Philip, Chairman, John Mowlem and Co. plc.

Benson, Christopher John, for public services.

Bowness, Alan, Director, Tate Gallery.

H G Rees, ch vet offr, MAFF; J A Scott, sec, Scot Educ Dept; J W Stevens, und-sec, Cab Off; J H Thompson, und-sec, DES; J H Willcox, clrk of publ Bills, House of Cmns.

ORDER OF THE BRITISH EMPIRE

DBE

Clayton, Miss Barbara Evelyn, (Mrs W. Klyne), professor of chemical pathology and human metabolism, University of Southampton.

Dench, Miss Judith Olivia, (Mrs Michael Williams), actress.

Kellett-Bowman, Mrs (Mary) Elaine, MP, for political service.

CBE

J D Allen, chm, Cwmbran Dev Corp; K A Allen, ltly dir gen of printg and pubg, HMSO; K H A Allen, grade 4, Dept of Env; J A Alston, v-chm, Norfolk Cnty Ccl; P W Barker, chm and c

The Times of 31 December 1987.

Henry Mee, artist.

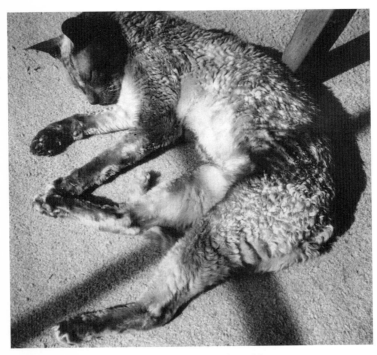

Trelawney, 27 March 1988.

Lady Antonia Fraser, 27 March 1988.

Sir Nicholas Henderson, GCMG.

Lady Moser, Dame Jennifer Jenkins and Lord Jenkins, 22 May 1988.

Snooks's arrival, 1 July 1988.

V.S. Naipaul, 31 July 1988.

Kingsley Amis, 26 September 1988.

AP, 27 October 1988.

The Countess of Longford CBE, 26 October 1989.

Harold Pinter, Alison Lurie, Antonia Fraser, at the Chantry, 1989.

Christmas at the Stables, 1989: Archie Powell, Harry Mount,
William Mount (invisible), Georgia Powell and Virginia Powell.

Lord Hutchinson QC, Lord Jenkins and AP.

Evangeline Bruce.

Hillier makes the point that Betjeman, who (I was astonished to learn) had difficulty in passing Responsions, was always jealous of Bowle's scholarship. Interesting details are provided about Betjeman's marriage to Penelope Chetwode. The latter is always said to have wanted a 'good' conventional marriage, and took Betjeman as second best. This may have been to some extent true. Also undoubted fact that she seems to have fallen for Betjeman on sight at the *Architectural Review*, tho' also involved with Johnny Churchill (Winston's nephew, an infinitely minor painter). Another of Penelope's boyfriends was Sir John Marshall [1876–1958], married, Indian archaeologist. Marshall possibly seduced her. Marshall discovered Mohenjo-Daro, the 3000 BC Indian city V and I visited with Mortimer Wheeler (Wheeler perhaps slightly similar character to Marshall).

The Chetwodes were understandably unkeen on having Betjeman as son-in-law. That admitted, their behaviour was unpleasant and above all stupid. When I met Lady ('Star') Chetwode staying with the Sitwells (who were some sort of cousins) at Renishaw I thought her far from attractive in personality. Roger Chetwode (who seemed a reasonably nice Lower Boy, was a contemporary of mine at school) apparently played a malign part in anti-Betjeman behaviour after the marriage. An interesting aspect of this is that Roger Chetwode, if hearty, was also by no means a fool, even tho' lacking in Betjeman's poetic 'cultural' gifts, an extrovert, jolly in manner, a terrific social snob and climber, go-getter in business (he made a fortune on Wall Street in his early twenties), he was at the same time, like Betjeman in many of these characteristics, also deeply melancholic. Indeed, for no apparent reason, he committed suicide at the beginning of the war. No doubt Betjeman's poetry and his religiosity kept him from suicide, as similar characteristics might have done for Roger Chetwode *mutatis mutandis*.

V recalled that when Betjeman was staying with the Clives at Whitfield, the house was not yet 'on the grid' for electricity, so Betjeman could not use his electric razor. Someone therefore had to drive him to the nearest house in the neighbourhood (in fact on outskirts of Hereford), which had electricity laid on. (Betjeman was then not Poet Laureate, tho' widely known from TV, other public appearances.)

V told this story to Ronnie Knox (Katherine Asquith's chaplain at Mells), who burst out: 'What a hypocrite that man is!' It turned out that an electric carillon had recently been installed at Mells Church and Betjeman had been invited down to speak in celebration of its arrival. His speech fiercely inveighed against modern, especially electrical, technology, regretting the old days of bell-ringing by hand. A slightly piquant trimming to this story is that the Mells chimes played hymns, which Ronnie had more than once mentioned greatly disturbed him, possibly hymns reminding him too vividly of his own apostasy from the Church of England.

Talking of melancholy, I have been reading W. M. Praed, another melancholic poet, Etonian and superior in gifts to J. K. Stephen (the latter KS; Praed, an oppidan). Probably wisely, Praed usually restricts himself to what's known as *vers de société*, which he wrote with immense elegance, yet one notes that later poets quickly caught on to something worth imitating when Praed tried his hand at other lines; e.g. Swinburne:

> So perish the leaves in the arbour,
>   The tree is all bare in the blast!
> Like a wreck that is drifting to harbour,
>   I come to thee, Lady, at last:
> Where art thou, so lovely and lonely?
>   Though idle the lute and the lay,
> The lute and the lay are thine only,
>   My fairest, on Valentine Day.

or Macaulay ('Naseby'):

> 'Tis noon: the ranks are broken along the royal line,
> They fly the braggards of the court, the bullies of the Rhine:
> And Rupert sheathes his rapier with a curse and with a frown:
> And cold Newcastle mutters as he follows in the flight,
> 'The German boar had better far have supped in York tonight.'
>
> (Praed: 'Marston Moor')

Snook, undoubtedly intelligent, has picked up the Chantry cat routine in twenty-four hours.

Friday, 8 July

Henry Mee rang about 12.45, saying he could not find Rodrigo Moynihan's studio. He had written the telephone number down wrong, could I help, as he was supposed to be having a sitting for Rodrigo's picture that morning. I took the opportunity of mentioning that various people, while liking the portrait of me in the NPG show, had thought the black impasto on the forehead a trifle heavy, had to stand well back from picture to get best effect. I suggested that might possibly be worth attention. Mee seemed to take that all right. After all, there was nothing Augustus John liked better than one suggesting something might have gone a bit wrong in some passage or colour, which he would at once take steps to rectify, not in the least offended, on the contrary he'd say 'You've got a good eye', something like that.

A film (not TV) has recently been made of Waugh's *A Handful of Dust*, regarding which Bron Waugh wrote a feature in *Sunday Times Colour*, saying John Beaver (who seduced Tony Last's wife Lady Brenda) was 'dead ringer' for John Heygate. In fact Beaver no more resembled Heygate than Evelyn Waugh resembled Tony Last, owner of vast neo-gothick mansion, woken by a footman every morning, whom he asked: 'Has her Ladyship rung yet?' So far as that went at all, the boot on the other foot, Heygate, heir to a baronetcy, country house, ex-candidate for the Diplomatic Service, invited to deb dances; Waugh penniless adventurer determined to make his way in 'society'.

As a matter of fact Evelyn Waugh himself told V that Beaver was lightly modelled on combination of Hamish Erskine and Murrough O'Brien (whom she knew; I never met; so far as I am aware still alive). This wholly inept statement by Bron evoked a letter of protest from Richard Heygate (John's second, and favourite, son), saying his father not in any respect like Beaver in *A Handful of Dust*. Richard added the picture of himself Heygate liked appeared in *Agents and Patients*.

I had not looked at the book for ages, accordingly reread. It might reasonably be called a frivolous novel, even bordering on farce, I suppose, but not altogether without 'serious' implications, I think quite well put together. What struck me, however, was, within its convention, how astonishingly 'like' were the 'real people' there adumbrated, notwithstanding a fair sprinkling of private jokes: Maltravers (John Heygate); Chipchase (myself, merely a cog in story); Sarah Maltravers (Evelyn Gardner); Mrs Mendoza, 'Mendie' (Varda); Reggie Frott (Freddy Mayor); Fräulein Grundt (Thea Struve, the poor girl died in a Nazi concentration camp, I believe); Inglethorne (Donald Calthrop); Commander Venables (Captain Turle, RN); the Duchesse de Borodino (Violette, Princess Eugène Murat); Gaston, Marquis de la Tour d'Espagne (Jacques, Comte de Maleissy): the last two, of course, belonging to totally different world from the others, which I only encountered marginally myself.

Basil Hambrough had met Jacques de Maleissy. I remarked that I believed he had a very good war record, Basil said: 'Certainly he was always telling one that.' When short of opium Jacques de Maleissy's state, conversation, were just as described, but of course horrifying rather than funny, which might be a legitimate criticism of the novel; pre-Hitler Berlin infinitely sinister.

That perhaps comes over a bit in the blow-by-blow account of the city's queer night-club (Hermann, hat-check boy at Eldorado, etc.), Heygate, employed at UFA film company, had just the same relationship with the German producer (called, I think, Dr Berger). Heygate life in Canonbury Square, Evelyn Gardner and her speedway riders, was just as described, above all Varda and her near-fiancé Captain Turle RN. When critics write about *Dance* they are apt to dismiss the pre-war novels as light-weight, which in a sense no doubt they are, but have bearing, I should have thought, on what came later. They also suggest profound melancholy. I see from the paper the Editress of *HG*, the magazine for which the Russells interviewed me, has moved elsewhere, nothing more probable than that the piece will never appear, knowing what American publications are like.

Sunday, 10 July

Notwithstanding the foulest weather Hilary and John Spurling drove from London and back in sheets of rain to lunch here. Hilary recounted adventures in India (Bombay and neighbourhood) researching the Paul Scott biography (to be delivered 1990). She managed, after great difficulty, to contact the somewhat anglicized Rajput lady who played a considerable part in Scott's writing about India. After considerable riding off in first instance, Hilary managed to see her; was then asked to luncheon, then actually to stay, the last of which Hilary did not accept. She also talked with an Indian General, whether or not in the Mess I am uncertain.

She was much impressed with the country, and said one felt presence of the Hindu gods all the time. Hilary would not be unsuitable herself as avatar of, say, Durga. From there she went to Australia, Tasmania, the latter a pretty place but sunk in untold middle-class philistinism and self-satisfaction ('Why shouldn't we cut down the bloody trees if we bloody want to'), not a book in sight. Australia, on the other hand, Hilary liked, 'country of the future', everything booming. Snook showed off to the Spurlings. John cooked chilli con carne; V did summer pudding. We drank Tristram's Château Léoville-Poyferré '66, first rate. Enjoyable party. Later in evening Snook managed to slip out, causing panic for a short time by his mysterious disappearance.

Monday, 11 July

I saw Lister, no action. I finished my reread of *The Mayor of Casterbridge*, a series of beyond words improbable events, like a strip cartoon, something extraordinary happening in almost every chapter; obeying to the full James's admonition to novelists 'Dramatize, dramatize'. I believe *The Mayor of Casterbridge* did make a good TV film. In the end one does accept the character of Henchard, the Mayor, if few others, especially his step-daughter Elizabeth Jane. (Was Elizabeth Jane Howard named after her?) A slick of oil is reported on Lake by the Syndicate (Mr Oatley), which they are lodging complaint about. John caught a 2lb trout which he took to London.

Tuesday, 12 July

I reread *The Merry Wives of Windsor* with enjoyment. Dawn of the Aldwych farce, good phrases 'Be not as extreme in submission as in offence', 'You orphan heirs of fixed destiny' (Anne Page, as Fairy Queen, to the fairies, near the Eliot line in *The Waste Land*).

Sunday, 17 July

Both of us have been having throats and colds. I was in bed last week, V today. Tristram, Virginia, Archie, to morning drinks, also Jane Keller, American girl who entertained the Dulwich players when in Boston. She seemed nice, if rather grumbly, Virginia said 'very game'. I found a leather two-vol. (1855) copy of Thackeray's *The Virginians*, which I tried to read but broke down after fifty pages. Nothing to be said for it, arch, longwinded, badly put together, characterization rubbish. It had belonged to D. R. Jefferson, my great-uncle, victim of melancholia, as a young man, spent his life in Ticehurst, the well-known upper-class bin. Various passages marked, one about irrational melancholy, having two lines drawn beside it.

Thursday, 21 July

Mark Boxer obit. I never saw a great deal of Mark, and first got in touch when he was still at Cambridge, or just sent down. I did that at once when I went to *Punch* with a view to his working for the paper. Saw him on and off ever since. His covers for *Dance* were far the best of any other paperbacks. Never went into the paperback department of Hatchard's without their standing out immediately from any other series on the shelves. Mark was also capable editor, perhaps unusual for someone of his particular gifts, no doubt fired by his own immense preoccupation with the power world and money as such, rather than for himself particularly.

Monday, 25 July

When Spurlings were here Hilary mentioned that Paul Scott had written on back of a photograph 'The Silence of Dean Maitland', obviously title of book (vaguely familiar), Hilary asked if I could identify the quotation. I said I would make enquiries, one of which to Tony Quinton, now Chairman of the British Library, in any case something of authority on obscure novels. Tony rang to say *The Silence of Dean Maitland* was by Maxwell Gray (pseud. Mary G. Tuttiett (? American), 1886, 3 vols, Kegan Paul. Tony said he never could have done it without resources at his disposal. However, Rupert Hart-Davis also knew. I passed this on to Hilary.

Finished *Coastwise Lights*, the second vol. of Memoirs by Alan Ross, as he prefers to call them, a background for poems written during that period, interspersed with prose. Some poems are better than others, one would say, the prose always of a high standard. Alan is an elegant writer and fills in details about various areas of life one is glad to know about. The whole book a little out of the ordinary in tone for a poet and editor of literary magazine, perhaps owing to cricket, racing interests.

I reread Christina Rossetti's *Poems, New Poems*, found nothing of great interest except the three or four well-known ones, notably 'Goblin Market', one of the really extraordinary inner fantasies of the mind, comparable with, say, 'The Ancient Mariner'. Some of its elements, sisters, fruit juice, entrapment, crop up often in lesser poems; then in 'Goblin Market' she suddenly released something deep inside. It is very moving.

Wednesday, 27 July

Bevis Hillier was delighted with my Betjeman review, which Max Hastings (holidaying in Devon) actually wrote to say he had enjoyed, an Editorial bouquet. Rupert Hart-Davis sent an inscribed copy of Max Beerbohm *Letters*, which he has long been editing, and I shall probably review. [In the event it was sent by N. Shakespeare to Harold Acton, a piece of half-bakedness on N. Shakespeare's part.] As usual admirably edited by Rupert, many interesting points, notably a letter to Florence Kahn (whom Beerbohm married) delicately explaining he did not want physical relations, this was after some apparent unhappiness on her part; the ultimate implication being that she did not want sexual relations either. When she knew this was his own attitude, all was well for the marriage to take place. Considering the number of men who hate women, but love sleeping with them (Malcolm Muggeridge, and many confirmed womanizers), there is really no reason why a man should not love women but hate sleeping with them in the light of how varied are sexual tastes. Beerbohm seems always to have been devoted to his wife (in fact an unusually boring woman, Ada Leverson, the Sphinx, emphasized, the only occasion I talked to her). That seems to have been the general view. Beerbohm had experienced passions for other women, usually actresses, before that, probably platonic, tho' David Cecil thought Constance Collier might have lured Max into bed, an experience he had not liked.

In September 1903 (writing to G. B. Shaw, with whom he was eminently able to deal and keep in his play) Beerbohm said he thought H. G. Wells's books were like 'cold rice pudding'. Just fifty years later, September 1953, he wrote that he had brought tears to Wells's eyes by praising *Love and Mr Lewisham* (1900), when all the critics abused it. However, none of us is on oath talking to other writers about their works. Rather surprisingly, Beerbohm could not read Jane Austen, but liked Arnold Bennett, Galsworthy, also Trollope, then completely out of fashion, but on verge of a great revival. He could not manage Proust or T. S. Eliot, except *Prufrock* read aloud by Sydney Schiff (novelist, Proust translator), nor did Max like the Diaghilev Ballet (1912).

There is an amusing account in one letter of a verbatim conversation with Aubrey Beardsley, showing it should be called The Yellow *Book*, rather than The *Yellow* Book. When Eddie Marsh said that Henry Moore's sculpture had put England on the map, Beerbohm remarked that after that no one would be able to say 'Roll up the map of Europe'. Rupert's notes as usual lively. He mentions Gosse, writing to a French author, referring to Swinburne's 'widow'; what could Gosse have had in his mind? Thinking of another poet? But Rupert notes the fact that members of the Orleans Club (for gourmets) paid nothing at the time, then received a bill quarterly, perhaps half-yearly, 'to food £268', whatever it was, no possible means of checking. I remember, when a boy, my father pointing out the Orleans Club in King Street, St James's, as a gourmets' club, but I don't imagine he had ever been inside. [Rupert told me later he often dined there with his father, E.V. Lucas, etc. The food was wonderful, and after dinner a conjuror.] I do not find essays easy to read as a rule, good as are some of Max Beerbohm's, but 'Enoch Soames', 'Maltby and Braxton' (*Seven Men* 1919) hold up supremely well, *A Christmas Garland* (1912) contains brilliant parodies. One notes that Beerbohm's parodies are so good for the same reason that the caricatures are good, that is to say his intense interest in both the minds and bodies of the persons concerned.

This passionate interest in the individual could not be claimed in the same way, for instance, by Osbert Lancaster or Mark Boxer; Osbert's thoughts were always filled with his own fantasies of what the people he drew were like, indeed what everything was like, sometimes wide of the mark; Marc (a considerably lesser draughtsman, indeed sparkling amateur) was keen on fashion of the moment, but both he and Osbert rose above the contemporary tendency to caricature by a more or less photographic face imposed on an absurd body. Beerbohm, understandably, never appreciated the greatness of Kipling, yet even the Kipling parody and caricatures are none the less superb for being unfriendly.

Beerbohm did not think he had ever read a play by Shakespeare all the way through (he must have seen many performed as dramatic critic). This accords with a certain anti-intellectualism, complete detachment from everyday life (to which latter Shakespeare so much belongs). This detachment did not preclude unusually warm condolence letters from Max. Osbert described Max's conversational tone as one of extreme precision, avoidance of any subject to be supposed at all 'unpleasant'. This cut-offness from life is sometimes rather daunting in the letters, when Max was old perhaps even a shade creepy, but all part of Max Beerbohm's perfect grasp of what, as an artist, he could and could not achieve.

I finished a reread of *As You Like It*. There is a wonderfully good interchange between two girls alone together (Rosalind and Celia). In fact the first half is splendid, then tails off. It never seems mentioned that Orlando and Jaques are brothers, perhaps understood by a contemporary audience through the way they speak to each other: 'Let's meet as little as we can', 'I do desire we may be better strangers'. Much academic heavy weather has been made about Jaques's 'melancholy' as then 'fashionable' (true, Elizabethan jokes were made on the subject), but Jaques is also like lots of people today. I found Charles Cotton's *Collected Poems* not very readable; for some reason my edition did not include 'Anthony feigns himself sick today', which Lovat Fraser illustrated and is naturally a favourite of mine.

Saturday, 30 July

Georgia rang last night to say she was back from Spain, where she seems to have had a lively time. All the suitable experiences of that age, such as quarrelling with the girl (Miron Grindea's granddaughter) who accompanied her, etc. On arrival in Barcelona they fetched up in an hotel in the Barrio Chino (brothel quarter), and had to escape surreptitiously. I received a letter from an Eton boy, Joseph Altham, asking for contribution for St Andrew's Day 'ephemeral' he is editing (refused). He added some relation of his attended the private school St Cyprian's, possessed a programme of the school play for 1916, in which the Pickwick play included Eric Blair as Mr Wardle, Cyril Connolly as Miss Wardle; another play, Cecil Beaton as Little Buttercup.

Driven by John, we lunched with Vidia and Pat Naipaul at The Dairy Cottage, Salterton, other guest were Mel and Angela Gossow, he Dramatic Critic of the *New York Times*. They had driven down from London (notwithstanding recommendation to come by train as much easier), where he is seeing a play every night, on Monday lunching with Pinters. He said President Reagan insisted on telling Gorbachev in detail plot of *Persuasion*. V knew this to be a movie about Quakers and Peace, but the story caused me some confusion as I supposed Miss Austen's work was referred to. That would have been much more enjoyable; probably for Gorbachev too. Vidia was in great form, having finished his book about Slavery (September). Pat is still rather thin, but also in good form. Mrs Gossow seemed a bit bewildered by it all, V thought possibly on account of Vidia's being so essentially part of the British social and intellectual life. Americans are always so acutely conscious of racial tensions.

Vidia has now bought a car (Saab), after years of existence in taxis. His great interest is now wine, which he buys at Marks & Spencer, where it is apparently very good. We drank two Margaux, Château Notton (Vidia said second wine Brane Cantenac) '73, perhaps a shade thin but excellent, and another Margaux '85 (which V preferred); salmon; raspberries. Vidia too said he much enjoyed my Hillier/ Betjeman review, possibly what people liked was quoting Guy Warrack's remark (a favourite with Constant Lambert): 'I'll try anything once, except incest and folk-dancing.'

Monday, 1 August

Mr Mosley brought the new car (a Maestro), pretty well identical with former one. I found and read Arnold Bennett's *Anna of the Five Towns* in a sixpenny or shilling red cheap edition. From signature it was owned probably when I was at school. Enjoyed the story, of which I did not remember a word, except (on coming to those incidents) when Anna's young man asks her father for a second helping of cold beef at supper (cf. Max Beerbohm's parody of Bennett in *Christmas Garland*); and the ominous sneezes heard on the way home from the rainy school treat. Curious what the mind retains. It's really not a bad novel, tho' the twist at the end should have been implicit rather than explicit. Anyway, there seems no reason why Willy should not have gone to Australia, rather than commit suicide. The whole novel really not at all unlike D. H. Lawrence with Dark Gods omitted. Probably Lawrence got a good deal from Bennett. Virginia Woolf always beefing about Bennett, but her own novels are far less alive than this (not to mention the *Old Wives' Tale*, incidentally Max Beerbohm thought the latter the best novel of his own lifetime), tho' admitted V. Woolf's *Diaries* and *Letters* are superior to Bennett's in expression, feeling.

Sunday, 7 August

Some weeks ago Anthony Burgess was reported as saying Graham Greene was a third-rate imitator of Conrad, complaining of emptiness of his serious novels, etc. Conflict thereby portended has now taken shape in an interview given by Graham. One does not know Burgess's motive in going out of his way to be rude (apparently on the French radio and literary paper called *Lire*), tho' one would agree what Burgess says is largely true. Apart from rows when he was my publisher, I have always got on reasonably well with Graham (who thrives on polemics), tho' never able to read his books. I remember one night after supper in the Waugh parents' house Evelyn Waugh laughing with me about the publication of Graham's first novel on account of being (if it was) about smugglers. (He did not know Graham until after the war, when their RC friendship was much advertised.) Anyway, there never seems to have been any reason for saying publicly that I don't like Graham's books, any more than he has said he doesn't like mine, which I should suspect.

This may be just wish for publicity on Burgess's part, possibly staking claim to be premier RC novelist, a subject Burgess appears to know a good deal more about theologically speaking. Graham, quite unused for decades to being criticized by anyone, gave an unusually silly interview, no doubt anything to relieve his *ennui*. I am not clear whether or not he knows Burgess personally, which would certainly have bearing on the row. Graham was very contemptible in speaking of his friendship with traitor Philby, saying 'only a few hundreds' political prisoners in Soviet Union (just what defenders of Stalin, for that matter Hitler, used to say), so far as Graham knew 'no British agents' were betrayed by Philby, 'only Albanians'. Why that should be less base, if they were on your side, is not clear. One looks forward to further developments. Perhaps this is just a single eruption for both parties to keep in the public eye.

I finished *Little Dorrit*, which I don't think I had ever before read, except Marshalsea prison at the beginning, far the best section. Dickens can do exceptional circumstances marvellously well (later on when travellers are arriving at monastery in the Alps; Mr Dorrit, just before death, having the illusion at a grand dinner-party in Rome that he is back at the Marshalsea). What Dickens is quite unable to depict is the ebb and flow of ordinary upper-middle-class life, or for that matter working-class life, except in the case of the latter through a thick veil of sentimentality, *Little Dorrit* makes particularly virulent onslaughts on what would now be called 'The Establishment' (the Circumlocution Office, tentacles of the aristocratic Barnacle family).

Dickens, one need not add, of course sent his own sons to Eton. I read a few weeks ago that a piece of silver with the Dickens arms on was up for auction. Were the arms thus authorized by the Heralds? In any case their use seems rather a pretentiously 'Establishment' practice, it might be thought. There is a Dickens family of baronets, which the writer may have satisfactorily linked himself on. I do not know, no doubt it would have been possible.

Wednesday, 10 August

Virginia, gardening at The Stables, to dinner, chicken Maryland, bottle of fizz, as V and I had suffered colds and Virginia trouble with a tooth. She recounted Georgia's adventures at Clarence House helping with the birthday post. The Queen Mother's Treasurer has a chip on his shoulder, 'Of course you're at Oxford, won't find any of us very intelligent, very much Below Stairs here.' The birthday letters Georgia opened were all that might be expected in way of lunatics, beginning 'Dear Mother', enclosures of nougat, white heather, etc. These packages are first tested for potential letter-bombs. The Queen Mum herself is still very spry, a couple of stiff pink gins when drinks handed round; various minor royalties appeared. Georgia goes to Thailand with Oxford friends in the near future, now somewhat in the news with neighbouring states trouble, Mrs Thatcher's visit, and so on.

Sunday, 14 August

Foul weather. Driven by John, we lunched with Rachel and Kevin Billington at Poyntington. Both were in good form, Kevin still looks a bit battered from the car accident of two years ago, Rachel blooming. Two nice children were present, Chloe, twelve, full of charm, Caspar slightly younger. Kevin recently was in North Pembrokeshire filming some fictional subject. The local farmer was incapable of understanding that actors playing agricultural parts did not really know what to do when a cow calved, etc., sending them off on specialized jobs of that sort. This Pirandellesque situation is really true of actors in most, if not all, of roles they play.

We talked of the Hillier/Betjeman biography, about which Betjeman's daughter Candida Lycett-Green is unenthusiastic, apparently she said: 'You know we're not making a penny out of it.' We agreed that all art must be selective, certain horrors and obscentities do not extend the literary understanding. In fact retailing them is a special kind of pornography.

Thursday, 18 August

Mr C. R. Eastwood, bookseller (Puriton, north of Bridgwater) came for a hundred or more books cleared out for space reasons (£120). He said it is difficult to get books in the country now as they all go to London even from local sales. Eastwood was formerly head of the Somerset Public Libraries. Copies of *A Question of Upbringing* in Portuguese arrived and *The Acceptance World* in Dutch. A letter from Hilary Spurling about *The Silence of Dean Maitland*, which she read on their Welsh holiday. The Dean was high-minded Victorian clergyman, who seduced and murdered, let his best friend serve twenty years, then confessed all from Westminster Abbey pulpit. The Spurlings' aggressive cat, Biggles, who insisted on their taking him on in this neighbourhood five years ago, disappeared, then turned up after they had left for London. John Spurling is now paying another visit to the Welsh Marches to collect him, although Biggles is the terror of Holloway.

I am running through all the art books, taking each as it comes in the shelf. Glancing at a couple of works on Poussin I noted that *The Music of Time* (if you prefer, *Dance of Human Life*), *The Arcadian Shepherds* (*Et Ego in Arcadia*), *Truth Revealed by*

Time, are all believed to be subjects suggested by Cardinal Respigliosi (later Pope Clement IX). The first, of course, gave title to *Dance*; the third, *Truth Revealed by Time* (existing only in a copy, which I have not seen), is mentioned in the novel as a piece of sculpture bought by Mr Deacon (sculptor, Bernini, seen in photograph); the second, *The Arcadian Shepherds*, occurs in *The Fisher King*. I seem to share some sort of taste in pictorial symbolism with Clement IX.

Friday, 19 August

I reread *Othello*. It was obviously necessary to sack Cassio from Othello's staff, if he could not carry his drink, and no business whatsoever of Desdemona's, unless she had indeed developed a fancy for him. Desdemona is usually played as a helpless innocent, but, even from doubts expressed at time of her elopement, evidently she had some reputation for inconstancy, or at least light affections. An interesting point: 'To hear music the general does not greatly care.' Perhaps that was because Othello did not find the local music up to his own standard, as at one moment there are echoes of the Deep South (whence perhaps he came), for instance Othello addresses Desdemona as 'Honey'. I also read (first time, I think) *Under the Greenwood Tree*, really no more than longish sketch of rural life, complicated only by a girl saying at one moment she will marry the Vicar, when already engaged. This difficulty is almost immediately cleared up. Hardy on the whole is greatly preferable when not harping on the inexorability of Fate, our all being playthings of the Gods, etc. Here he is even quite funny at times.

Saturday, 20 August

Freddie Ashton obit. Tremendous showing in the papers for his choreographical works. Fred was terribly gloomy during his latter years (always that to some extent), notwithstanding immense professional and social success, honours, smart life. The latter is much more routine adjunct of music than the other arts. Fred, of course, had a considerable interest in smart life, Billy Chappell used to stay at Fred's Suffolk residence occasionally as Fred's oldest friend, and always complained that he had to do all the cooking. Fred died in his sleep, having worked until the last moment, always desirable. In ancient days he rented (or considered taking) flat in Bloomsbury (Brunswick Place perhaps), where his mother was also to live. Barbara Ker-Seymer, another very old friend, went over it with him. Fred was worried that nights shared with lovers might disturb Mrs Ashton. Accordingly Barbara shut herself into what would be his mother's room; Fred closed door of his own room, then threw himself on to bed, simulating sounds of orgasmic delight. I think Barbara reported all was well, she could scarcely hear anything.

Sunday, 21 August

Georgia drove down from London for lunch, John doing his chilli con carne. She related her Spanish trip and Clarence House experiences. She is going to Thailand on Tuesday. I finished reread of the *Collected Rochester*. One gets rather sick of all the Chloe stuff, I remain fond of:

> Ancient person, for whom I,
> All the flatt'ring Youth defy;
> Long be it ere thou grow Old,
> Aking, shaking, Crazy Cold.
> But continue as thou art,
> *Ancient Person of My Heart.*

I suppose increased age helps the appreciation of the subject.

Tuesday, 23 August

John and Rosemary Monagan gave us luncheon at the Bridge House, Nunney. They have taken The Old House, Rushall, Nr Pewsey, Wiltshire, for some weeks, with various members of their family, grandchildren, etc. We excused ourselves from going there on grounds of the longish drive. The Congressman is a bit aged, but in good form. He wanted to do a kind of interview with me after lunch for some reason, his tape-machine battery turned out to be down, so he just took a few notes about my parents. One had always imagined him of purely Irish origins, on the contrary they visited a place in Somerset where an ancestor named Minor had set out for Massachusetts (Salem) in 1629. They presented me with cassette of various tunes that occur in *Dance* played and sung by the Monagan family: 'South of the Border', 'Pale hands I loved', 'Guide me, O Thou Great Jehovah'. It was all a rather refined rendering of the down-to-earth singing of the Welsh troops, but interesting to hear collected together.

Thursday, 25 August

Elizabeth Burke, from the BBC World Service (Bush House), tall, rather pretty, quite bright, came to hear our T. S. Eliot reminiscences for his Centenary. She left to pick up her husband, a barrister, at Bristol. They were then going to Dorset. She said she thought Eliot's reputation was at a record low at the moment. I said I remained always attached to *Prufrock*, *The Waste Land*, some of the early ones, which to my surprise appears to be the fashionable view. I tried to convey the occasions when we met Eliot after introduction at the Claridge's luncheon by Margaret Behrens. Eliot dined with us once or twice at Chester Gate, but we saw him chiefly when he stayed at Lee (near Ilfracombe). We were there for two or three months after I came out of the Army and was working on Aubrey. She asked if Eliot ever said anything about my books. I had never particularly thought about that (he was known to have a taste for middlebrow fiction, especially by Faber's female writers). I think the answer was Eliot never mentioned them. When I got my CBE he wrote some formal approval like 'well deserved'.

I am reviewing Vol. 1 of his *Letters* (not yet finished), Lyndall Gordon's *Later Years of TSE* (good), so difficult to remain uninfluenced by what occurs in these, I mean keeping one's own recollections clear. Letters give that peculiarly immediate sense of the writer (even one's own letters reveal feelings long forgotten). So far from disliking the Bank, some of the work there positively enjoyed by Eliot. He made desperate efforts to join the US Navy/Army in Intelligence, but was thwarted by American bureaucracy worthy of the French, perhaps greatest exponents outside Communist countries.

Much light thrown on Vivienne Haigh-Wood, Eliot's first wife. She might easily have been the wife of a regular soldier (like his brother), in my view. I can well imagine (as a child) my parents' rather disapproving comments, my mother making the best of it: 'Captain Eliot's new wife came to tea. Of course she smokes, as all young women do now, slightly bad style, I thought, she *loves* dancing, but *very* interested in books, I could imagine her a friend of Aunt Vi's, picked up in some hotel, perhaps at the seaside. I didn't at all dislike her' etc. (my mother's verdict).

Sunday, 28 August

Pansy, staying with Helen Asquith, came to tea. She now looks very like an untidy version of the Pakenhams' grandmother Lady Jersey. She seemed in good form, comtemplating a formidable series of visits over here among relations.

Wednesday, 31 August

Helen Fraser of Heinemann lunched, having indicated she would like to see us again. This turned out to have no bearing on any particular publishing matter, at the same time probably a good idea to keep in touch. Helen is sensible, exceptionally intelligent, and recognizes a joke. Hilary Spurling lunched with her a month or two ago. Hilary said she had made clear to the Paul Scott relations from the start that if she wrote his biography that would be without reticence should she come across matters they might find undesirable to make public. Hilary was glad she had done this, as something fairly hair-raising turned up. Hilary would not reveal what that was. Helen Fraser had seen Anthony Burgess about the second vol. of his memoirs. The interview took place in an hotel bedroom, clothes lying about, space made on the bed to find somewhere for Helen to sit, cassette playing some composition by Burgess himself, shouting arguments with his Italian wife, general air of confusion. Burgess is dissatisfied with all publishers he dealt with; 'So-and-so, a *bad* man', 'Someone else, a *bad* man'. Helen Fraser has two daughters. She lives at Brook Green, Hammersmith.

AB South & West Carriers (Cardiff) collected a box of odds and ends for the Welch Regiment Museum in Cardiff Castle, mostly revolver holster, compasses, spurs, etc., belonging to my father; map-case, leather swagger-stick, blue side-cap, of mine; silver-lace cross-belt, buttons, of my grandfather from the Leicestershire Volunteers, to which Museum will give a home.

I reviewed the two Eliot books; in the *Letters*, during legal negotiations about launching *The Criterion*, Eliot writes (to Proust's translator Sydney Schiff): 'I have seen Mr Broad.' This seems likely to have been Reggie Broad, solicitor (old enough to have been in the first war), friend of the Lloyds, passionate balletomane, drinker, who looked rather like Stroheim. At Sadler's Wells, Reggie Broad always had left-hand aisle seat, second row of stalls, when, the moment the curtain descended, he made for the bar, where *two* drinks (doubles) were always waiting for him to consume at each entr'acte. Broad used to walk, probably with friends, from his flat (somewhere in Bloomsbury), matter of about a mile and a half perhaps, certain pubs on the route compulsory, certain voluntary. He was well known in queer circles, but I never heard of him having a specific relationship with any individual. He also used to frequent Castano's. Seems extremely probable it was Reggie Broad who arranged the legal side of *Criterion* affair in 1921. In his way Broad was a richly comic figure, and it is a real addition to the Eliot story.

Thursday, 1 September

The Vice-Chancellor of Oxford, barrister called Sir Patrick Neill, asked if I would lend my name to an Appeal for the University. I took the opportunity of saying that, after Oxford's behaviour in refusing an hon. degree to the Prime Minister (Mrs Thatcher), one had to think twice about allowing oneself to be associated with the place. On consideration, I would allow that, tho' unlikely I should be able to attend meetings, which might rule me out. [He seemed quite happy about this, and gave the appearance of heartily agreeing with me.]

Friday, 2 September

Selina Hastings drove from London to discuss Evelyn Waugh, about whom she is writing a book. She arrived at midday, gave us luncheon at Bridge House, stayed for tea, then went on to her parents at Beaulieu, Hampshire. I was curious as to why she wanted to write about Evelyn, several people are already on that track, finding the subject was simply put forward by her publishers Hamish Hamilton. Selina, now in her early forties, attractive, intelligent, cuts through wide area of social life, to some extent perhaps consequence of her father Jack's final marriage being to Selina's mother Margaret Lane. Margaret Lane is a very capable journalist, formerly married to Edgar Wallace's son Brian (we met him years ago in Madrid where he was Hon. Attaché at our Embassy).

Selina has rather surprisingly never married. She possesses the immense advantage of immediately knowing who and what one is talking about. She has been given a passionate unsigned love letter(s) to Evelyn Waugh, of which she will send me photostat for possible identification. She suggested Evelyn was not really at all highly sexed. This is possibly true.

We covered good deal of other than Waugh gossip. Selina staying some few years ago at Faringdon (left by Gerald Berners to Robert Heber-Percy, The Mad Boy), went down to the pool with The Mad Boy after breakfast when he had awful hangover. The Mad Boy got in, said: 'Oh God, I shall die, I've forgotten to bring my cigarettes.' Selina offered to fetch them from the house. The Mad Boy said: 'When you return, I will give you anything you ask.' Selina brought cigarettes. The Mad Boy enquired what she wanted. Selina said to be left Faringdon. This he promised to do, adding: 'Remind me from time to time, I swear on my honour as a gentleman I will leave the house to you.' The catch was obviously in the latter qualification, as he never did. Selina brought messages from Elizabeth Jane Howard, Andrew Devonshire and Billy Chappell, which suggests her wide social coverage. Enjoyable day.

Monday, 5 September

I finished (not without a degree of skipping) Samuel Richardson's *Clarissa*, something I never expected to do, it is round about a million words. One must admit it is a remarkable novel, if much too long, Laclos (no doubt owing a good deal to Richardson) brought off a much more amusing job at normal novel length in *Les Liaisons Dangereuses*. At the same time, there are many good things, especially the relations between the two girls, Clarissa Harlowe, her friend Anna Howe. These are convincing, as also the circumstances of former's elopement with Lovelace. Here behaviour begins to be doubtful. If Clarissa were in the unusual position of possessing property of her own, the possibility of a minor lawsuit with her father seems unlikely to have kept her from accepting this strong financial position. The consistent odiousness of the whole Harlowe family could probably be paralleled, even Lovelace drugging and raping Clarissa (important point that she was never actually seduced by him), also her consequent temporary madness, final decline and death. None the less her death (to a lesser degree) causes Lovelace's own death in duel, lessens the realistic strength of the story. One feels there would be little danger of this attractive, lively girl, with property of her own, not finding a husband she fancied, in the light of her passions being sufficiently strong to have run away with Lovelace in first instance, then turned against him for his bad behaviour. That would have been far more interesting. The plot is all contrived to fit in with conventions of period, every bit as hypocritical (e.g. Harlowe family after Clarissa's death) as supposed Victorian behaviour. All the same there is a lot of force in *Clarissa*, which I am glad to have read. Some of the action takes place at an inn in Hampstead called the Flask. There is, one presumes, or at least was, a pub so called in Flask Walk.

Wednesday, 7 September

Juliet O'Rourke obit. She must have been eighty-five. Juliet could be inimitable in her own line. I remember her saying of her small son, then perhaps five or six, 'He is the most ignorant person I have ever met.' There were still traces of her funniness when she came here a year or two ago. Sad story. I did not exactly have a pang but felt poor Juliet's career had been depressing for one so gifted in her own way.

I reread *The Satyricon*, also J. P. Sullivan's book on Petronius. The translation of former by Paul Dinnidge is good and fluent. Sullivan, as a don, is rather worried as how to categorize the work, which does not accord with classical idea of satire. This point perpetual stumbling-block with many critics in quite other areas too, who find difficulty in grasping that the world, realistically surveyed with even a minimum of irony (simply naturalistically, so far as that can ever be done), turns out to be a grotesque place, human beings even more so. After all, Nietzsche points out, the Greeks knew that well. Decently translated, *The Satyricon* holds up amazingly well, especially Trimalchio, who, one feels, could have been exactly like that as a Roman *nouveau riche*. Even the picaresque adventures are scarcely exaggerated.

Thursday, 8 September

Henry Mee rang in evening, saying the National Portrait Gallery are likely to want portrait in the view of his contacts there; accordingly he would need more sittings to replace it among the twenty-four planned for his show. Rodrigo Moynihan gave him a couple of sittings, then went abroad, painting to be continued on return.

Saturday, 10 September

V went to Whitfield for the weekend. Tristram and Virginia were at The Stables

(Archie is doing his Houses of Parliament guiding, Georgia in Thailand), where John and I dined. They had been in France (St Rémy, Dordogne). They came on Angus Wilson and his long-time boyfriend, who live there in a high block of flats in the market place, where the lift periodically goes out of order, and gets stuck. The boyfriend (agreeable) always carries a telephone to report they are stuck in the lift. Angus Wilson somewhat disorientated these days. Asked Virginia, 'Are you alone here?' She indicated Tristram. 'Are you engaged?' 'Married, actually.' By that time Archie and schoolfriend had arrived. Angus Wilson enquired of Tristram, 'Which of those boys do you live with?' Tristram replied that he lived with 'that one' (indicating Archie) for about three or four months in the year. Tristram and Virginia also visited Stephen and Natasha Spender, who have a cottage there.

Sunday, 11 September

John cooked chilli con carne for luncheon to which Tristram and Virginia came. There was a somewhat disparaging piece in the *Sunday Telegraph* by Andrew Sinclair (still in College at Eton when Tristram was an oppidan) about Cyril Connolly (linked with the republication of *Enemies of Promise*). In this various improbable remarks are attributed to me, and Peter Quennell is described as an Etonian. One is staggered by the unnecesary howlers made in writings of this sort about recent events.

I reread *Love's Labour's Lost*, the beginning is lively, then the play tails off. I am struck by how much Berowne's backchat with Rosaline resembles Beatrice/Benedick in tone. One wonders whether this is based on the actual way Shakespeare himself talked to self-assertive girls, or (with which one is personally familiar) the shape into which the writer's dialogue fell naturally. Perhaps not quite the same thing. 'At the first opening of the gorgeous east', cf. Wordsworth.

Monday, 12 September

V returned from Whitfield, nice weather, enjoyable, Evrilda Fleetwood-Hesketh was there with her child by an American journalist (the father now dead) and her child's friend. Also present Penny Graham, George's long-time girlfriend. V much wanted to see Penny. I am rather curious to see her myself.

Wednesday, 14 September

Jeffry Spencer, whose collection of E. M. Delafield material he handed over to V for her biography (accordingly dedicated by her to him), came to a lateish tea, driven over by Michael Parker, somewhat younger. He is a genial old person in his early seventies, an authority on railways and sometime Director of the Railway Museum, Clapham. He and friend were on their way to Devon. V gave back certain E. M. Delafield items he had lent her; in return he presented her with his book of photographs of Victorian and Edwardian railways.

I reread Graham Greene's *The Power and the Glory* (not opened for years). I tried to analyse why I find Greene novels so distasteful, while being perfectly prepared to meet Graham as a man, which I should indeed find amusing after so long. There is a kind of falseness in his writing, which I also dislike in Ford Madox Ford's work (which Graham so much admires), tho' Ford's falseness is of a somewhat different order, usually based on some imaginary code of gentleman's honour to which he personally laid claim. He invested his heroes with similar misfortunes due to behaving in a high-handed manner. Graham's heroes are not at all like that, tho' equally soaked in self-pity. His characters, puppets constructed to appeal to his particular public, are shown in their processes of thought, every cheap novelistic trick used in narration, to appeal to sentimentality. As David Cecil said: 'Formula, plenty of religion, plenty of sex.'

Graham is not in the least interested in what people are really 'like', the Priest a most improbable figure as a Mexican; the Lieutenant scarcely less so. At the same time the book, in technique, must be admitted to be economically written. It had immense international success, somehow plumbing levels of religious belief and disbelief, combined with sex, which went straight home. Graham possesses an enormous vitality, allied to infinitely low spirits, a state quite different from melancholy. He is determined to impose this condition on the reader, which obviously some people find sympathetic. Also, always present, is Graham's chronic love of conflict.

Friday, 16 September

I read in Court Circular (which I have taken to scanning through since appearing there for my CH audience) that the Prince of Wales was attended somewhere by Mr Richard Arbiter. Is the latter a modern version of Petronius Arbiter at Nero's court, who will write a *Satyricon* of our own day, then be threatened by the jealousy of another royal favourite (perhaps Colonel Laurens van der Post) and will he then open a vein in his bath, while commending and censuring his servants? John tells me that Mr John Arbiter is, in fact, a media figure, attached to the Prince in some PR capacity. Very suitable.

Wednesday, 21 September

Selina Hastings sent a photocopy, dated February [1938], of the letter to Evelyn

Waugh from an unidentified woman, recalling a passionate adulterous love affair with him, apparently ending two years before (spring 1936), just before Evelyn proposed to Laura Herbert. One assumed the letter must have been found by Bron, who handed it over to Selina for her biography. The writer's husband is called Don (conceivably Dom), two children, apparently boys, prep-school age. 'Holiday cottage' (farm) at Milton Abbas, Dorset. London residence recently changed to Hampstead. Handwriting (one would judge) is sophisticated, narcissistic, rather dotty, the style typical of one sort of fan letter writers receive. A scrap of similar letter also exists written from Brussels. Evelyn's committing adultery is interesting in the light of the tremendous to-do he made about adultery committed which involved his own wife; indeed, in the case of his friends, as indicated in his *Letters*, and *Diaries*, for that matter his novels.

Saturday, 24 September

Anne Lancaster to luncheon. Perhaps rather tired after a longish drive. More probably the reaction after working twenty-four hours a day during Osbert's last few years, the sudden release, coupled with his loss. She said Richard Ingrams is poised like a vulture for death of Malcolm Muggeridge, when he hopes to clean up on his Muggeridge biography. Malcolm shows no sign whatever of demise, nor will for many a long year in my opinion. In fact, if I had to put money on it, I'm not sure I wouldn't regard Malcolm's as the better life of the two. There is also the question of how many will remember Malcolm, when he does pop off. Anne never seems greatly interested in the activities of her son Max Hastings as Editor of the *DT*, however did allege Mrs Thatcher cut him because he sacked her daughter Carol. Such pieces as I have seen in the paper written by Carol Thatcher seem no better, no worse, than other female journalists of her kind, but I was reminded of Adrian Daintrey's experience when Camouflage Officer (Major) in Egypt on Corps HQ with Persia/Iraq Force (I can't remember which), when sent Field Marshal Alanbrooke's son as Assistant Camouflage Officer. This was not a success. Adrian (who can get on with many unpromising people) could at last stand it no longer. He went to the officer in charge of such things, saying Brooke must go.

The Colonel (possibly Brigadier, even Major General Administration) listened carefully to Adrian's complaints. Then he (more or less) said: 'Daintrey, I absolutely see what you have suffered. Every effort has been made to find some niche in the army where Brooke will not cause trouble. He has eventually been dumped as your Assistant. We have orders that he is not to be moved again. There are men fighting for their lives in the sands of the desert, in the jungles of Burma, among the islands of the Pacific, in the air, under the sea, often in frightful conditions. They are having a worse time than you. Your war, Daintrey, will be to put up with young Brooke.'

Anne praised the Notton, Cantenac '73, at luncheon, which I thought a shade disappointing.

Monday, 26 September

Kingsley Amis and Neil Hughes-Onslow to luncheon. Neil seems the only person nowadays who can persuade Kingsley to take a train to see a friend. They are a slightly odd pair together. Neil is perfectly competent to talk about 'books' though really a pictures man (National Art Collections advertising management side), but what he most likes is dishing up Eton shop and upper-crust gossip (subjects on which he is often exceedingly funny). None of that is at all in Kingsley's line. His new novel, *Difficulties with Girls*, was out last week, which we possess, not yet read. Its newspaper coverage is being extensive, on the whole good, with one or two violent exceptions. Kingsley brought off a notable double by having an obsequious piece written about him by John Mortimer in one Colour Supplement, and Kingsley himself being egregiously rude to Mortimer in another on the same day. Among other things, Mortimer stated in his interview was that Kingsley 'hit his son with a hammer', when in fact Kingsley had said he 'hit his thumb with a hammer'. Mortimer also instanced as Kingsley's literary admirations 'Wodehouse, Waugh, Greene'. I was rather surprised at this, Kingsley having never been greatly besotted about Graham, or for that matter more than reasonably about Evelyn. Quite unprompted, Kingsley mentioned that he had never said anything of the sort. *The Old Devils* has been dramatized, and is to be played somewhere in North Wales; presumably as enjoyable satire on the drinking habits of South Walesians. *Ending Up* will possibly be done by Thames TV. Kingsley is slightly self-conscious about being handled by Thames TV after the IRA Gibraltar incident.

Neil said Nicko Henderson may outwardly give a feeling of relative political wetness, in fact it is entirely due to Nicko's appearances on American Breakfast TV that the Falklands campaign was so successful owing to comparative American co-operation. Nicko is being given all sorts of jobs now, Neil thinks he might easily end up with the Garter. Snook recognized Kingsley at once as a cat-victim, sat on him, then to show off jumped up on the lintel of the library door. I asked Kingsley if a pub exists called the Flask in Flask Walk, Hampstead, where some of the action in *Clarissa* takes place. There is. Must have been there since at least the 1740s, probably much earlier. Prawn mayonnaise; Breton cold smoked chicken, red kidney beans, beetroot, lettuce salad; gâteau; Château Couronne de Gaie, Pomerol '78, good, Calvados. Enjoyable party.

Tuesday, 27 September

I saw Lister. See him again in a fortnight's time to get my lower plate relined.

Saturday, 1 October

Tristram to luncheon. He has to come down for talks with Mr Millard and Mr Fricker about building matters at The Stables, where they are making certain alterations. Snook arrived at The Stables, attempted to disrupt these consultations by jumping on people's knees, also using Ruth's tray in an aggressive manner. The *New Yorker* cartoonist Charles Addams obit. He is said to have had affair with Barbara Skelton, who looks remarkably like the vamp in his pictures. His cartoon of man in cinema audience roaring with laughter, everyone else in the house weeping, V says represents me.

Sunday, 2 October

Dick Blacker, who acts as keeper/water bailiff on strength of being allowed to shoot over our land, his wife Dolly our former daily, reported Foster Yeoman shooting syndicate's keeper trespassed in the wood on far side of the lake recently; a man with two or three dogs coming down as far as the water. Mrs Foster Yeoman, now chairman of company, lives at Southfields (rather a pretty house) mile or two away. Her husband died some years ago. There are two sons. I rang at once, Mrs Foster Yeoman was very civil, put me on to one of sons, who apologized, said he was surprised, would speak to their syndicate.

Sachie Sitwell obit age ninety. He was, I suppose, my last link with authors of ancient days in Duckworth's. Sachie was possibly most talented of Sitwells, undoubtedly handicapped by having to grow up with Edith and Osbert, never really sharing their passion for drawing attention to themselves and making trouble. Sachie simply wanted to get on with his writing, travelling, and smart social life. I always found Sachie agreeable, tho' he lacked the warmth of the other two, even if saner; saner certainly than Edith. I never greatly cared for Georgia. There seemed an innate chilliness, tho' she too always perfectly agreeable when we stayed with them and they came here.

Sachie is probably underrated these days as a poet, even if his poetry a trifle wooden; he did pioneer work on baroque art, other sides too in that field, but he was incurably careless. I remember being left to see one of his books through the press, probably *German Baroque Art*, Sachie himself having disappeared abroad without address. I found he had used words 'painted altars' and 'painted pulpits', indiscriminately in same long paragraph, no means of knowing which he was talking about, tho' of course both might have existed. I just had to settle arbitrarily which he meant in the context. If Freddie Ashton and Charles Addams are still waiting on shore for Charon's boat, Sachie will make an agreeable companion for them. Chronologically the Sitwells could perhaps be termed Art Deco Poets.

Tuesday, 4 October

I finished Kingsley Amis's *Difficulties with Girls*. Kingsley always has moments that make one laugh aloud, the first description of the man who has allergy to cats' fur, and the character looking like a 'career torturer', but the novel as whole cannot be called a success. Kingsley might well defend his position by saying he has to earn a living and is not concerned with such aspects as the end being dreadfully sentimental. One is really back with Arthur Mizener's dictum that 'a good newspaper article is not the same thing as a good novel', something not always grasped by reviewers. If you try to write a book about a married couple, 'the author fair to both sides', adultery, etc., you are bound to come out with *Woman's Own* sort of stuff. Although many years ago I once did to a small extent (*From a View*) write through a woman's eyes, it is a mistake for a man to do that in my opinion. I did not care for *Take a Girl Like You*, whose heroine, Jenny Bunn, reappears in *Difficulties with Girls*. Were I a feminist I should find Kingsley's sentimentalities far more insulting than his acerbic estimations of female behaviour.

Thursday, 6 October

I reread *The Return of the Native*. The early part, the description of Egdon Heath, comic peasants, the character of Thomasin and Eustacia, are all good. Wildeve as a come-down-in-the-world pub keeper is unconvincing. Yeobright, selling diamonds in Paris, even more so. The reddleman, wandering about stained all over red, mummers, etc., are good. Then everything goes wrong, sometimes even ridiculously contrived. This is Hardy's persisting fault. Thomasin, widowed, marries the reddleman, now a successful dairy farmer, Hardy adding a note to say that was not originally intended but altered for serial publication. His own preferred version was the reddleman disappearing mysteriously with his van from the countryside, which, if everything is to go wrong, has something to recommend it.

I reread *Troilus and Cressida*, one of Shakespeare's best. 'Two traded pilots 'twixt the dangerous shores of will and judgement': 'Time is like a fashionable host'. Struck by the way the protestations of love in the letter (photostated by Selina Hastings) from an adulterous wife to Evelyn Waugh resemble Cressida's speech to Troilus: 'If I be false, or swerve a hair from truth', just before returning to the Greek lines, then immediately starting off affair with Diomedes, who conducts her back. Did Pandarus obtain some monetary reward for arranging Troilus and Cressida affair in the first instance? This is never mentioned, yet seems implied by the soliloquy which closes play.

Wednesday, 12 October

Hugh Massingberd rang saying Adrian Daintrey dcd, would I write a short memoir for *DT* obit, which I did. Last week I ordered a case of wine for Adrian (twelve assorted Italian) as a Christmas present. I rang IEC Wine Society to cancel, found they had already sent it. I rang the Master of the Charterhouse, who turned out most agreeable, called Eric Harrison, knew the late John Lloyd (The Widow). We agreed The Widow is greatly missed by both of us, particularly the sort of joke only The Widow appreciated. The case of wine had arrived that morning. I thought best thing to deflect it to some other friend in London, rang Spurlings, who will get in touch with Harrison and arrange to pick up wine. It turned out that John Spurling's great-grandfather had been Master of the Charterhouse, a post John himself always coveted to end his days.

Apparently Adrian had a binge (Harrison's term) to bring to a close his life, luncheon, champagne, cigar, died that afternoon, when resting, so his passing was as satisfactory an occasion as can reasonably be expected, charming young women visiting him to the last. Harrison said the latter phenomenon not uncommon among the Brothers. Strange after Adrian's wife leaving him (no particular reason beyond genuinely not liking being married to him, tho' she did marry again quite a long time later). He himself never tried again so far as one knows. Perhaps he realized deep down that marriage not for him. Anyway would have been handicap to the sort of social life he really enjoyed. Adrian in many ways was not at all 'cynical', indeed in some respects profoundly sentimental. True, of course, the two characteristics are apt to go together. He had that curious power of attracting women, which seems quite unconnected with any wish on their part to remain continuously with the man concerned. One supposes process in some way connected with Adrian's extreme solipsism, tho' he combined this conviction, that only he himself existed, with occasionally making shrewd comments about other people. Again he would be disturbed by some generalization, often humdrum enough, on the subject of the failings of human nature, rather in the manner the generation before one's own would be shocked by flippant comments of that sort.

I suppose in the end Adrian had, probably like most people, the life that best suited him. He belonged to a very early period of my London life, we seeing something of each other on and off through the whole of it, except the interlude of the war. I always wished I liked his paintings a bit more than I did. The last few years in the Charterhouse inevitably shut him off (something of an ordeal to go there, also one was visiting London less), Adrian's own routines continued to the end, even if he was often pretty bored. All in all things might have been much worse.

The OUP paperback of John Meade Falkner's *The Nebuly Coat* (1903) was sent by its latest editor, Christopher Hawtree. I had never read the novel and enjoyed it as a late-Victorian romance, written, oddly enough, by an armament tycoon/poet. I sent Hawtree (not met, he edited *Night and Day* anthology well) a line saying I was surprised Falkner, obviously knowing a good deal about heraldry and genealogy did not make the Blandamer peerage heritable through female heirs, which would have rounded off story of illegitimacy, murder, more neatly, something demanded by that sort of book. Mr Sharnall, the bad-tempered, tumbledown organist at the Cathedral is the best character, probably drawn from life. One presumes the Bishop who insisted on lunching with Sharnall on an episcopal visit to the Dean and Chapter, had a homosexual affair with him as undergraduate at Oxford.

Thursday, 13 October

V took Snook to the vet for his operation. In characteristic cat manner he stayed out for about eight hours yesterday, returning with a slightly injured back leg. About 9.15 a.m. foreigner rang talking unintelligible English, equally unintelligible French, which he alleged himself to be. He said he was a 'scholar', and continually spoke of 'Monsieur Jacques'. V, listening in on this, diagnosed a maniac, so I told him to write and hung up. It did not occur to me till later that he was talking of Mr Jack in *The Fisher King* (which he did not mention), rather than *Dance*. He was undoubtedly a dotty fan.

A longish session with Lister in the afternoon. He spoke about his flying. Dentists would make an interesting study in their hobbies. There is a tendency to be keen on something. Snook turned out to have broken a bone in his leg. This will be pinned. It is not yet announced when he will return home. Oddly enough that is just what happened to Trelawney at about the same age. I am running through all the art books in order they appear on the shelves, just looking at pictures. George Gross collection called *Ecce Homo* is a splendid portrayal of Germans, especially Berlin in 1920s. Raking molehills on the lawn, I leant on rake for moment reminding myself of Millet's peasant listening to Angelus. The rake broke and I fell down.

Monday, 17 October

Snook returned from the vet (female, Judy Quig). He is slightly lame still. The pin will always remain in. Snook is showing all the same excellent form. His goodness was commented upon in the surgery. Adrian Daintrey's niece (Mrs) Philippa Wallace rang to say the Memorial Service for Adrian on the 31 October, Christ

Church, Chelsea. She asked would I say a few words? She had much liked the brief memorial at the end of the *DT* obit. I refused on the grounds of stiff joints, and no longer visiting London but agreed to suggest someone who might do it. After consultation with V, we put forward Alan Ross, Lees Mayall, Ferdie Mount, Algy Cluff (tycoon I do not know, who bought Daintrey pictures according to John). Adrian left his body for dissection. This ought to make medical history.

I read Barbara Pym's posthumous novel *A Few Green Leaves*, best of her books, I thought. She cannot manage the 'dramatic' side of plots; her thing, amusing village scenes, unmarried ladies, clergy, doctors.

Wednesday, 19 October

I saw Dr Rawlins about 'throat' that developed after my visit to the dentist (not uncommon consequence) and was given penicillin tablets. My electric typewriter broke down. Office International usually do repairs, but referred me to National Technical Services (Bath), who sent their man this afternoon. He turned out to come from Cardiff. We talked about South Wales, the Welch Regiment. He then revealed that the representative of his firm from whom he had just come on, in the neighbourhood of Stratton-on-the-Fosse, knew this house, that it was associated with an ironmaster, and a writer lived there. The Cardiff man asked what novels I had written, which I always find rather embarrassing. A strange little episode.

I looked at a book about African Sculpture. Struck (1) how extremely good much of it is and how varied in different areas of Africa; (2) how much 'modern' sculpture slavishly copies African, but quite pointlessly, if the African background and African sensibilities are missing. It is, in fact, just as artificial as Victorian sculpture copying classical Hellenic realism.

I reread *A Midsummer Night's Dream* with certain amount of enjoyment. Bottom and his fellows remain funny. The play within the play is in a sense preparation for *Hamlet*; Oberon's relations with Puck, for Prospero's with Ariel. Constant Lambert once described to me how he had to discuss a production of the *Dream* at Covent Garden with David Webster, who was homosexual (also perhaps a shade sinister), the manager there. 'Of course I knew the question would arise sooner or later in our conversation,' said Constant, 'I just hoped I would not break down into helpless laughter.' It came at last. Webster said: 'Now Bottom . . . How do you yourself feel about Bottoms? I myself have seen some surprisingly good foreign Bottoms. All the same I always prefer an English Bottom. What I never like is an *old* Bottom. One of the best Bottoms,' etc.

Saturday, 22 October

The Fisher King is to be translated in Spanish (Versal, Barcelona). Christian Bourgois asks for suggestions for the jackets of French translation of *Dance* (he does not want Boxer). Very unlike the French not to have their own ideas about that sort of thing. Yet again one is struck by how things have changed in France, particularly Paris, in such matters. Anyway, why not Boxer? Not unFrench in a way, I should have thought. Repair of mowing machine to cost £406. I suppose one will have to go through with it, in some degree to keep David Moore happy, as he is such a perfect tenant for The Lodge, useful in all sorts of ways, and a nice chap.

Sunday, 23 October

Driven by John (through a marvellous autumn countryside) we lunched with Kevin and Rachel Billington at Poyntington, as Frank and Liz Longford staying there. Frank with a cold, Liz a shade battered when we arrived, but both in excellent form. Liz cheered up after some talk. She is editing the Letters of Princess Louise. Frank is writing a book on House of Lords. From time to time he thinks V is his daughter. I have been landed with three books to review about C. S. Lewis, whom I find a tedious figure. I asked Frank if he knew him as fellow Oxford don. It turned out he only spoke once to Lewis, nevertheless he recently addressed the C. S. Lewis Society.

This is an interesting piece of negative information, as one would have thought that as fellow dons, both youngish, they would inevitably have come across each other. I have no recollection of Lewis's name being mentioned by Maurice Bowra, tho' Henry Yorke always grumbled a great deal about his tutor at Magdalen, who at one moment at least seems to have been Lewis. We watched Tristram's production of Michael Palin's *No. 27* on TV in the evening, very funny and well cast, a lady of ninety to be evicted by property developers was played by the actress Joyce Cary, herself ninety; therefore slight fear she might expire on set in the course of filming. It was good and we laughed a lot.

Monday, 24 October

A tiresome development about Adrian Daintrey's case of wine. The Master of the Charterhouse could not find it, so John Spurling had a wasted journey. The Wine Society tell me the case was delivered and the signature appears to be 'Daintrey', Adrian having died week before. Eric Harrison is looking into this apparently suspicious matter.

Tuesday, 25 October

It now transpires (to use the phrase disliked by Henry James) that the Wine Society muddled the order with that sending Adrian wine in June for his birthday, so a case of mixed Italian wines has been rerouted to the Spurlings as a Christmas present. This mistake caused a good deal of trouble to the Master of the Charterhouse, who was extremely nice about it. Bob Conquest rang in the evening. He is over for four days, somewhat jet-lagged. But said he and Liddie had tea with Kingsley Amis (rare meal to partake of with Kingsley), who was in rather a bad temper. Bob also met elsewhere Neil Hughes-Onslow, who described himself as courier to Kingsley for visits to the Powells. Bob suggested Neil might ferry the Conquests down next time. Excellent idea.

Bob told his publishers to send me his *Collected Poems*, which they had omitted to do (with several other presentation copies). The Larkin Letters are apparently being carefully sorted by Anthony Thwaite, so probably a censored version will appear. This seems a pity, all the same one sees it is a bit early, if there are really embarrassing ones with early homosexuality and later flagellation in them. The American election is still uncertain. Bob says Bush is pretty awful, even if better than Dukakis. Anthony Wagner replied to my congrats on his eightieth birthday (he is now blind), saying he had enjoyed *The Fisher King*, apparently available in Talking Books.

Wednesday, 26 October

V and I lunched with Lees and Mary Mayall at Sturford. They are recently back from their US trip. They were fairly exhausted, but in good form. The tour of the Grand Canyon, etc., by bus was a trifle gruelling; then Tulsa, Oklahoma, where Mary's son by Robin Campbell, Bogey (Gerard), is a waiter, living with an (apparently fairly opulent) hospital nurse. Bogey, as the only Briton in Tulsa, is a famous figure. Something called the Five Hundred Acre Fair was in progress, including a sale of hats bearing slogans, one of these saying simply: SHIT HAPPENS (how profoundly true).

Lees said Nicko Henderson was the man responsible for detecting Donald Maclean's spying activities in the Foreign Office, which is interesting.

Thursday, 27 October

Eric Anderson, Headmaster of Eton, wrote saying he would like to call, so we invited him and his wife Poppy to luncheon. Anderson made a good impression. He is very tall (so characteristic of Eton Headmasters, perhaps a rule instituted after Keate), a Scot, looks young for fifty-two. He kindly brought a bottle of Lynch Bages '78, one of a dozen given him by an Arab, whether hospitality in the desert, or to prevent his son at Eton being sacked, did not transpire. Anderson is an authority on Walter Scott. Poppy Anderson, also Scotch, bossy though quite agreeable. She teaches at Eton, where their son was formerly in College. Like Alington, Anderson came from being Headmaster of Shrewsbury. He seemed to like the job, and was well up in Eton lore. He is keen on international exchanges of boys, also that promising boys should give 'leaving portraits', as in eighteenth/early nineteenth century; how paid for nowadays I'm not sure. Presumably boys' parents. I gave him a signed set of *Dance* paperbacks (American edition with unbelievable covers) for the School Library. Anderson seems to have energy, humour, grasp of being up to date without a lot of nonsense. Enjoyable party. Melon and spiced ham; lamb chops; gâteau; Château Notton '73 (drank one and a half bots).

Monday, 31 October

V's check up with Mr Lloyd Williams. All well, not another till next year. She is rereading Bevis Hillier's *Young Betjeman*, about which we have been talking a lot. When Betjeman worked as an adman I went to see him in his office to explore the possibility of breaking into that calling myself. I was told to produce some ideas and send them in. This I did, to be returned with the comment that they were those all novices come up with. Two of my suggestions were in connexion with a series called *Old & New*, already advertising Shell: two contrasted figures drawn by the *Punch* artist (or rather three collaborating persons) called Anton, with a two-sentence caption. I put up an Army one: old-type Sergeant saying: 'Fall in defaulters'; new-type Sergeant: 'Fall in trigonometry candidates', and a Stage one: old-type Actor: saying: 'I trod the boards with Irving', new-type Actor: 'Noël's practically promised me the part'. Both these were, in fact, subsequently used in the series, but I was never given a halfpenny when, say, a guinea each would have been most acceptable.

I always thought that rather discreditable on Betjeman's part. He was also not good on people he ragged ragging him back. There were two brothers John and Terence Greenidge, who come in Evelyn Waugh's early *Diaries*, where John Greenidge is called The Bastard (some joke about getting drunk on burgundy, therefore Bastard of Burgundy), who was an architect. Terence Greenidge, the younger brother, was at Hertford with Evelyn Waugh. Terence was absolutely dotty. When he went down he did occasional jobs as a film extra and wrote various crazy novels, one of which, *The Magnificent*, was about being in love with the (heterosexual) actor Anthony Bushell. The Greenidges had a little money of their own to keep them going.

When I was Literary Editor of *Punch*, Betjeman ran into Terence Greenidge somewhere, who had just written one of his crazy books (some ravings about universal peace). Betjeman told Terence I would like to review it in *Punch* (where there was not nearly enough space to review books that really ought to be noticed). I sent Terence's book to Betjeman, saying no doubt, as he was so keen on it being reviewed, he would like to do it himself. Naturally nothing happened so Terence (who really was very dotty) began to ring me up morning, noon and night, asking when the review was going to appear. I told him John Betjeman had the book, he was the man to ring. As he was by temperament indolent, he, Betjeman, liked being kept up to the mark about his work. It was real kindness to pester him, as he did not like being forgetful.

This resulted in a somewhat irritable Betjeman asking me to call Terence off. Accordingly I said that, if Betjeman would return the book, I would find another reviewer. This I did; in fact another Oxford contemporary of Terence's called Bernard Causton, almost equally dotty, one of the characters Malcolm Muggeridge involved *Punch* with. He had mushrooms spilt on his dinner-jacket at the *Punch* dinner, and talked of suing. I don't think Betjeman ever really forgave me for this incident, but it was just the sort of tease he often perpetrated himself.

Wednesday, 2 November

John Saumarez Smith, of Heywood Hill Bookshop, Curzon Street, rang saying he had been approached by a New York bookseller (called Horowitz, I think) on the subject of a large American corporation, which wished to buy the archives of well-known British writer, to be presented to the library of the writer's own choice. My name has been mentioned, the sum in the neighbourhood of £40,000. I replied that my MSS, etc., had been made over to Tristram and John; if some such deposit were ever made, I regard Bodleian as the preferable place. These propositions are always slightly unsettling, even when one does not wish to take advantage of them. The mere thought of the administration involved makes one dizzy. Hilary Spurling in the evening, rang to thank for the wine, which reached them at length. She said John Spurling had greatly enjoyed his talks with the Master of the Charterhouse, in anticipation of taking over job like his, John's, ancestor.

I suggested the post might be comparable with that of the Priest of Nemi, who slew his predecessor and reigned until he himself was slain by his successor. I told Hilary of Snook's misadventure, allowing him to purr down the telephone. She said they had a cat called Henry, thought to be female, but turned out male, with only one ball, which, for compassionate reasons, they felt ought not to be removed, consequently he fathered kittens. This was a characteristic Spurling gesture and result. Biggles is worse than ever after his Welsh exploit, bad-mannered, aggressive, unfriendly.

Friday, 4 November

George Clive is staying one night at The Stables with Penny Graham, whom I had not met. She has been with George for perhaps five or six years, pretty and elegant. Penny acts as hostess at Whitfield when Mary is absent. I thought her, in principle, decidedly attractive, tall, thin, rather little-girl voice that makes her seem like girls in the past one used to know, not of today. Her father was a famous upper-class racing correspondent called The Scout, she herself having journalistic connexions with glossy papers and the rag trade, organizing models and the like. Penny arrived under her own steam, George (whom I have never seen in better form) appeared later. He kindly presented us with a bottle of Château Pavie, Medoc '61. Tristram (in an aside) told me he was ferrying Penny up here from The Stables, inspissated darkness, so Tristram had to take her hand. He had a sudden vision of George driving up at that moment, seeing this scene across the lawn in his headlights. Later, headline: SON'S MURDER BY COUSIN AT WRITER'S HOME.

I read *The Nigger of the Narcissus, Typhoon, Falk,* all good. *Falk* is perhaps best. I am struck by how Conrad resembles Vidia Naipaul in his writer's temperament. No doubt Vidia was influenced by Conrad, but then so was Graham Greene to an inordinate degree, while Graham's temperament could hardly be further away from Conrad's ironic detachment. Graham is full of every sort of prejudice, *parti pris*, desire for publicity, not to mention all lack of Conrad's technical knowledge of doing a practical job; in Conrad's case a sailor's. It might be argued that Graham is potentially able in most areas and Vidia, too, lacks extraneous technical knowledge but like Conrad his books are uncontrived. Conrad perhaps has slightly routine appearance of villains at appropriate moments. Graham's on the other hand, one feels are not anything to do with his own life except for a few characters rather crudely taken straight from observation.

Wednesday, 9 November

In the American Election Bush walked it as President. Will Sir Claus Moser ante-up bottle of '75 claret?

I reread *Romeo and Juliet*, some of the Bard's best language, young men wisecracking, tragic passages. Old Capulet one of Shakespeare's splendid dotards, a category he felt strongly about, and was adept at depicting. He makes his old men at once futile and poetic: 'Death lies on her like an untimely frost . . . Death is my son-in-law, Death is my heir.' This remarkable scene (when, in fact, Juliet is not really dead), which contains so much good stuff about Death (the Nurse, for instance), is followed by longish extremely funny, quite pointless row between Peter, the Nurse's manservant, and the musicians hired to play at the wedding feast.

Was that just to get the play the right length, or did the Bard want to use up those passages of dialogue?

Monday, 14 November

Tristram is down to oversee alterations at The Stables and lunched. We discussed Peter Webb's biography of David Hockney, which I am reviewing. Tristram said he thought Hockney's experiments in photographic cubism more interesting than successful. (I'm not sure they are even very interesting.) He had seen the Hockney décor for Stravinsky's *The Rake's Progress*, which he confirmed as no less excellent than appeared from illustrations. We talked of producing, and how to avoid actors 'doing their own thing' in the Bedlam scene by the use of stylized inmates in cells. I was much struck by this (having seen *Marat-Sade*, as an example of naturalism not really working with real lunatics). Artifice would be preferable, tho' I did not grasp what was wrong at the time. Madmen in *Duchess of Malfi* similarly need to be stylized to make effective, rather than just jump round the stage. This is the old triumph of Art over Life.

Saturday, 19 November

Selina Hastings came to luncheon for further talks about the Evelyn Waugh biography. She arrived about midday from Hinton Charterhouse (some ten miles from here), where she is staying with Pamela, Lady Harlech, widow (American second wife) of Mary Mayall's late brother, David Harlech. Selina was in good form. She knew Alec Waugh well, friend of her father (indeed only time V and I met Jack and Margaret Hastings, later Huntingdon, was dining with Alec W. before the war). She said how amazed she was at the age of about fourteen to learn that Alec was a tremendous womanizer. Apparently he also actively liked studying bores, so that Alec would be welcomed by friends with bores on their hands, whose various forms of tedium Alec would investigate. It came as a complete surprise to Selina to learn that Evelyn Gardner was (no doubt still is) an excellent housewife, making any place she lived in a model of neatness and good organization, also, I think, a goodish cook.

Selina retailed a picture of Quennell family life. The Quennells have moved to a flat near her in the Regent's Park Road area, Marilyn (apparently Kingsley Amis's pupil when don at Swansea) rang recently, asking Selina to come round at once, as she was in great trouble. Selina complied, found the place in considerable disorder, Marilyn Quennell (never met by either V or me) complaining that they had only just moved in and could not find a builder. Selina asked when they took over flat. It turned out to be December, that is ten months earlier. Selina recommended two

East End young men, who do her building jobs. Peter Quennell, just out of hospital, looking like Death, arrived on doorstep. Later she said: 'He likes me to read Beatrix Potter stories to him in the evening.' Quennell: 'No, he doesn't.' Apparently Jim Lees-Milne remarked to David Beaufort: 'You must ask poor Peter down to Badminton to cheer him up,' to which David Beaufort replied: 'Never again.' Tomorrow Selina lunches with the Roy Jenkinses at East Hendred. Here we had lamb, Spotted Dick with treacle, which Selina said was her father's favourite pudding. I heartily agree. Until I went into the army I thought you had either Spotted Dick, or suet pudding and treacle. It was in the army I learnt the Lucullan combination.

Wednesday, 23 November

At long last National Technical Services fitted a repaired component to the electric typewriter, the Cardiff man arriving in afternoon. He is called Roy Spikit, as he remarked, unusual Welsh name. He spoke of the Welch Regiment Museum in Cardiff Castle, knew that one 'Service' battalion in first war had been called 'The Cardiff-Pals'. In evening V went to Mells to meet the new incumbent, the Revd Dan Olive, the Diocesan architect who took Orders about six years ago. He, in fact, built the new rectory in the garden of former Mells Rectory (the latter is quite grand eighteenth-century house). V returned rather tired about 9.15, reserving judgement. She said Olive looked rather like the politician Dr David Owen.

In consequence of reading Scott's *Journal* (presented by Eric Anderson, after his visit here), I got through *Old Mortality* (never read before), not without copious skipping. It is clearly a very original novel to be published in 1816, curiously looked forward to Victorian tastes, just as Surtees (the R. S. Surtees Society set of whose complete works I have been reviewing) looks back, if you prefer, a century forward. *Old Mortality* cleared my mind about the later seventeenth-century history of Scotland, previously never intelligible to me. The fact is the Civil War continued there, one side being, as it were, Roundheads, the other, as it were, Cavaliers; which in a sense went on until the Stuarts were out of the way. *Old Mortality* (its eponymous character scarcely appearing) the model for innumerable later historical novels, by no means least those of R. L. Stevenson.

Saturday, 26 November

The dotty fan rang about 7 a.m., again about 9 a.m., V hanging up on him on both occasions. Sir Claus Moser's secretary is in touch, so good prospect of claret for winning bet. V rang Rosie Goldsmid to talk about Chloe Teacher's ball (to which we were invited) to find that Chloe has had an awful hunting accident, possibly fatal. Rosie is naturally shattered by this. She really has suffered tragedies about her daughters (both delightful girls), Sarah drowning, now this happening.

I reread *The Comedy of Errors*. I dislike plays and books about misunderstandings, which upset me, grate on the nerves, but the humour and economy with which this play is written is most impressive, it is also essentially Shakespearian. ('Far from her nest the lapwing cries away' is referred to in one of the other plays too [*Hamlet* V.2].) The manner in which the subject is stripped down is most interesting, without any of the sense of 'seriousness' contained even in the other Shakespeare comedies. Some years ago the BBC put on an excellent, uproariously camp (the Dromios) performance, which seemed right way to do it.

Sunday, 27 November

Joff and Tessa Davies were about to have their beautiful grey Burmese cat, Amelia, operated on to have no kittens, when she was seduced by an unknown stranger. V and I went over to see kittens, born last Monday or Tuesday. They look like tiny moles. I took some photographs. Joff told me he always reads Dumas in bed, about seven or eight of them, then begins again at the beginning. I meant to ask whether he restricted himself to *The Three Musketeers*. I must enquire later. We returned to one of John's chilli con carnes.

Monday, 28 November

Tristram and Virginia down to oversee alterations at The Stables, lunched here (chilli con carne recycled, rather nice Anjou table wine, Pinot Noir). Virginia is suffering from a cold. Tristram is going to India to prepare a film about the Indian poet/musician Ravi Shankar. I finished Bruce Chatwin's novel *On the Black Hill* (1982), about two old Radnorshire twins, who lived together all their lives, sharing same bed, a couple described to him by Penelope Betjeman who knew them when she lived at Cusop, a cottage high up just the other side of the Wye from Clyro. I really only got hold of the book on account of the Radnorshire connexion, as not much attracted by what I heard of Chatwin's writing. Tristram said the film made of *On the Black Hill* was not very good. Tristram knows Chatwin, who worked at Sotheby's, an anthropologist, interested in nomads, extremely intelligent, accordingly a tremendous show-off. Chatwin is married to rich American, but suffers from AIDS, being bisexual. *On the Black Hill* is undeniably competent, if a trifle lifeless, the upper-class characters, especially, are dreadfully stylized and stereotyped. The Radnorshire place names (of which I have some genealogical experience on paper) are well done, but misarranged, which gives a confusing effect. *On the Black Hill* is one of those novels (perhaps Hardy influenced) in which everything has to go wrong and somehow never strikes a spark.

I reread Bernard Berenson's *Diaries 1947–1958* (reviewed by me on publication 1964). I found them more interesting than twenty-five years ago, perhaps chiefly because Berenson was about a year younger than I am now when *Diaries* begin, and they go on to death at ninety-two. (From which age one hopes to be preserved.) Extremely intelligent, conscious of his own failings, in fact an obsession with himself, his own dishonesties, little if any humour. Berenson had rather middlebrow tastes in novels (tho' he mentions I. Compton-Burnett with approval) and indulges in frequent banal descriptions of beautiful views. His conceit is so colossal that he cannot understand individuals because he thinks he knows all about all people. He remarks that in the end he lost interest in 'Old Masters' (except for obscure attributions) and preferred French painting from David to Degas. He had inordinate vanity, especially about his successes with women. He was much put about by Eric Linklater saying in a newspaper interview that he, Berenson, looked 'foxy', Berenson insisting that he was neither foxy in appearance nor character. In fact photographs make him look almost like a fox wearing clothes, as if he were one of Beatrix Potter's vulpine characters (Mr Tod, I think) come to life. Osbert Lancaster, who did not like Berenson when he met him at I Tatti, said he spoke in precise Ninetyish accents, emphasizing every separate syllable.

Berenson perpetually notes how much old friends and old loves bore him when they come to see him, or write, while equally noting how much he depends on a stream of relatively distinguished visitors to stimulate his mind. He mentions a throat specialist he came across who, with no memory for faces, always recollected the throat of anyone he had previously examined, when he had another look. One would wholly agree with Berenson that the most exasperating burden of old age is feeling one's mind and imagination, apparently no less vigorous than when younger, at the same time being too fatigued to put them into practical motion.

Tuesday, 29 November

My eyes tested (not done for two years), a very slight deterioration in my 'bad' eye, no need for any change in specs. I can still read (with specs): 'If you can read this print your vision is exceptionally good.'

Thursday, 1 December

The anniversary of our wedding. We had a bottle of fizz for dinner (Veuve Cliquot Ponsardin '80) and discussed the correspondence in the *New York Review of Books* on the subject of Tom Eliot's alleged anti-Semitism. It must be agreed to have existed with him in the form of obsession about 'world Jewry', etc., but there is good deal of humbug nowadays about how Jews were spoken of before the war; true, there existed anti-Semitism for no apparent reason (e.g. Henry Lamb, possibly some flotsam of his Manchester upbringing), together with infinitely more people (not least Jews themselves, like Gerald Reitlinger, for instance) who made endless Jewish jokes.

People too young to have grown up before the war simply write as if they would never have dreamt of making a Jewish joke, perfectly legitimate, unless, as in totalitarian countries, jokes are not allowed at all, jokes of all kinds forbidden. I was irritated about ten or fifteen years ago when an American reviewer (with a name like Milburt Mudrake) complained that *Afternoon Men* was anti-Semitic, chiefly on grounds that Verelst (in fact surname of English landed family, presumably of Netherlands origin, which I did not know at the time) is described as *not* looking like a Jew (which he was), depicted as rather attractive middle-aged man who gets the girl in the story. (Incidentally, recently reading Berenson's *Diary*, Berenson, himself Jewish, almost always notes whether a Jewish visitor 'looks like a Jew' or not.)

It now occurs to me that another element in *Afternoon Men* might be held to stamp the novel as overwhelmingly non-anti-Semitic, that is to say Pringle, certainly rather a ridiculous figure, was modelled on Gerald Reitlinger (whom I then barely knew except for many anecdotes about his oddities, general grotesque behaviour) was given surname not even ambiguously Jewish, in fact, so far as I can remember, described as a North of Ireland family, where the name is certainly found. In other words I went out of my way not to appear anti-Semitic in days long before the Nazis.

Sunday, 4 December

Driven by John we lunched with Vidia and Pat Naipaul at The Dairy Cottage, Salterton. It was really our turn to have them here, but Vidia leaves for India for three months tomorrow and they had already invited James and Margaret Sutton. Sutton is a typographer and stone-cutter, contemporary of Vidia's at Univ, Oxford. He seemed agreeable, his wife pretty, slightly arty. He is building a dolls' house for a grandchild, dealing with the problem whether the lights should switch on and off in every room for the whole house. Sutton had also been setting a passage from *Dance* for specimen type of some kind, the sort of thing that is always gratifying to a writer.

Vidia is now a Heinemann author, Heinemann has commissioned a book about India, a prospect that must make the hearts of the Indian Government sink, as they will probably get some fairly caustic criticism. Told Vidia we had recently read 'Rednecks' (reactionary Southern farmers), excerpt from his forthcoming book on Slavery in the US, in *New York Review of Books*. An interesting point is that the *New*

Yorker, serializing most of the Naipaul book, omitted the 'Rednecks' section, presumably on account of *New Yorker* (indeed, American) traditional nervousness about giving offence in any area whatsoever; which is now a virulent American disease. The present *New Yorker* Editor is said to read few books of any kind. Vidia was as usual in great form, he delivered terrific diatribe against rich Arabs, indeed Muslims in business anyway, their dishonesty in financial matters, conviction that it does not matter swindling 'Unbelievers', in fact is a praiseworthy act. The food good, if rather oddly assorted, lobster soup, odds and ends of crab, almond crumble; excellent Pauillac (missed the Château) '76.

More in the papers about the threat to Avebury, its vulgarization through various forms of commercialist development. I rang Jim Lees-Milne, as a former National Trust official, who recommended getting in touch with Jennifer Jenkins, now in charge there. Jim did not know she and Roy were friends of ours. I made various efforts to telephone, then wrote to Jennifer. As biographer of John Aubrey (who first discovered and recorded the Avebury Stones after finding them when out hunting) I feel specially responsible; awful as such depredations are in any case, where historical monuments and beautiful country are concerned. Sharks who plan such things always speak of 'giving employment'. No doubt it would 'give employment' to have a Stonehenge Disneyland.

Tuesday, 6 December

The American Election claret bet has become an inextricable tangle. Nicko Henderson's original document, as croupier, stated:

Dukakis	*Bush*
Lady Moser	Dame Jennifer Jenkins (in fact Lady Jenkins)
Sir Claus Moser	Mr Anthony Powell
Lady Violet Powell	Mr John Powell
Lord Jenkins	Sir Nicholas Henderson

John and V are agreed to pair, so nothing happens. The first action was taken by V ringing Nicko at Hambro's (where he is now working) about herself and John pairing off. Nicko, who appeared to be delighted to have something serious to do, someone to talk to, said he was informing everybody how they should act. The next thing was that Sir Claus's secretary rang me to enquire what was John's address and telephone number. I took this to mean Sir Claus thought it the best manner of conveying a bottle to me via John, but it now seems likely he thought John himself ought to be recipient. A postcard came from Roy this morning saying he regards himself as owing me a bottle, may he deliver this when he comes to Somerset in near future (about SDP matters)? In short some confusion seems to reign between a former Chancellor of the Exchequer, a recent Ambassador to Washington, and Paris, and a former director of N. M. Rothschild's. John put forward the interesting theory that all this really reflects is the war between Rothschild's and Hambro's.

Saturday, 10 December

Tristram and Virginia to dinner. Tristram's Indian trip for the moment is suspended. Archie now working as packer in a wine shop in or just off Lamb's Conduit Street, round the corner from Great Ormond Street, where we began our married life, and I think occasionally used the shop for the odd bottle or drink. The conditions are somewhat Dickensian (*Tale of Two Cities*), as a crate broke and wine dripped through the rafters on Archie toiling in the cellar.

Sunday, 11 December

The new incumbent, the Revd Dan Olive, with wife (Margaret), came for a pre-luncheon drink, attended also by Tristram and Virginia. Mr Olive, as V reported, is slightly like pictures of Dr David Owen, with a touch of some old-fashioned comedian (Dan Leno?). V says he obviously expects great things from this living. Both Olives come from the West Country. They should fit in well.

I finished Dante's *Divine Comedy*, after reading a canto a night, never wholly got through before. My copy was given me by Alick Dru during the war. It has Italian one side, English the other, an old-fashioned translation with rather skimpy notes. The *Inferno* is comparatively easy going; the *Purgatorio*, less so; *Paradiso*, somewhat unintelligible. I find T. S. Eliot helped himself fairly liberally in *The Waste Land*: 'I had not thought Death had undone so many' (Eliot), 'I should never have believed Death had undone so many' (*Inferno* III, tr.); 'Your shadow at morning striding behind you / Or your shadow at evening rising to meet you' (Eliot), Dante's shadow (he being still alive) thrown before him (*Purgatorio* III), etc.

Saturday, 17 December

V to London for wedding of Rebecca Fraser and Edward Fitzgerald (said to be a left-wing barrister). All seems to have gone well. The reception was in the House of Lords, where V and Rachel Billington used the loo marked *Peeresses*, but V assured me they did not scribble graffiti on walls, which must have been tempting.

I reread *Victory* (1915) and *Lord Jim* (1900) in that order. Both are linked with *Falk* by Schomberg, the German-Alsatian hotel-keeper at Sourabaya, at first mainly a tiresome gossiping hotel proprietor, finally actively sinister. One feels Conrad could have been additionally effective had he done more of this enlarging of the canvas, fitting characters in together against the vast South-East Asian background. Both *Lord Jim* and *Victory* begin well with the convincing characters of Jim and Heyst (the latter regards 'all action as harmful'), both tailing off into less good stuff about an island, a girl and invading desperadoes.

Gentleman Brown (son of a baronet), Mr Jones (disgraced clubman), are really the same character, Jones having the additional trait of being obviously homosexual. One takes it that Jones is jackal. Ricardo is bisexual, 'rough trade', contracted at some stage and kept on as a henchman, who accordingly falls for the girl, maddening Jones with jealousy. Ricardo is, perhaps inevitably at that period, allowed to become a somewhat absurd figure. In neither of the stories do the girls come off, Conrad's chronic failing. Lena defeats Ricardo when he tries to rape her, but inexplicably she does not tell Heyst. Are we to understand that she was really quite attracted to Ricardo? Her standing remains undefined throughout. One presumes by that period in her career she had *faute de mieux* more or less become a tart, in which case why was she worried about living with Heyst, except for becoming pregnant, an obvious danger? General arrangements for life on Heyst's island strike one as presenting all sorts of practical problems, even if nothing compared with unclear nature of their mutual relationship.

This starting with brilliance, then descending into melodramatic muddle, is typical of Conrad, even if action, as such, is always well done. No doubt difficult to avoid obliqueness in getting his novels published at that date. Frequently things he wanted to imply. Even so, the women are rarely well conceived. Marlowe (who tells most of the story in *Lord Jim*) seems almost to have had a homosexual passion for Jim himself, but cf. manner in which Kipling (other nineteenth-century writers) speaks of young men. It is difficult to know to what extent Conrad rationalized sexual relationships in his own mind, quite apart from what he committed to paper.

Monday, 19 December

V and I celebrated my birthday, in anticipation, with caviar, Veuve Cliquot Ponsardin '80 at dinner. I read *Richard II*: a good play. 'The setting sun, and music at the close'; 'Those banished and forbidden legs'.

Wednesday, 21 December

My eighty-third birthday. I don't feel too bad. V gave me a shirt chosen by John. We dined with Tristram, Virginia, Georgia, at The Stables. Georgia was recently mugged, held up at knifepoint in Stockwell neighbourhood, not far from the house. Really too much. In the course of the morning Gerry de Winton rang from Maesllwch to wish me Many Happy Returns. He talked of various things, including the sixteenth-century magician Fludd (typical surprising knowledge Gerry suddenly turns out to possess). Gerry didn't think much of Bruce Chatwin's Radnorshire novel, not in the least like people of whatever class round there (Gerry is technically in Brecon, I think, but essentially a Radnorshire landowner). I agreed about Chatwin, there is a kind of lack of life about his books. James Sandilands sent two bottles of Bollinger '83, a kind act. Evangeline Bruce rang from Washington. Apparently Nicko Henderson arranged claret bets on the American Election in the US too, also confusing who should pay whom, Evangeline (although a Democrat) thought Bush would win, but no bottle yet.

Christmas Day

Warmish. V, John and I lunched at The Stables, where are staying Ferdie, Julia and the Mount children William, Harry, Mary, last recovering from flu. Extremely good classical Christmas dinner (I think the right term), Virginia making the pudding herself, certainly an improvement on most bought ones. Ferdie brought down a magnum of Santenay '83, of which I partook with extreme moderation after a couple of glasses of Tio Pepe. Ferdie also presented us with magnum of Château Nenin, Pomerol, '77. Archie gave me Il Favot (Piedmontese) '83 for my birthday, Château Phélan Segur, St Estèphe, '75 for Christmas, both from the wine shop (H. Allen Smith) in Lamb's Conduit Street, where he worked. V gave me another shirt (chosen by John). The Mount boys made good impression, William, dark, rather like Bill Mount so far as I remember him; Harry, fair, possibly more intriguing figure, tho' both lively, gave one idea of what present-day Oxford intake is like, Harry has just got into Magdalen (where William already is), both from Westminster.

Ferdie said he lunched with Evangeline Bruce in Washington, expecting to meet *le tout Washington*, in fact found John Saumarez Smith, of the Heywood Hill bookshop. Julia thought I let Edward Lucie-Smith down lightly when reviewing his not over-brilliant *Osbert Lancaster Anthology*. I didn't want to crab Osbert, hard not to do if one pitched into Lucie-Smith too hard. Julia had known Lucie-Smith when in Christie's. Jolly party.

Boxing Day, 26 December

Tristram, Virginia, Ferdie, Julia, lunched here: turkey, Christmas pudding, mince pies, Mouton Cadet '79. Ferdie met Reagan before becoming President. He seemed very old, if quite impressive; although a B movie actor, Reagan was at one moment the highest paid star. Ferdie claimed to have had some influence in getting Hugh Massingberd appointed to run the *Daily Telegraph* obits, which Hugh does with great éclat, transforming what was formerly a somewhat inadequate aspect of the paper into one of its main features. Drinks party at The Stables in evening: Lees and Mary Mayall, with assorted grandchildren, friends. Mary in great form, discussed medicine with me: 'What was that stuff they gave one as a child to make you shit – syrup of figs?' Lees with a stick, rather arthritic. Alexander Weymouth and his very ebullient Hungarian wife Anna, and daughter Lenka. Lenka pretty, and at Univ with Georgia. Alexander is still dressed as a hippy of twenty or more years ago, patchwork coat like Harlequin, straggly beard. Joff and Tessa Davies, both daughters now engaged. Mary Anne (Foreign Office) to Richard Charrington (Captain, 9th/12th Lancers), Lucinda (City) to John Sunnucks (former Life Guards, now City), last not present. V and I withdrew towards eight, party still in full swing.

1989

Made a curry for luncheon just for ourselves, not done for some time, thought I should keep my hand in.

Friday, 6 January

Henry Mee asked if he could look in, arrived about 4 p.m., bringing a large gâteau from his local Tesco's. He wanted to explore possibility of my writing comments for the catalogue of his show for 'portraits of distinguished persons', Hugh Casson is doing an Introduction, Mobil Oil possibly mounting it. He takes photographs of sitters, among which is an amusing one of the Queen talking to Mee in front of her own portrait, taken by Henry with interval lens. After Henry Mee left, I had a word with Hugh Casson, who seemed to think no more than 'long captions' were required for the catalogue. At same time Casson agreed about the considerable difficulty in composing these. He said 'like writing twenty-six obits', especially as some, if not most, portraits of individuals about whom I know nothing. I shall have to think it all over.

Tuesday, 10 January

I reread the whole of *Dance*. This prompted various reflections on the sequence as whole. The novel, for better or worse, seems to me quite on its own in content, construction, as far from *A la recherche* in one direction as from *The Forsyte Saga* in another. Nor does its tone or style appear to me in the least like Evelyn Waugh, except in most superficial connexions. Balzac, again, on a far wider scale, deals with aspects of life *Dance* leaves untouched, also Balzac is far less systematized. Everything 'serious' in Waugh is confronted with the Roman Church; less serious matters, as often as not reduced to farce, no doubt on the whole effective (tho' when Evelyn is not funny, he is painful to a degree). The last method is avoided in *Dance*.

These comparisons reflect quite extraordinary incomprehension of novels, and novel-writing technique, on part of reviewers, sheer literary ignorance or stupidity. On the other hand, complaints about the use of coincidence do require consideration, although reference to any of the 'great' novelists of the past reveals coincidences right and left (Fielding, Scott, Dickens, Thackeray, Trollope, Hardy, not to mention Dostoevsky, Proust, *et al.*). My comments on this subject: (1) Extraordinary coincidences do take place in life, of which one could give innumerable instances; (2) Coincidental meetings in a novel seem much more improbable if telling a story 'forward', rather than 'backward', e.g. the fact that I drew Gerry de Winton in the School Chess, because someone put my name down as a joke, then met him again just after the war because Osbert Lancaster had known his wife Pru (then a widow) in Greece, invited by Gerry to stay at Maesllwch largely because of shared interest in Radnorshire, then Gerry rang the other day because he saw my birthday announced in paper. All this would sound far less probable if Gerry's last telephone call had resulted in some dramatic incident in a novel, had to be planned at an early stage why we knew each other, then traced forward in narrative. Reviews would say: 'Of course de Winton had to be the boy Powell played chess with'. (3) All novels have to accept certain conventions as to why author knows what is recorded. Simplifying meetings, marriages, and so on, of large group of people, many related, described in the course of about sixty years, including a world war, seems as legitimate as any other convention, provided social, psychological improbabilities are avoided (as they are not, for example, in Hardy).

One does not really believe that the young Marcel climbed up the wall and through a glass panel watched M. de Charlus buggering Jupien (or vice versa). That is merely a simplified manner of describing incontrovertible known information on the subject which Marcel acquired. Having said all this, I would admit coincidence does play some considerable part in presenting *Dance* conveniently, tho' not, I think, untruly. With regard to individual volumes, *Upbringing* gets off to quite a good start, together with fairly copious introduction of characters to play later part at a stage when the precise number of volumes remained undecided.

Monsieur Dubuisson originally intended to have known Farebrother in the First War (later only lightly hinted) and play some part in Second-War Free French affairs. This closer involvement seemed on examination by me too contrived. *A Buyer's Market* presented a far more formidable problem in creating the broad basis of circumstances, characters, incidents, on which to build future developments. Here should be mentioned the chronic anxiety as to speed in inventing material (only to be effected by 'inspiration'), getting it down on paper in a desirable manner, pressing on with the narrative, while at same time keeping clearly in one's head what has already taken place.

From the very beginning I was painfully aware of the necessity of speed, which would, in fact, continue for twenty-five years (settling down after this second volume to volume every two years), deciding how much time could be allowed for perfecting things, without danger of delay, running out of steam at the close of the sequence. These pressures resulted in *A Buyer's Market* having too many phrases like 'as it turned out', 'I did not understand at the time', which reflect uncertainties as to how the story would go forward, several such phrases better omitted. At same time, except for vagaries as to which year is described (1927–8, I think, no more than when someone recounts a reminiscence) nothing went badly wrong in light of future development, action, necessary explanation in introducing new matter. All these continue reasonably smoothly through *Acceptance*, and *Lady Molly*.

Good beginning to *Casanova*, but overlong explanatory passages follow, probably unavoidable to establish new characters and changing atmosphere of the period. At same time all rather lacking in action until Mrs Foxe's party, visit to Maclintick, his death, events leading up to these, both episodes satisfactorily dramatic after rather long somewhat rambling descriptions. *The Kindly Ones* again opens reasonably well, hard to know how to treat neatly, effectively, the vague shapeless period leading up to outbreak of war, perhaps inevitably amorphous.

The Valley of Bones and *The Soldier's Art* both flow in a lively manner, with right sort of interplay of action and character. *The Military Philosophers* opens all right, but followed up by a rather formless explanation of Allied Forces in Exile, again scarcely avoidable in contemplating wartime circumstances unknown to future readers. This, too, is relieved by later action, Embassy party, tour of Military Attachés, Victory Service, all of which come off pretty well.

Post-war conditions set an acute problem for *Books*, not entirely unlike those posed in *A Buyer's Market*, accordingly all rather more discursive than one would like. A recovery is made in *Temporary Kings*, perhaps the best constructed vol. of sequence, plenty of action and character play. *Harmonies*, one would say, opens reasonably well, then rambles a bit owing to the necessity for tying up loose ends in the final volume, which I decided the twelfth must be, both as a neat number and avoidance of risk as to declining powers. I am not sure that Delavacquerie wholly comes off. The concept of PR man, also poet, somewhat derived from Laurence Cotteril (who was both those). I met him arranging matters when awarded W. H. Smith Prize; superimposed on Cotteril is the well-known poet/businessman Roy Fuller, plus the rootlessness of V. S. Naipaul. Vidia has his touch of mystery, which Roy shares a bit in his own manner.

I told Roy the suggestion of himself was intended, to which he replied he had supposed Delavacquerie a certain Canadian poet, whom I did not know. Roy seemed to find the character perfectly acceptable. The question of models is immensely complicated, as one's own view of one's own work changes. Both Hugh Lloyd-Jones and John Bayley, dons themselves, suggested Sillery owed something to Maurice Bowra. Bowra was never in the least in my eye when writing, however in this last reread, irrespective of whatever I intended, Sillery did once or twice recall Maurice to me. One phrase Hugh Lloyd-Jones picked on as Bowra-esque was 'won golden opinions'.

In the same way Hilary Spurling always insisted (in face of direct denials by me) that Bagshaw represented Malcolm Muggeridge. This too never intended, Bagshaw in my mind combination of Bobby Roberts (when drunk), and Malcolm's journalist friend Cholderton, obsessed with dialectic of Communism (Cholderton had been a correspondent in Russia and Eastern Europe) while hating Communism itself unreservedly. Again this rereading brought Malcolm to mind more than once in case of Bagshaw, quite involuntary on my own part. These last comments indicate the degree to which a writer lacks absolute control over a novel, therefore sections of *Dance* criticized above, in fact, may be less unprofitable than they seemed to the author.

Speaking subjectively, one wonders, had there been world enough and time, whether these discursive, relatively rambling passages could have been broken down into set pieces of incident, explanatory dialogue, such latter seeming to oneself more effective aspects of sequence. This would undoubtedly have made the whole undertaking longer, perhaps created danger of obscuring narrative and historical background. Pilate's principle (what he had said he had said) was probably right in avoiding too much afterthought rewriting and redrafting, tho' certain amount absolutely necessary at the time. Henry Yorke himself put about that he was the model for Stringham, impossible to imagine anyone less like Stringham than Henry.

Friday, 13 January

Henry Mee is delighted with 'long captions' for portraits, which I continue to compose.

Sunday, 15 January

Tristram took photographs in morning for the sculptor William Pye, who is supposed to be doing head of me. Tristram photographed my head front, back, sideways, apparently all Pye needs. The project is initiated by Hilary Spurling. Other heads by Pye stand in the Spurling garden at Penn Road, where perhaps mine too will come to rest for Hilary to pronounce witch's spells in front of. I should like that.

I reread *Henry IV Part 2*, Worcester speaks of having 'trained on' Hotspur, expression used in contemporary racing language. I am still moving rather lethargically through the art books. Owing to some volume about Surrealism being out of place, I looked through it after Rubens, then turning to Brueghel. I was much struck by Brueghel's 'Surrealism' being every bit as fantastic, inventive, as anything conceived in heyday of Surrealism, while infinitely more accomplished as pure painting. Oddly enough Brueghel at moments greatly resembles Cézanne in small passages of landscape.

Saturday, 21 January

Benjie Fraser, staying with the Baths at Job's Mill, asked if he and Silvy Thynne could come over for a drink. This they did. After working on the Borders as a journalist, Benjie is now a merchant banker, like everyone else. Specs, rather teddy-bearish in appearance, very much Fraser rather than Pakenham, in fact I could see no trace of Pakenham, rare in Pakenham ramifications.

I followed up Brueghel by returning to Hieronymus Bosch at whom I was looking some months ago. Bosch was born about seventy years before and no doubt influenced Brueghel. Bosch has nice colour, on the whole not so various in imagination as Brueghel, one would say. What an immense absurdity of Roger Fry stating Brueghel not an artist, a mere illustrator, when one considers Brueghel's Cézanne (perhaps even Utrillo) roots, insets of still life and peasant groups. The half-bakedness of Bloomsbury is well exemplified. Probably in consequence of reflecting on these pictures, I dreamt that V and I went to see a church, rather like the Cloford church (Horner tomb), where some of the locals were tossing a man in a blanket in the field outside.

Tuesday, 24 January

John and Suzanne Keegan to luncheon. This was somewhat delayed because V had scruples about asking them before we returned the luncheon of Michael Carters (former High Sheriff, Batcombe House), as we met the Keegans there, notwithstanding John Keegan being military correspondent of *Daily Telegraph*, where anyway in theory I might come across him. As we could for the moment think of no obvious fellow guests for the Carters, their entertainment here is postponed *sine die*. John Keegan was always lame, not as I supposed a war wound. She is taller than I remembered, attractive.

We talked a lot about army matters. I asked about General Kitson (who spoke at Johnny Walker's Memorial Service, on strength of which I recommended him as a military portrait for Henry Mee). Keegan described Kitson as immensely brave, now retired. Had been C-in-C troops in Great Britain, now paralleled with C-in-C troops on the Rhine, from one of which the Chief of General Staff is normally chosen, Kitson not getting the latter appointment. He is a former Commandant of the Staff College, a job usually leading to high rank. The Commandant of the Staff College is expected to be reasonably chatty with the students to explore their capabilities. Kitson's only recorded remarks while there were 'Good morning' (pronounced in drawling grudging tones) and 'Why aren't there any more of those pink biscuits?'. Lady Kitson, old-fashioned soldier's wife, equally out of the ordinary, a great rider, also paints. She is rumoured to have been invited to some official ball, which she forgot about until she came back late from riding, hurriedly put her ball-dress on over jodhpurs and attended the ball. I asked about the fussiness one now hears of in the army. John Keegan said army professional puritanism began about fifteen years ago, when those who had fought in the war came to the top. The theory that six months is quite enough for Sandhurst. Those views are now changing as to the necessity for giving officer-cadets some educational training. Keegan said that Field Marshal Bramall is a good man. Avocado, Welsh chicken pie, gâteau. Château Notton, Margaux, '73, which Keegan praised. Certainly good bottles. Amusing party.

Wednesday, 25 January

Professor P. M. W. Thody, Head of the French Department, Leeds University, sent a piece called 'The English Proust', written for a *Festschrift* to which he was contributing. My heart sank at the title, because comparisons with Proust, if flattering, are rarely made with intelligence. Thody's, on the contrary, was exceedingly well done, pointing out certain similarities, and a great many fundamental differences in most respects. It seemed to me an intelligent and subtle piece of criticism, fitting in well with my own appraisal of *Dance* earlier this month.

I reread Delacroix's *Journal* (tr. Lucy Norton, rather a jolly fat girl, who used to frequent rackety parties in ancient days, had, I believe, a great passion for the pretty model Hodge). Delacroix is always intensely serious, at same time makes acute and ironic comments. An interesting contemporary view of Balzac: 'I have been reading that dull book *Eugénie Grandet*. Works of this kind do not stand the tests of time; the muddle and lack of skill which are the incurable defects of the author's talent will relegate all such things to the scrap-heap of the centuries. No restraint about it, no unity, no proportion.' One sees what he means, but Balzac's sheer vitality eventually triumphs. (As it happens, phrase about 'scrap-heap of the centuries' almost exact words used by Malcolm Muggeridge of my own works.)

Sunday, 29 January

The Sunday papers have been delivered for the last six years or so, about four of those in company with her sister Charry, by Jane, now retiring to do her A levels, the job being taken on by 'her boyfriend's father'. These two – later one – pretty little girls ornamented Sunday morning, as they were always chattering to each other all the way up the drive, jolly, high-spirited. Latterly the boyfriend had been driving Jane in his car. For administrative reasons I enquired the address from which the Sunday papers would come. This Jane did not know, but gave a telephone number. I then asked the name (in fact, Brown), which she also did not know, presumably surname is unnecessary these days, even in boyfriends.

I have never properly read J. L. Borges's *Fictions*, at which I had another go. Borges is obviously extremely intelligent and one would suppose a rather nice man, but I can't really get on with philosophic short stories about the unreality of human identity, personality, time, etc., interspersed with scenes of violence. Unlike, say, Pirandello, whom I like (especially *Six Characters*, *Henry IV*), preoccupied with somewhat similar themes, the Borges stories for some reason do not hold my attention. At same time, considering some of the writers awarded the Nobel Prize, Borges might reasonably have been given it.

Sunday, 5 February

Tristram, Virginia, Virginia's cousin Christina Noble (as she prefers to be called, rather than Mrs Singh), with the latter's daughter Tara (nice little girl), Joff and Tessa Davies, to pre-luncheon drinks. It turned out that Tessa was at school with Suzanne Keegan, but did not know her as they were different ages.

Tristram brought an additional copy of Thody's 'The English Proust', passed on by Anthony Verity, Master (i.e. Headmaster) of Dulwich (assistant masters are referred to as teachers), friend of Philip Thody's, also fan of mine. Tristram said that until comparatively recently all Masters of Dulwich had to take the name of Edward Alleyn, founder of the school, actor, contemporary of Shakespeare. Tristram and Virginia were in Paris last week, Archie is comfortably fixed with room on the ground floor, with his own front door, the rest of the (French) family on the sixth floor.

On return Archie will go to New Zealand for a month or two and visit friends known to Virginia during her time as Lady-in-Waiting to the Governor General's wife, a Grenfell cousin married to Bernard Fergusson, sent to rule New Zealand by Andrew Devonshire, when Dominions Minister.

Reread Benvenuto Cellini's *Autobiography*. Enjoyable, rows with Cosimo di Medici, immensely reminiscent of Henry Lamb, Adrian Daintrey, all painters, bickering with patrons, no doubt the same with all painters and sculptors since beginning of time. At one moment Cellini was given special access to the Ducal Palace, apparently causing him to go through rooms which included that used as the Duchess's loo, Cellini complaining (as no doubt did the Duchess too, as she did not like him) that he was always coming upon her at 'inconvenient moments', which can have done little to improve relations between them. This is even more amusing when one recalls that the Duchess was Eleanor of Toledo, painted by Bronzino, looking highly disdainful, in a splendid dress with her little boy. She looked decidedly attractive and comes into Cellini's book quite often.

The switch-over of the Sunday papers seems to work. They are delivered for the moment by an infinitely gloomy small boy called Mark, while his parents sit in a car in the background.

Monday, 6 February

Tessa Davies to tea after the Women's Institute meeting at The Stables. Tessa revealed that she was expelled from school for celebrating passing of her A levels by running down the village street (frequented, she assured us, only by a few cows) with another girl, neither wearing anything but gum boots. The Headmistress asked her parents to come over, as offence was too heinous to be mentioned on the telephone.

I recently reviewed Tommy Lascelles's *Letters and Journals Vol. II*, which gives a devastating picture of the awfulness of the Duke of Windsor, to whom Tommy was Secretary when the latter was Prince of Wales. In Canada, Fruity Metcalfe, a notorious member of the Prince's entourage (late Skinner's Horse, I think, certainly in the Indian Cavalry), visited a brothel, from which, having insufficient funds to defray expenses of his entertainment there, he was expelled into the street without trousers. One of the illustrations in the book misidentifies Prince George with Fruity Metcalfe, which I pointed out in my review. In consequence of that I received a letter from Fruity Metcalfe's former tailor (Mr Whilley, premises in Cork Street next to my own tailor, Taylor & Gardiner, in more spacious days), who agreed the photograph certainly was not Metcalfe. Tessa pointed out that Mr Whilley essential aspect of the story, as he no doubt had to cut a new pair of trousers in place of those sequestrated in the Canadian house of ill fame.

Talking of brothels, when I was looking through some Van Gogh volumes among art books, I was interested to read that after the painter chopped off his ear, he delivered it in a parcel to the *maison tolérée* at Arles. Van Gogh seriously toyed with a project of joining the Foreign Legion (which takes recruits up to forty, he remarked), because he liked a life of routine. Why not? Van Gogh might have added to the school of North African painters like Fromentin. After all Renoir served with the Cuirassiers in the Franco-Prussian War.

Thursday, 9 February

A letter from Ania Corless (Higham) arranging the translation of the first two vols of *Dance*, in one vol., into Catalan (a series called *Best Works of Universal Literature in the 20th Century*, Editions 62, Barcelona). This apparently will not prejudice either Spanish translation, nor subsequent whole sequence in Catalan.

Sunday, 12 February

Roy and Jennifer Jenkins to luncheon. This arose in first instance by Roy's request that he might call with the claret bottle owed for American Presidency Election bet, when visiting the West Country. I pointed out that Sir Claus Moser had already ante-ed up a bottle via John, but Roy seemed determined, so eventually it was arranged that they should both lunch here, which would anyway give an opportunity to talk that one does not get at biggish luncheon parties with the host. We invited Rachel Billington (Kevin not available), then, notwithstanding about three weeks' notice, Rachel ran out on grounds of Kevin needing the car to go to London.

In the event, party turned out equally lively without her, as Roy and Jennifer seemed to like being on their own, no doubt rare in their high-powered social life. The night before Roy rang to say he was on the wagon during Lent. This was an unexpected blow, as I had planned to drink the Château Pavie '61 (given to me by George Clive) and Château Phélan-Segur '78, presented on my birthday by Archie, to whom I hoped to report Roy's claret-experienced judgement. ('Don't open anything special for Jennifer,' Roy said. I wasn't sure V would have liked me to give a similar injunction *mutatis mutandis*.) He brought a bottle of Château Mouton-Rothschild '76 and I passed on to him Moser's Château Haut-Bages Libéral '78. This curious interchange I think satisfies Roy's political/bureaucratic side, in preference to Jennifer (who backed Bush's chances) and Roy himself (Dukakis) cancelling out; perhaps some residue of being Chancellor of the Exchequer, taking a penny off VAT, adding tuppence to Income Tax, some such financial transaction.

Roy was amusing about some of his official travels. In Senegal the President, Léopold Senghor, is a man of letters, and translated (among other works) the poems of Gerard Manley Hopkins. He also married a wife of minor Normandy *noblesse* (good Proustian theme). Roy asked which twentieth-century French poets Senghor thought the best. Senghor named a couple Roy had never heard of. In return Senghor asked Roy which twentieth-century French novelists Roy thought the best. Roy said: 'Proust and Simenon.' Senghor replied: 'Why Simenon?' As Roy remarked, the more chic answer would have been: 'Why Proust?' They discussed Proust, but neither was able to remember the name Proust gave the seaside resort based on Cabourg. On the way out Roy recalled that was Balbec. The following day the insignia of Grand Officer of the Legion of Honour of Senegal (bright green sash) arrived for Roy, with a letter that seemed to imply the decoration had been awarded for literary services, notably for calling to mind Balbec.

Roy brought an inscribed copy of his *Brussels Diary 1977–1981*, about to be published. This looks amusing stuff. Welsh pie (made with turkey instead of chicken). Christmas pudding. Château Notton '73, Roy abstaining, but saying Notton '73 was the best claret available on the House of Lords Wine List. Jennifer, I noticed, showed no sign of not appreciating the bottle. Enjoyable party.

Wednesday, 15 February

V to London. Ayatollah Khomeini, dictator of Iran, has sentenced the British novelist Salman Rushdie to death for Islamic blasphemy (Rushdie having been brought up a Moslem) in his new book *The Satanic Verses*. It is now the duty of every other Moslem to kill him. As usual Shakespeare has an apposite quotation: 'Tear him for his bad verses' (*Julius Caesar*). Rushdie is a tedious writer, publicity-seeking in a distasteful manner, but this seems going too far on the Ayatollah's part. Iran one of the few countries I have visited where the population, high and low, seemed uniformly disagreeable. Awful as the Shah may have been, he was preferable to this murderous savage; typical of the Left (also *Private Eye*) to go on nagging about some ruler, as they did about the Shah, until something much worse was substituted.

Henry Mee rang. He has got into his head that the set of portraits with my captions would 'make a book', having, like all painters, not the least idea of books and publishing. I tried to explain all this to him and that the best he could hope for was an illustrated catalogue sponsored by some rich organization. This Henry doesn't seem to have fixed up yet. He seems incapable of understanding (as so many people are) who buys books, how many they sell, etc. I was interested to hear how his painting of the Queen's portrait arose. In first instance, the Press Club got in touch with him to do a portrait of the Prince of Wales for the Club. Buckingham Palace approved of the result. Mee, finding himself at a bar somewhere (possibly at the Press Club itself) talking to Sir William (Bill) Heseltine (agreeable Australian Secretary to HM, met at my audience, fan) was asked by Heseltine if he would like to paint the Queen. This naturally Henry closed with. Interesting that a commission should be arranged this way.

V returned from London. She visited Heywood Hill bookshop, where John Saumarez Smith gave her a catalogue of modern first editions produced by him and (more substantially) the American bookseller Horowitz. Information is given about individual books within. This is full of grotesque howlers such as Cyril Connolly meeting Cecil Beaton (Harrow) at Eton; Christabel Aberconway being left her North Audley Street house by 'Sir Samuel Constable' (in fact left her by Samuel Courtauld, the name Constable perhaps dim memory of Constable who was Director of the Courtauld Institute); Evelyn Waugh described as writing to Cynthia Asquith (née Charteris, married to Beb Asquith), when EW's letter is in fact to Katharine Asquith (née Horner, married to Raymond Asquith). Among other items *Caledonia* (Hugh Kingsmill's copy) at $3000, the same price as first edition of *Prufrock* and *A Shropshire Lad*, so one can't grumble.

I am rereading Matthew Arnold rather sporadically. I have just finished 'Sohrab and Rustum'. Why on earth did Arnold write this poem? No reason to suppose he was in the least interested in legendary wars in Central Asia. Was the attraction that a Father killed Son unknown to him? Does this reflect conflict between Poet and Dr Arnold, or is it pure *Boy's Own Paper* stuff? One suspects a bit of both. I'm always fond of *The Scholar Gypsy*. Incidentally Arnold ('Sohrab and Rustum' 1855) seems to have had a go at Macaulay (*Lays of Ancient Rome* 1842) 'sword that only he could wield': while Fizgerald (*Omar Khayyám* 1859) helped himself to Arnold with 'I came like water and like wind I go'.

Saturday, 18 February

We were lined up for the traditional picnic brought down by Tony and Marcelle Quinton and Evangeline Bruce, when Marcelle rang about 9.30 a.m. to report that Evangeline had developed a 'throat', just as she did at first picnic attempt last year, so everything off. As it happened I slept abominably last night and the foulest weather today, the combination of these somewhat mitigating disappointment at missing what is always a good party by offering the acceptable alternative of a quiet day.

I reread *Henry IV Part 2*. I had forgotten 'Sneak's Noise', name of band ordered to play for entertainment of Falstaff/Quickly/Tearsheet at Boar's Head party. Constant Lambert would have greatly liked this name for an orchestra. He probably knew it already. The play full of good stuff. A suitable stockbroker's comment: 'Those white investments figure innocence' and motto for hostesses at deb dinner-parties of the past: 'Give me spare men, and spare me great ones.'

Tuesday, 21 February

I finished Roy Jenkins's *European Diary*. An entertaining picture of the EEC world. There are some convincing portraits, notably Giscard, a somewhat unattractive figure, who, one feels, could well be accommodated in fiction. At first I was unable to put a finger on which novelist (for Giscard) when I wrote to Roy. Giscard's alleged affair with the Sorbonne student suggests perhaps a potential Stavrogin, tho' clearly he is without Stavrogin's (characteristically Russian) willingness to throw everything overboard according to mood. On reconsideration, Giscard is essentially a French figure, Stendhal or Balzac. Giscard's apparently phoney claims to *noblesse* are typical of characters in novels of either of the last. Proust less so. One certainly does not see Giscard in Proust's grand circles, nor Marcel's family, nor for that matter the Verdurins, where he would essentially have been regarded as a 'bore'. Perhaps M. de Norpois might have made some revealing comment on him as an ambitious young politican.

Roy's self-portrait is amusing, his taste for the arts, good living, smart society, appreciating such things as being given the Spanish Order of Charles III, because its blue-and-white riband often figures in Goya pictures of Spanish royalties and notabilities. That is absolutely the right reason for wanting the decoration. One recognizes that Roy was born into the purple of the Labour Party, even so his ease, unaffected pleasure in the *beau monde* is remarkable in its total lack of strain, to which I can think of no parallel on the Left; often missing in those of a higher social bracket. At one point Roy's *Diary* records going to the loo with James Callaghan, then Prime Minister, after some dinner. Callaghan 'made me a most fanciful offer'. I think Roy deliberately worded the entry so that one would think Callaghan suddenly gasped in a broken voice: 'Roy, have you never guessed after all these years what I feel for you.' It was, in fact, proffer of the Governorship of Hong Kong. Interesting that appointments are made in such circumstances.

On reconsideration, I suppose Giscard would fit fairly well into *Education Sentimentale* (1857), just reread (tr. Anthony Goldsmith), when characters like Monsieur Damoise were no doubt common at that period. There are distinct Giscard overtones. Flaubert is always praised almost religiously for the purity of his style, yet on several occasions (so far as one can see quite unnecessarily) the narrative is suddenly recounted from point of view of some character other than the hero, Frédéric, whose eyes survey the vast bulk of the novel.

I am struck by how much Maupassant appears to have been influenced by *Education Sentimentale* in writing the extremely unsentimental education of *Bel Ami* (1885), the characters of which, whatever people say about Maupassant's vulgarity, are on the whole much more convincing. All the same, the reality, the down-to-earthness, of *Education Sentimentale* must be agreed remarkable, when compared with contemporary novels of, say, Dickens, appearing in this country. The quality of

Flaubert always strikes me as lacking in making the reader feel at home, in a manner that Balzac, Proust, for that matter Shakespeare, do, managing to give conviction that the story being told is true, however improbable. This perhaps to the same extent due to a determination that things *must* go wrong; in short what Richard Cobb calls being a miserabilist. (Already a French term, I believe.)

Friday, 24 February

Evangeline Bruce rang to say goodbye, mentioning she was still eating pâté, chocolate gâteau, destined for picnic. Mr Joyce (Cooper & Tanner), rang. The proposed TR4 Road through Dead Woman's Bottom (no less) seems unfeasible, as always appeared likely. An eye must be kept on this, however, till proved certain. While Joyce was on the line, V told him about the 'small print' proposal from the Rural District Council to dump 'bad neighbour' rubble in disused quarries, a sinister scheme that needs watching. Mrs Lloyd (our four-times-a-weekly) rang to announce one of her daughters had a son, not in wedlock, but she takes the view preferable to marriage in haste, there being ample examples of both in her family already.

Saturday, 25 February

A letter from Philip Ziegler, Chairman of Society of Authors, asking for my signature to group letter from Society to *The Times* about the Rushdie affair, saying the Society is 'appalled' at the threat of death to a writer by a supposedly responsible Head of State. This I was prepared to sign, as having a direct connexion with writing, and as indication to Moslems in this country (some of whom are showing signs of concurring with the Ayatollah's murderous proposals) that, if they live here, they must obey the laws of this country like everyone else. If they don't they must get out.

Today another letter arrived from Mark Le Fanu, Secretary of Authors' Society, asking for my signature to a 'World Statement' on the same subject, drafted in windy terms characteristic of the professional protestor of the Rentacrowd order. This I thought a lot of waffle, and did not sign. I sent a letter to Le Fanu (who always seems a sensible fellow) explaining why; i.e. that I did not approve of phrases like 'calling on World Opinion', etc., which do not have the slightest effect on anybody, merely inflate the ego of individual signers. I rang Kingsley Amis to co-ordinate, Kingsley turning out not to be a member of the Authors' Society. He said, if asked, he too would sign first letter, not second.

Tristram and Virginia, at The Stables for a night, came to drinks. Tristram was recently in France on a TV project. He stayed near Cabourg and had memories of the whole family's 'practical Proust' trip there (as Tristram called it at the time) nearly thirty years ago. He said the Prince of Wales is now a bosom friend of Billa Harrod, with whom he visits Norfolk churches. In evening V, John and I watched a goodish TV film, *Colonel Redl* (producer Szabo, actor Brandauer), the Austro-Hungarian Chief of Secret Police just before First War, a homosexual, who shot himself in somewhat mysterious circumstances, possibly having betrayed secrets to Russians. Tho' latter is uncertain. Impressive, if certain points in story insufficiently clear, perhaps owing to the German dialogue dubbing. It was entirely owing to the alertness of John that we did not miss the play, which I knew about, but did not mark down.

Thursday, 2 March

I reread Keith Douglas's *Complete Poems*. The pre-war poems are efficient, if wholly obscure. Douglas did not really get going until the war gave meaning to what he wrote: 'Simplify me when I'm dead' (he was certain of his own death), 'Vergissmeinicht', 'Aristocrats'. He drew the design of Death riding behind the horseman (Horace) for the cover of his *Poems*. I am struck by how much the style of this drawing (others by him I have seen) rather resembles Peter Quennell's self-executed decorations for his first book of poems (which I possess, inscribed 'for darling Tony', tho' nothing could have had less queer, or even affectionate, implications, and my having bought the Poems myself, for that matter no one less queer than Quennell). One suspects Douglas may have possessed a somewhat similar narcissistic temperament to Quennell, even if differentiated by Quennell's lack of any wish to be absorbed into military life at any stage; Douglas, on the other hand, was certain that he was destined for death in that way. He was apparently a good soldier. I had a somewhat Surrealist dream: a car without driver passing slowly through garden, not our own garden either, I think.

Friday, 3 March

I was a little surprised by V reporting that BBC News (confirmed by John) giving Kingsley's name among those supporting the 'World Statement' about Rushdie. The *TLS* arrived with names of the better-known signers. Kingsley's name was not among these and hardly would be among 700 or so omitted. Is this characteristic BBC muddle, a complete lie, or Kingsley not thinking what he was doing? [I think, in the end, it was Kingsley not really caring much about how he behaves in this sort of situation.]

Wednesday, 8 March

Archie (using Virginia's car) stayed for night before going on to Bristol University for a potential entrance interview. He described some of his Paris experiences living with family of a Breton naval officer (children with Celtic names, the daughter Morgan), food bad, insufficient, passionately nationalistic, Bonaparte was never defeated, and so on, however on balance the experience was enjoyable.

Friday, 10 March

Reread *Henry V*: rather mixed bag. The Death of Falstaff is, of course, superb (one is unwilling to accept various fancy alterations to mere green fields, which is so marvellous, whether Falstaff was trying to repeat the 23rd Psalm or not). When Fluellen says: '. . . I warrant you, you shall find the ceremonies of the wars, and the cares of it . . . and the sobriety of it, and the modesty of it, to be otherwise,' he is exactly like Horace Probert, my Company Commander in the 1/5th Welch who was fond of laying down the law on military matters. I thought of Fluellen at the time, and reading this, Probert immediately brought back. Henry's wooing of the French Princess is infinitely embarrassing, one of the most awful passages Shakespeare ever wrote.

Sunday, 12 March

We lunched with Joff and Tessa Davies at Whatley House for the now traditional celebration of Tessa's and V's birthday tomorrow. V, John and I, Mary Anne Davies, Lucinda Davies, Mary Anne's fiancé Richard Charrington, John and Suzanne Keegan, Simon and Elizabeth Heneage. Heneage is retired from wine trade, living at Wanstrow, where he has turned a barn into a gallery for a cartoon collection. Both seemed agreeable. Lucinda's fiancé (name Sunnucks) not present, formerly in the Life Guards, did escort behind the coach at the Yorks' wedding. On that occasion his servant forgot to put the foam-rubber lining into Sunnucks's helmet, so that it was a difficult balancing act to keep on during the procession. His name (derived apparently from Sevenoaks) is known in the regiment as Snooks, so Lucinda was amused at Snook being name of our cat. A long wait before luncheon (Vino Nobile Montepulciano '79, which we have on occasion had ourselves, not bad). Delay was perhaps cause of V and I being exhausted on arriving home, V in any case having had upset inside the previous day. Virginia, down for gardening at The Stables, to dinner. Cold meats, Crozes Hermitages '86. Archie was eventually interviewed at Bristol University 5.30 p.m., everyone tired, so he felt depressed as to result. Georgia in goodish form after Mods.

Monday, 13 March

V's birthday, caviar for dinner, bottle of James Sandilands's Bollinger '83. I reread F. G. Lorca's *Elegy for Bull Fighter and Other Poems* (tr. A. Lloyd). I can see Lorca may be all right in Spanish, but not particularly sympathetic to me in English. One suspects a good deal of rubbish talked about him.

Wednesday, 15 March

Both V and I saw Lister in the afternoon, she for a broken tooth, me for usual slight adjustment of lower plate. There was a medical character with beard in the surgery to monitor Lister's back, with which, like all dentists, he has trouble. I reread *A Farewell to Arms*. It seemed wonderful when published in 1929, the period when I was seeing a lot of John and Evelyn Heygate. We used to talk a good deal of Hemingway language together. I must have read the novel at least once since those days. The scenes in mountains remain good, the love affair awful twaddle, also some of the hero's prolonged stretches of endurance; such things as tolerance of the Swiss police, when they would certainly have been on the look-out for spies, money arrangements in wartime, regarding which there seem to have been no difficulties. In short a great deal of it is terrible magazine stuff. There has been talk about an unpublished Hemingway novel (possibly by now published) containing equivocal scenes regarding the hero and heroine having their hair cut same length, to minimize difference of sex between them. This also comes in *Farewell to Arms*, Catherine suggesting Henry grow his hair longer, she shorten hers. Curious obsession; one imagines narcissistic in basis, rather than homosexual.

Thursday, 16 March

Myfanwy Piper rang to enquire if V or I could pronounce on which of Alice Astor's several husbands was reigning in 1944, when John Betjeman caused Alice to give a luncheon party at Hanover Lodge, Regent's Park, for the architect Ninian Comper. V certain Alice then married to Philip Harding. Myfanwy remarked that as a survivor one was perpetually being asked questions like this (for some article), for which she was apologetic. 'John [Piper]', she added, 'doesn't remember a thing.' She sounded in goodish form herself. Dr Rawlins came in twice to talk on the subject of the projected TR4 road, only three objections to which seem to have been registered by the Rural District Council, among what, in fact, are dozens, not least from V and myself. These last remain for some reason unrecorded. This is most unsatisfactory, if not actually sinister. Rawlins's solicitors are going into the matter.

Sunday, 19 March

At rather long last, we returned Michael Carter's High Sheriff luncheon, Joff and Tessa Davies (who know the Carters from Carter wanting to be selected as Tory MP) being the other guests. Carter is believed to make a living from selling pictures. He made no reference to any of those on the walls here, either in praise or blame, tho' V saw him steal glance at the Sickert. He had just returned from Texas, which he intensely disliked. Camilla Carter is large, overflowing, quite jolly. She described the holiday she recently took in The Gambia as enjoyable, nice people, food not at all bad, lots of fish from the Atlantic. The Carters' house at Batcombe was originally a spacious rectory, then had a period of being owned by an army crammers, who went bust in 1920s, during the moment of bottleneck for officers' promotion. Although Carter is occasionally mooted as Tory candidate one doubts whether he is quite up to it in personality, tho' that sort of thing is his line. It turns out that Joff Davies is half-American, mother born in North Carolina. For some reason not uncommon for clergymen (his father was vicar in Hastings, Bournemouth, some South Coast seaside resort) to marry Americans.

Graham Greene's life story, still running in the *Sunday Telegraph*, continues to be hilarious. Today's instalment dealing with the affair of La Glover, consequence of taking a room to write in, then seducing the landlady. Malcolm Muggeridge used to say The Glover was the second occasion when this situation occurred, but Malcolm may, as so often, be inaccurate. Not having read *The Confidential Agent*, I was unaware that Graham had given a blow-by-blow description of Dorothy Glover in that novel, even to point of stating that name 'Glover' to be inscribed on door of her flat, which I rather think was actually in Mecklenburgh Square, Bloomsbury.

The serial represents this as taking place in 1938, possibly to some extent the previous year, when Graham asked us to dinner in their Clapham Common house (Queen Anne), soon after our return from Hollywood. We were then extremely hard up and had no car, so on receiving the invitation I expressed hope that we should not be required to change, to which Graham concurred. The night before the dinner-party he rang up saying: 'I find we *are* changing.' This immensely inconvenient, as a taxi to Clapham and back would have been untold expense, in bus or underground one looks like a conjuror, in a dinner-jacket. In fact I think a bus did go moderately near the house. V flatly refused to wear a long dress, so we set off, she in some sort of evening-dress compromise, me in a mackintosh (it was warmish weather), looking like an orchestral player, taking about an hour, I think. We supposed at least the fellow-guests would be of fairly high grade. Not a bit of it. They turned out to be a minor civil servant and wife of infinite dreariness, who lived in a house two doors up in the same row as the Greenes. Vivien Greene, a woman of considerable pretentiousness, middlebrow views, was presumably responsible for insisting on evening dress. One is surprised Graham managed to stand living with her as long as he did, which, indeed, was not long.

Monday, 20 March

Georgia drove down from London (Virginia's car) for the night. She was in excellent form and goes to the French Alps for skiing next month, when the result of Mods also comes through. She is not hopeful of any great things, she said. Sometimes a good sign. I was slightly appalled that she had never heard of *The Scholar Gypsy*, which I gave her to read. Roy Fuller sent *Available for Dreams*, latest vol. of poems. Roy, now seventy-seven, has been going on about his age, health, generally decrepit condition, since his fifties. Now that old age really has come, he writes about that state well, his essentially individual manner, interesting, funny, ironical. Series called *Kitchen Sonnets* includes:

> Above the sink: a beverage, it seems,
> For summer evenings – 'mild green fairy liquid'.
> And next to it a phrase from sterner verse –
> 'Intensified tide': some unknown Hopkinsese.

Monday, 27 March

Tristram, Virginia and Archie, on their way back from Mounts' Pembrokeshire residence, looked in, with V, John and I lunched at the Bridge House, Nunney, excellent roast beef, Yorkshire pudding. Tristram said his photographs taken for the William Pye head of me for some reason are wholly unsatisfactory. Pye doing a West Country tour at some future date, will get in touch. Texas appear to be paying for the work, Tristram thought; why, inexplicable. The *New York Review of Books* reveals that Kingsley Amis did indeed sign the 'World Statement' in Rushdie's cause, so I must withdraw objurgations regarding the BBC News, but not regarding Kingsley.

Thursday, 30 March

Janet Adam Smith, staying with friends in Mells, to tea. Janet is within a few days of my own age and known since my early Duckworth days when she was working on *The Listener*. Janet comes from a Scotch academic background (nothing whatever to do with the economist). She married first Michael Roberts, poet (proletarian origins, I think), who died youngish, then John Carleton, Headmaster of Westminster. When we met them in Italy he drove us somewhere or other with great kindness. Then he too died.

Janet said she thought John Hayward might have been distinctly *de haut en bas* to 'Miss Fletcher', merely secretary at Faber's, then thunderstruck to hear Tom marrying her and leaving their flat. (Apparently Eliot, when Janet's first husband died, was very generous and paid for the education of one of her children.) I mentioned I recently read Walter Scott's *Journals*, adding what a nice man Scott seemed to be. Janet said: 'Yes, he was the only nice novelist.'

I read *Henry VI Part 1*, and revised the opinion that Shakespeare was not the author, anyway of most of it. I think Sir John Falstaff (alleged to have behaved in a cowardly manner, tho' history seems not to confirm this) to be thought of clearly as Fastolfe, totally different conception from Falstaff (originally Oldcastle) of *Henry IV/Henry V* plays.

Saturday, 1 April

V to Whitfield. John and I lunched at the George, Nunney, not too bad in pub manner, vast helpings. The saloon bar is the epitome of horse-brasses/galleons/warming-pans and usual pub interior decoration. Tristram and Virginia are at The Stables for a day or two. They saw Archie off to New Zealand. At London Airport Virginia said she would stand everybody a glass of champagne. Champagne was unprocurable there except in bottles.

Sunday, 2 April

The *Observer* carrying more biographical matter about Graham Greene, this time by his official biographer Norman Sherry, notably Graham's martyrdom at school, Berkhamsted, where his father was Headmaster. Graham never seems to have moved a yard without a pair of compasses sticking into him. Morning drinks at The Stables. John cooked the lamb with great success.

Thursday, 6 April

V attended the Public Enquiry in Frome on subject of the Frome Plan, notably the question of the objectionable TR4, proposed through Dead Woman's Bottom. So far as could be seen this went reasonably well, Dick Lomer giving evidence more or less to the point.

I finished *The Amis Anthology*, which I was too stingy to buy (anyway we have dozens of anthologies), but having been sent unreviewable book called *Adultery* (supposed examination of that subject, utter rubbish), which the *DT* did not want back, V swopped it in part-exchange for the Kingsley volume in a Frome bookshop.

The Amis Anthology is a strange collection, extremely enjoyable if one knows Kingsley, who has certainly been open about putting in awful stuff which, in his day, he liked (Ralph Hodgson's 'Time, you old gypsy man', Alfred Noyes, 'The Highwayman'), of which all of us have a store hidden away.

I certainly had 'Time, you old gypsy man', tho' not 'The Highwayman', which was in *Poems in Action* in use at my prep school, sometimes read by me, but never bothered to learn. My poetic skeletons would be rather different ones (Poe, for instance, to this day), almost always I should have made choices other than Kingsley in poets we both like (e.g. Matthew Arnold, anyway some, whom Kingsley omits entirely). He also provides some very funny notes, saying, for instance, that W. B. Yeats usually writes nonsense, sometimes 'vicious nonsense, like "Easter 1916". Some of the early poems Kingsley dug out often decidedly good.

David Cheshire, pretty jumpy, rang to ask if I could help about information regarding John Keegan, on whom he is doing a TV programme, being a great admirer of Keegan's books. Explained I knew no more than having met Keegan at luncheon, then had them both to lunch with us, and usually read his *DT* military pieces.

Friday, 7 April

Helen Fraser (Heinemann) wrote that she had lunch with Bruce Hunter, and discussed doing a collection of my *DT* reviews. Question of reprinting *TLS* 'fronts' and 'middles', a few other things like Amiel, in book form dates back at least forty years. I have always been opposed to this, because never sure that people want to read short bursts like 1000-word reviews (even long ones for that matter). However, it might be worth consideration as I have nothing else on the stocks, nor am likely to have. Preferably a *fat* volume, including most of what there is, but that may not be on offer, so far as being published. V suggested she might edit it. This would be excellent, tho' I pointed out would mean a lot of work, some of it tedious.

Monday, 10 April

I talked to Bruce Hunter about the proposed collecting of reviews. I was surprised by how keen he was on the project. On reconsideration I feel pretty sure I shall have to do the editing myself, almost impossible for V, or anyone else, to cope with problems of selection and dovetailing that will arise.

Thursday, 13 April

Hilary and John Spurling, driving to Cornwall, stopped off to give us luncheon.

This was to have taken place at the Bridge House, Nunney, but the Edgeleys who run the place turned out to be on their holiday, so the Spurlings booked at Oakhill House, about seven miles away, between Shepton Mallet and Bath. This hotel was formerly a private residence of people a party of whose V and I attended in early days here, we could not remember who. [Eventually we thought it to be Colonel and Mrs Cooke-Hurle, but uncertain whether Oakhill their house.] V first recalled this on the way there, while sitting in the dining-room some recollection of place came back to me. Several of us ordered duck off the menu, but only one portion remained. By general consent this was voted to V. My own melon, beef, apple pie, was tolerable, salad rather unappetizing. The latter John Spurling designated as *nouvelle cuisine*.

I thought Hilary was for once a little subdued; V judged her no more than tired after writing the Paul Scott biography, children, housekeeping. She talked of Tulsa, Oklahoma, which she had greatly enjoyed and said there was an Englishman employed in the town's best restaurant, of whom everyone locally was very proud, correct accent. This seems undoubtedly to have been Bogey Campbell, Mary Mayall's son, believed to live in Tulsa. Hilary is rather keen for me to meet American academic Tom Staley, of Austin, Texas, but as I don't want to sell my papers (which appears his object) there seems no special point. It does appear, however, that Staley's university has a large collection of busts and heads of British writers, so they might buy William Pye's head, for which Hilary continues to make arrangements.

She said when *The Jewel in the Crown* was adapted for TV the chief of Granada (Foreman) roughed out whole scheme of adaptation personally, sticking up pages of book on his office wall, only then did Ken Taylor get to work. In short it was not Ken Taylor's arrangement of scenes in first instance, only dialogue. This I found interesting in light of KT's adaptation of *Dance*, so far as it went. Hilary said with great truth that in any question of things like a TV adaptation for relatively uncommercial works no amount of pushing gets the thing done; the moment just arrives when it goes through without effort. I am sure this is true in almost all spheres of that sort. The Spurlings left here at 4 p.m., Hilary borrowing paperbacks of Martin Amis's *Money* and A. N. Wilson novel. Enjoyable jaunt. Both V and I thought how pretty and charming-looking (not quite the same thing), Hilary remained.

Sunday, 16 April

Jonathan Cecil rang last night to say his cousin Lady Cranborne was collecting pieces on his father for a David Cecil memoir; would I contribute. I agreed to that. One of the weeping willows (which I put in on the drive some years ago) blew down.

This is annoying, as they were just reaching a reasonable height. It was blocking the garage entrance, but John cleared some away, making an efficient support for what remains, so the tree may possibly recover. [It died a year or two later.]

Wednesday, 19 April

Ali Forbes rang from his Swiss hideout, asking if I had once told him that Pamela Digby (Churchill, Harriman, etc.) looked exactly like the description Aubrey gives of Venetia Digby, famous seventeenth-century beauty. I replied that was extremely improbable, as, so far as I knew, I had never set eyes on Pamela Digby, nor could remember off the cuff what Aubrey says about Venetia Digby. I would look this up, if Ali would hold on. He said that would be too much of a business (no doubt also cost a fortune, now I come to think of it). He would ring later in the morning. He rambled on in that curious torrent of gossip-column material, personal items spiced with a certain degree of malicious comment and at times dubious intimacy, with which he talks.

Ali's general manner has become rather like that of a slightly eccentric dowager from days when I was going to deb dances. When he called up again later in the morning V answered, she also remarking how old-fashioned (in the literal sense) Ali sounded, which in V's case reminded her of Peter Fleming; interesting parallel. Peter no doubt had his dowageresque side. I read aloud Aubrey's account of Venetia Digby to Ali, which did not bear much resemblance to what he recalled. He remarked that he always had long complicated dreams about all the people he knew, everyone talking, 'scarcely anyone holding a spear', when he woke up he could not remember in due course whether things had happened to him in dreams or real life.

He said Georgina Ward (now Tritton, Ali's second wife briefly) was rather under the weather at the moment. She had a hip pinned as a child which was now going wrong. She would much appreciate a postcard. I have, in fact, sent Georgina postcards from time to time without the smallest response, so I shall do so only if in the mood. Ali has never met Georgina's husband, Patrick Tritton, who, a fellow member of White's Club, knows Ali by sight, which irritates Ali. I enquired what Tritton did. Ali said Georgina was very secretive about that, but he thought Tritton sold groceries from a van in Mexican villages. Eventually Ali hung up. He must be now about seventy-one (I estimate). Ali is a strange figure, American by nationality with strong British affiliations, once supposed essence of male attraction and intellectual brilliance.

Friday, 21 April

Colin Walters rang from Washington saying he was arranging for the *Washington Times* (not, it shall be noted, the *Washington Post*) of which he is Literary Editor, to have a series of articles by distinguished people on a past book, a thousand words, would I contribute. Nothing wanted till September. Walters claimed to be friend of John Monagan. I replied I'd consider that and suggested Jocelyn Brooke, John Aubrey, as subjects. That was when I could see light in relation to my collected journalism project. Walters (who left this country only thirty years ago) seemed pleased at this. He said he would send copies of the paper.

I reread *Henry VI Part 2*, enjoyable play, tho' one regrets no comic scenes. I wonder whether 'who finds the heifer dead, and bleeding fresh / And sees fast by a butcher with an axe' (III.2), and 'Then sin is cut down like an ox, and iniquity's throat cut like a calf' (IV.2), refer to Shakespeare's alleged butcher apprenticeship, calf-killing, noted by Aubrey.

Sunday, 23 April

Tristram and Virginia at The Stables. One of the balloons which float over fairly frequently descended in field at top of the Lily Pond above the Lake, west of Butler's Mead. A support car, with which radio connexion is made to keep in touch all the time, crossed the fields to remove it. A balloonist arrived at the house to apologize. His name, McCoy (no doubt real one), was worked on his sweater. I took a photograph of him.

Friday, 28 April

I sent the piece about David Cecil to Lady Cranborne. Before Rachel Cecil died she had been seriously ill for some time (nurse, etc.); David is said to have woken in the night to find her dead. He was holding her hand. I mentioned in the memoir that this at once recalled Larkin's poem 'Arundel Tomb'. Incidentally, someone wrote saying the Arundel tomb in question had been restored in the nineteenth century, when the hands had been remodelled as clasped together. This may have been so, tho' one suspects whoever wrote did so with passion some people have for wrecking, if possible, anything at all poetic or amusing. Whether true or not, I happened to have been looking through Lawrence Stone's *Mediaeval Sculpture*, in which at least two tombs show husband and wife holding hands, so in principle there is nothing whatever against it as a mediaeval practice.

Saturday, 6 May

Mary Ann Davies's wedding in Mells Church to Captain Richard Charrington,

9th/12th Lancers. V obtained permission from the Oxfords to park in their drive, a great convenience as there is a door through the wall from The Manor to the churchyard. Mells Church is big, but was very full, pages in Lancer uniform (which John alleges come from the Regiment, so presumably the pages are chosen to fit the uniforms, rather than vice versa), a regimental Guard of Honour with an arch of lances. All rather enjoyable. I was dropped off on the way home, wanting to avoid a lot of standing at the reception.

The Balliol Record (Mrs Clare Eaglestone, presumably College Secretary, or his assistant) asked for review of Vol. 1 of Norman Sherry's biography of Graham Greene. I should have avoided this for a newspaper, as not liking Graham's novels, being only moderately interested in his life (as opposed to that of several other contemporaries), while existing on relatively good terms with Graham himself. Also, I suspect it is not too well done and I don't want to pan Norman Sherry too much, whom I liked when we met. However, curiosity, coupled with a slight desire to express in public what I thought, overcame these objections.

Sherry wrote several excellent studies of Conrad, doing first-rate detective work which was much admired by Graham (me too). This resulted in Graham asking Sherry to write his, Graham's, official biography a dozen or more years ago. Writing Graham Greene's life is, of course, a totally different proposition from carefully going through and painstakingly collating files from Far East newspapers for snippets about Conrad in the twentieth century. Sherry is industrious, naive, nowhere up to analysing Graham's devious character and personality. Indeed, what it boils down to, not sufficiently shrewd.

To begin with, the book is much too long. Personally I like laundry-lists in principle, but pages and pages about Graham's parents, plots of the books, etc., are wearisome to a degree. Sherry never grasps that Graham is a master of publicity. Refusing interviews and acquiring the reputation of a hermit was all part of his publicity equipment. It is shrinking into the limelight as someone said of T. E. Lawrence. Sherry never takes this in, in spite of exhibitionistic accounts of having whores, on Graham's part. What strikes one about Graham's career as recorded here is his phenomenal energy, passion for rows, coupled with real ability in the journalistic field and films.

The Liberian and Mexican journeys must have needed a great deal of stamina and courage, tho' there appears to have been no great point in making either of them. When all this material is turned into fiction, which it always is, there seems to me that a kind of falseness gets infused, none of the people supposedly drawn from life is in the least like anybody one has ever come across. Clearly the world does not find that; as shown by Graham's sales, what seem to me capable, if self-consciously gloomy thrillers, rather portentous in tone, somehow appeal to highbrows (anyway a lot of them), as well as the general public.

Recently there have been some signs of Graham's more intellectual level of admirers faltering a bit. It is, I think, his sheer forcefulness which somehow comes over, determination to be a success, also his own particular form of remaining in touch with childhood, its fantasies, horrors, in principle no doubt key to all novel-writing, tho' greatly varying in final results. Graham's references in the biography to his having tarts (during early years of married life particularly), seem a shade unsavoury, as the experiences are not described clinically (or in the Latin manner of, say, Casanova), merely referred to under initials in a diary in rather a prurient tone.

Sherry was allowed to look over this document. If Graham wants such details about himself to be made public (no reason why he should not) he surely ought to state clearly what happened, not reveal just enough to titillate the curiosity of a certain type of reader. One gets back to that aspect of biography I always find important, that is to say to get straight in the mind: the difference between knowing that X had an affair with Y; and X stating in so many words that he (or she) had an affair with Y. The nature of the love affair (whatever it may be) is affected by the latter taking place. This is perhaps no more than a particular (professional) form of 'kissing and telling', which has always been looked on as somewhat weakening the essence of any love affair concerned. I sent off a piece on Jocelyn Brooke to the *Washington Times* (a paper which the *Spectator* columnist, Taki, praises this week as infinitely superior to the 'mendacious' *Washington Post*).

Tuesday, 9 May

V to London. She had a traumatic journey, as the train was an hour and twenty minutes late, but enjoyed giving luncheon at Lansdowne Club to Anne Lancaster and Virginia [Powell]. The dwellers in Bullen Mead (housing estate) complained that the wall on one side bordering my property shows signs of collapsing. This appears to be true and it looks as if this will cost £4000 or more to deal with. I am in touch with Mr Millard, builder, and Mr Joyce of Cooper & Tanner on this subject.

Wednesday, 10 May

V drove me to the Bath Clinic for a check-up with Mr Southwood, an annual business. He found another polyp, so I have to go into the Clinic to have that removed on Thursday, 18 May, with any luck only a twenty-four-hour job. We lunched at the Red Lion, Woolverton. The curried prawns were excellent, all cooked in a potato baked in its skin, a *specialité de la maison*. We went on to house of Mrs Sandy Bellaart, The Stable, Rode, who has been binding a copy of Lemprière's *Classical Dictionary* (1820), leather, one of my dearest possessions, bought in Charing

Cross Road many years ago for 1s.6d, far the best book of reference of its kind, now somewhat collapsed.

The Bellaart residence was an extraordinary small house with gothick windows, said to be the stable of a former rectory. It is set back beyond several other houses, rather attractive, the inside full of strange odds and ends – of The Netherlands origin of her husband, perhaps – causes a slight touch of a Pieter de Hooch interior. Mrs Bellaart prettyish, seems to have done job well (£35). It is not quite finished, but will deliver in couple of days. We returned to Chantry, looking in at Bullen Mead wall on way home. It is sad that this nice old wall will have to be reduced in height. So far as I can see there is no alternative to cutting down by about half and back with concrete blocks or fence, the latter decidedly cheaper than alternative (saving about £2000), so one hopes it will be feasible. I was in touch with Mr Joyce in evening, who will have meeting on the spot with Mr Millard. I asked Mr Joyce also to inspect the building at backyard beyond wall to make sure it is not dangerous.

Thursday, 11 May

I bought pair of 'summer' trousers in Frome. V showed me the Public Library, a much more comfortable, well-organized place than pictured; I had supposed a dark underground crypt with shelves round about. Hodges, where I bought the trousers, is staffed by immensely polite white-haired female assistants, reminding one of shopping at the haberdashers W. V. Brown in Eton High Street as a boy. I had my hair cut in the afternoon at Donna's, in Nunney, usually done by Nicki, who is leaving to get married. She will live in London (Finchley). Nicki enquired after Snook. I told her he jumped on the lap of a policeman (who called about some routine matter), but she did not find that funny. Now I come to think of it I believe V said she is marrying a policeman.

Saturday, 13 May

Driven by John, we lunched with Anthony Hobson at The Glebe House, Whitsbury. Guests: John Julius Norwich and Molly Philipps; Fram and Candia Dinshaw. We had not previously met Candia Dinshaw, of whom one had formed a somewhat doubtful impression from what appeared about her in the press and interviews, her own reviews, etc. I expected a certain pretentiousness; on the contrary, she seemed attractive and easy to talk to, distinctly amusing. She is very tall, obviously from photographs pretty, but her appearance greatly preferable to what photographs make of her. She had a baby ten weeks ago (male), called something like Michou [Minocher = 'Minoo'], a name with Parsee affiliations. Candia, née McWilliam, is adopted daughter of Lord Strathcona (who has six children of his own). She was formerly married to Lord Portsmouth, by whom she had two children.

It turned out she knew Adrian Daintrey. Adrian picked her up in Warwick Avenue on strength of having seen her once or twice in the local delicatessen. She was soon dining with him, cooking dinners for him subsequently on various occasions. She was quite funny about this, perfectly appreciating the situation. She talked about Adrian's harem, whom he would put individually on their mettle by saying: 'So-and-so cooks such-and-such better than you do.'

She asked if I knew Adrian had been married to a woman in Antigua. I replied that Adrian certainly was not married (having done that briefly only once). The Antiguan woman must have been the black girl by whom he had a child ages ago, before the war, I think. Apparently the son is now in the Antiguan Customs. I thought this would make good Victorian story. Adrian goes to stay with smart friends in Antigua. On his way through the Customs he is found to have drugs, or the like, in his luggage (in fact, so far as I know, Adrian has never touched a drug, throughout his life). There is a heart-breaking scene. 'You are my father.' Explanations take place: 'Having committed one crime by bringing me into the world, you commit another by importing cocaine . . .' 'Would you send your parent to prison?' 'You betrayed my mother, now you ask mercy of me . . .' The climax of this confrontation of father and son would have to be decided later. Perhaps the Customs officer dines at a smart house and marries the daughter. Fram was in great form. He said he met Salman Rushdie at dinner before his condemnation to death by the Ayatollah. Rushdie spoke of the recent demise of Bruce Chatwin: 'Even I, with all my powers of description, cannot tell you what a loss he is. He was one of the few people who really understood my books.' Fram designated Chatwin a kind of Dorian Gray, who remained all his life looking eighteen years old. Chatwin's earlier career was made in Sotheby's, its homosexual head Peter Wilson sending Chatwin abroad to charm Bronzinos out of elderly queers, which Chatwin always turned out able to do. Fram said he himself is toying with idea of writing life of K. Clark, a man coming from immensely unpromising *nouveau riche* origins, who turned out to have extraordinary aesthetic sensibilities. These, at same time, took an extremely practical go-getting form. I pointed out that several books written about Clark already.

He described dinner with John and Iris Bayley. Iris, while expressing some deep philosophic truth, removes the casserole from oven, and upsets it all over a beaded cushion. Without pausing in conversation, she reverses the cushion over a serving dish, gives cushion wipe, and dinner proceeds. The Bayleys are moving again to another North Oxford address to escape from noisy children who pervade all the houses round them.

John Julius was also in good form. He said his father liked reading Kipling's poem 'The Mary Gloster' aloud after dinner and always broke down in the middle, crying like a child. I wondered if that was at the moment when the poem suddenly caused Duff Cooper to wonder if it would have been better, rather than Eton and New College, to have sent John Julius to sea. Teddy Hulton's father used to cry when reading 'In the Islands of the Highlands' . . . Molly Philipps is really very attractive. Anthony seems to be holding up reasonably well after loss of Tanya. He showed us all round his newly designed kitchen (with an Aga), all presided over by trim young cook, introduced to everyone. Pheasant pâté (from Major Matthew Connolly's book of recipes), steak, rhubarb fool. Château Talbot '71. Enjoyable party.

Sunday, 14 May

Hilary Spurling rang to arrange that William Pye, sculptor, come here, take photographs (whatever his method), date made for 3.30 p.m. Saturday, 3 June. Hilary spoke of further administrative earthquakes at the *Daily Telegraph*, which always thrill her. I told her I was making second attempt to read Paul Scott's *The Raj Quartet*, which defeated me on the first round, but I am now quite enjoying. I still retain considerable reservations about technique and general style.

Reread *Henry VI Part 3*, rather patchy owing to chops and changes in Wars of the Roses, but at the same time gives a vivid impression of those; Queen Margaret and Henry himself, to some extent emerging as characters, anyway what Shakespeare thought they were like.

Thursday, 18 May–Friday, 19 May

V drove me to Bath Clinic, arriving 9 a.m. A little Iranian (mother British) nurse called Catherine (like in *A Farewell to Arms*), tiny monkey hands, gave me an enema. I had forgotten how awful that made one feel (perhaps it was a special Ayatollah variety); for about five minutes after it worked I thought my last hour had come. Dr Hill, anaesthetist, as before. I reminded him that he had said I was a disgrace to look so well in spite of taking no exercise. He remarked: 'My usual tactful way.' Mrs Roberts did the cardiograph. When I reached the theatre Mr Southwood appeared wearing light blue turban, a smock of the same colour, looking like Widmerpool clad as a pirate for a fancy-dress party. That might have made rather a good incident. I was struck by how much things have been ameliorated even compared with ten years ago, so far as feeling less knocked out when one comes to. The removed polyp was apparently quite large but harmless. Dinner: mushroom soup, plaice, chips, fruit salad, carafino Jugoslav Lutomer. V picked me up on Friday morning, was home by 10.30 a.m. I felt curiously better 'in myself'.

Previous day Mrs Judith Medlicott, a fan, called with her husband. She is a New Zealand barrister and solicitor. She rang from the neighbourhood. V asked them to call. Mrs Medlicott won a TV quiz on *Dance*, the prize being a visit to this country. They are going to a variety of places, so don't imagine all is paid for by the prize. They brought gifts of New Zealand Gewürztraminer and two sorts of honey. Traditional classical offerings. It was bad luck striking the one day in years when I happened to be absent from home. I shall write after sampling the wine and honey.

Tuesday, 23 May

There was a violent storm last night, thunder, lightning, followed by failure of electricity. V descended soon after 7 a.m., on the way down the stairs had a disaster pulling up the Venetian blind, thereby bringing down the plaster bust of Seneca, smashing the convex glass of the Empire mirror, noise like end of the world. V was mercifully undamaged.

Saturday, 27 May

A hitherto unnoticed Proustian item was revealed by the rereading of *A la recherche* now taking place. On one of the occasions when Marcel and Saint-Loup dined together, after their meeting at Balbec, at a restaurant in the neighbourhood, they saw a distinguished bearded man recognized as Elstir (the prototype of all Impressionist painters), to whose table they sent a note saying they both knew his friend Swann and would be honoured by meeting him. Proust adds that Elstir had known the place as still a farm, where he and fellow painters had stayed, eaten, when working in those parts, now become a fashionable restaurant.

In short, the Ferme Saint-Siméon is clearly meant, haunt of the Impressionists and earlier painters, where Adrian Daintrey and I lunched in the 1920s or early in 1930s, during an Easter spent in Le Havre and found astronomically expensive. Interesting that Proust describes the Ferme Saint-Siméon as expensive in a period before Dreyfus Case (1894), cf. what he also says of Guillaume le Conquérant Restaurant at Dives, where V and I went with Tristram and John in middle 1950s and could only afford drinks outside.

Selina Hastings (staying with Pamela, Lady Harlech, David Harlech's widow, at Hinton Charterhouse) to tea. She talked of various things. Selina said Nicholas Shakespeare for some reason got into his head that Evelyn Nightingale (Gardner/Waugh/Heygate) had died, so Selina wrote to Evelyn's son, Bendy, a letter of condolence. Selina recently dined with Billy Chappell, to whom Ed Burra's sister Anne Ritchie, left some money, five of her brother's pictures (worth something in neighbourhood of £1,000,000), which one is relieved to hear, as Billy has not been too well, in any case getting elderly for tagging round doing dreary theatrical directing jobs.

Someone is writing a life of Freddie Ashton and likely to approach me, Selina said, tho' I know nothing much more than what's in my Memoirs. Selina said Fred was really an obsessive snob: for some time recently quite mad on subject of Dowager Duchess of Devonshire (Mowcher), later the Queen Mum, could talk of nothing but one or other. This explains a lot I never quite took in about Fred, tho' I can't think why as he once refused a weekend here, explaining rather loftily that he was going to the Dudleys'. In any case interested only in his own subject, never read a book, at same time had immense physical magnetism with both sexes. In early days no one made much distinction between these two little Ballet boys, Freddie Ashton and Billy Chappell, camping round at almost all parties of a certain kind (not necessarily queer ones), tho' generally felt that Billy was much the nicer.

Tuesday, 30 May

I went down to lake to see what the Syndicate had constructed to prevent water from escaping from side by waterfall sluice, which has happened always to some extent. This turned out an excellent job, with a cement embankment, which should be great improvement. The leaning tree there on the slope will be held by support for the moment, because a wren is nesting in its hollow. On way back met (for first time) Mr Paul Lewis, brother of Mr Mervyn Lewis who runs the Syndicate. Paul Lewis is a builder in Bath. We talked of what had been done. His brother will see me in near future about expenses. I trust these will not be too high in light of the Bullen Mead wall rebuilding, but undoubtedly worthwhile. A marvellous spring afternoon by lake, which always imparts a peculiarly magical atmosphere.

Wednesday, 31 May

I dreamt I was spending a night in London at kind of hotel in Old Compton Street. I was at dinner at enormous round communal table, but only one other man could be dimly observed sitting a long way from me. The place seemed to be run by Mrs Thatcher, who was proprietress or manageress, 'There is meat pie for dinner,' she said. 'It's very good.' I ordered the meat pie. When Mrs Thatcher brought it in, the pie looked like large jam puff, meat within and tasted excellent. I asked where such pies came from. Mrs Thatcher smiled meaningly, indicating that she was unwilling to reveal that. I said: 'Very well, then I suppose my poor wife will have to try every shop in Soho likely to sell such pies.'

My rereading of Paul Scott's *The Raj Quartet* was spurred by its being among a pile of paperbacks recently brought by Tristram to The Stables. Felt that if I have to review Hilary Spurling's biography of Scott, which is fairly likely, I ought to know the books better than a failed attempt to read one. I have now finished the novel. My final judgement on the whole favourable. The ground plan of the narrative is well done, inventive and the narrative itself eminently fulfils Maugham's view that most important, also most difficult, problem for novelist is sticking to the point. The theme is people, changes, during period of years of handing over Indian Independence, also the time just before that began, to give some sort of launching pad. The characters chosen to illustrate all this are well conceived, if on the whole not greatly interesting in themselves. The exception is the District Police Officer, Merrick, a secret homosexual, who loses an arm and wins a DSO, after transfer to army when war comes. Like many – perhaps most – novels of any length or significance the author clearly begins with one story in mind, which subsequently fades into another, or others. In this book Scott evidently intended to contrast Merrick's modest origins, old-fashioned imperialism, sado-masochist homosexual tastes, physical bravery, with the public-school-educated, totally anglicized, somewhat cynical, Hari Kumar, of rich (tho' not Rajput) Indian upper-middle-class background, who is left penniless in India after his father's bankruptcy and suicide. Merrick behaves brutally to Kumar, unjustly thought to have raped an English girl (with whom he was having affair). Kumar is subsequently imprisoned, also unjustly, for suspected political unreliability.

The trouble is that Kumar never really comes to life. One does not altogether believe in him although no reason why an Indian of his sort should not exist. In fact he seems to lose the author's interest, too, as the book progresses. An even more unreal character, tho' useful to develop the narrative, is the White Russian emigré, also homosexual, Count Bronowsky, Chief Minister of the Maharajah in an independent Indian State. Bronowsky is a kind of *raisonneur* in the story, full of worldly wisdom, even if much more level-headed than any White Russian one has ever come across. He is perfectly acceptable in a Ruritanian romance, but not quite up to a novel of *The Raj Quartet*'s reasonable pretensions.

Scott, himself leftish, tends always to give Indians best of the argument and be more evidently sympathetic characters than the British. Indian failings in general are omitted, or minimized, tho' the author undoubtedly strives to some extent to balance this tendency. One will only know Scott's own background and prejudices when Hilary writes her book. She described him to me as 'in all societies an outsider', to whom India 'gave his first chance of measuring himself up'. Scott has no grasp of the real implications of the innumerable characters in the novel having been educated at 'Chillingborough', presumably a public school like, say, Cheltenham/Clifton/Wellington. This school question is treated far too romantically (tho' true he is writing of Indian army, Indian circumstances) yet emphasis somehow wrong.

On the other hand, the army characters are pretty well done *vis-à-vis* military life, especially Lieut.-Col. Layton, a PoW returned from Germany, whose neurotic reserve with his daughters is convincing. Scott does not always rise above the novelist's perennial problem how to impart interest to characters, and society, fundamentally uninteresting, unless brilliantly dealt with and some original slant on both is devised. Nor is Scott a master of dialogue, often continues at too great length, when essential point already made. On the whole army jargon is good, though ADCs, not Aides would be normal. No one not in-the-know would have used the word camp (homosexual behaviour) in 1945, which would immediately suggest familiarity with bohemian life. That was perhaps intended for Sergeant Perron, an intellectual Field Security NCO, but does not seem quite Perron's style. Perron himself, who refused to take a Commission, is a bit lifeless.

In short, Scott seems to have unusual novelist's gift of being capable, efficient, over wide canvas, while his actual writing is somewhat pedestrian and inelegant. He is the reverse of, say, Jocelyn Brooke, unrivalled in his particular manner of short bursts, but not able to plan over large areas. I don't care for the technique of presenting narrative in diaries and letters written by individuals of the opposite sex to the author, especially Indians, let alone a Rajput lady. It is impossible for a British author to know how her mind would work. One would prefer the 'God's eye' view, which at least has the blessing of long tradition, if not always a technique one likes best.

Merrick is by far the most interesting character and rather wasted because Scott sets out with view that Merrick is a villain, when Merrick's own nature would have been quite sufficient to work on. Scott himself evidently saw this to some extent later, because, having put in incident of the faked bicycle evidence, that is watered down by more or less implying the native police, rather than Merrick, were responsible. Nor is Merrick's type of homosexuality adequately worked out. On the other hand, Merrick's efforts to behave heterosexually are convincing, particularly when the widowed, rather dotty Susan, also her little boy, both adore Merrick during their brief marriage before he is murdered. In spite of these criticisms I found *The Raj Quartet* an impressive *roman fleuve*, as such, its qualities particularly appropriate to make the good TV film it did.

Friday, 2 June

Antonia and Harold Pinter to luncheon, bringing with them Alison Lurie. Antonia is doing something in the Bath Festival. The Pinters were in excellent form. Harold talked of his translated plays, now in almost every known tongue, including Urdu and South-East Asian languages. We discussed accuracy of translations. Harold said that in *The Birthday Party* sentence occurs: 'Who watered the pitch at

Melbourne?' (Apparently a well-known cricket incident, a watered pitch in a dry country having all sorts of implications.) This came (in German, I think) as 'Who pissed on the gates of Melbourne?', which has a rather Biblical ring. Harold had seen the Queen not long ago (occasion unspecified, conversation changed before that was ascertained). He said: 'Do you know, Ma'am, that vegetables were introduced into England very late? Henry VIII never ate a vegetable.' HM not impressed. 'Oh, yes?' she said. Harold put Philip Larkin up for MCC, so Larkin inscribed *High Windows* for him to the effect: 'For Harold Pinter, who gave me nets,' or some such cricket metaphor. When Harold was divorced from his first wife, Vivien Merchant, he left some of his books behind. He was horrified later to find this inscribed vol. of Larkin's poems in a second-hand bookseller's catalogue. In course of talking about cricket Harold wrote an extempore poem, which he handed to John:

> 'I knew Len Hutton in his prime . . .
> Another time, another time.'

Antonia said her father could make coffee (hot water poured into a cup which contained coffee preparation of some kind), but not tea, too complicated a process. The Pinters were going to Prague in a day or two to see dissident writers. Alison was perhaps rather subdued, a little deaf, but all right if you get her good side. She said her former husband Jonathan Bishop, now some form of RC monk, does not wear a robe, nor is he allowed to administer Sacrament, tho' he may handle its elements. He lives quite alone in their former house in Ithaca, now become gothick in decay, an overgrown garden.

I suggested William Faulkner mansion in the South. We talked of Faulkner, regarding whom I feel I must hold some coherent opinion before I die, rather than saying: 'Well, I quite liked *Sanctuary*, but have never really been able to get on with any of the other ones' in reply to any questions asked. To this end I borrowed *The Essential Faulkner* paperback from The Stables, edited by Malcolm Cowley. Found it at best hard going, in fact mostly unreadable, one's interest never really aroused. I can see pieces like *Old Man* (River), *The Bear*, etc., are well written in their genre, indeed struck by how much Hemingway (who called Faulkner 'old cornswilling mellifluous') took from *The Bear* for his *The Old Man and the Sea*, but I cannot accept Faulkner as in the top class, Proust, Dostoevsky, etc., just good original regional writer. This disturbed Alison, although no great Faulkner fan, who, like all Americans, dislikes hearing Faulkner belittled. She insisted that Faulkner's importance was in writing novels about connected families in long sentences, no writer ever having done this before in America (such as Hemingway, Dos Passos, of that generation), always just telling an immediate story. People, like the Snoopses, for instance, are described in complicated genealogical patterns. Alison put Faulkner forward as the greatest American novelist since James. If one concedes even this, it doesn't make Faulkner a top-class world figure as novelist. I remain unconvinced. Proustian luncheon: asparagus, *boeuf en daube*, strawberries and cream cheese (all excellent, Pinters refused last item). Margaux '73 (goodish bottle). Both Pinters drank Soave ('84, '86) as aperitif (of which Antonia, one way or another, drank a bottle). Alison drank nothing before, then about half-glass of Soave at luncheon (half bottle left). The Pinters presented us with Château Latour '64, bottle cowslip wine; Alison traditionally gave a box of Black Magic chocolates (name always fascinates her). Enjoyable party.

Saturday, 3 June

William (Bill) Pye arrived in afternoon to take photographs for the projected head. After various comings and goings as to the most suitable spot for this to be done, a kitchen chair placed on the grass in front of house. Snook, put out that he was not included, prowled about interfering. Bill Pye in his early fifties, somewhat puckish in manner, is easy to deal with. In principle he executes abstract sculpture usually for public places (Gatwick Airport, etc.), and does portraits as relaxation. After taking photographs he went down to The Stables to have word with Tristram and Virginia who are friends of his. He was then moving on to visit another sculptor in this part of the world. Pye said he would produce head in about six months' time.

Sunday, 4 June

Driven by John, we lunched with Roy and Jennifer Jenkins at St Amand's House, East Hendred. Guests: Evangeline Bruce, Michael Howard, Jeremy and June Hutchinson. The latter had driven from Sussex bringing with them Marie-Alice de Beaumarchais (former French Ambassadress, widow of Jacques Beaumarchais, who was descended from the dramatist). Beaumarchais was unscrupulously removed from the London post by Giscard, when he came in, for one of his own men. Evangeline in good form. She slipped away to catch a train immediately after luncheon, so we did not see much of her. At table Jennifer was on my left, June Hutchinson on my right. Met her rather vaguely once or twice years ago. She was née Capel, and married a Czech musician, who died young. Cecil Beaton proposed to her at one moment, then she finally married Jeremy Hutchinson, a barrister now retired (formerly married to Peggy Ashcroft).

I always liked June Hutchinson when met before. This time she brought a dog, Norfolk terrier, to sit on her knee during lunch, and released rather a flood of chatter, which, combined with dog (Rocky), I found a shade tiresome for a while. Then I came round to her again, and found her nice, amusing, attractive. She spoke of Ali Forbes, said that he was by temperament a nanny, entirely bringing up his own son himself (by some Scandinavian girl now married to someone else); in general liked looking after sick people and doing other charitable acts.

As it happens, a flood of postcards have been arriving lately from Ali, one of his communications enclosing an article on John Aubrey in some French paper, which surprised me that the French had ever heard of Aubrey. I used to find Jeremy Hutchinson rather over smooth (somewhat in manner of Rex Whistler), this time I came round to him. (There really is no objection to smoothness, I speak only of a personal prejudice.) I was fascinated to find he was directly descended from Colonel Hutchinson and his wife Lucy, who wrote *Memoirs of the Civil War*, from which I culled the name Widmerpool, a Cromwellian Captain of Horse, who occurs frequently there. Another Hutchinson ancestor was Byron's doctor, a position not without interest. Jeremy Hutchinson spoke of Adrian Daintrey, whom they knew quite well. They possessed a water-colour of Adrian's, which they managed to lose. Adrian obviously thought they had sold it, so whenever there was a meeting, without fail he always asked: 'Have you found that water-colour yet?' Very characteristic of Adrian.

We hadn't seen Marie-Alice for ages. She and Jacques lunched twice at The Chantry. On one occasion he was standing beside me, then suddenly disappeared, I found he had gone down on his hands and knees to play with Fum (Burmese cat), who very much took Jacques's fancy. Marie-Alice had scraped her hair back, a fashion I don't much care for in ladies of mature age, tho' sometimes charming in young girls. When Ambassadress she produced the enjoyable piece of information that there was indeed a broken gold chair (which she showed me), saying it was undoubtedly the one broken by Pamela Flitton. In this connexion (i.e. Marie-Alice reading *Dance*) I was amused to learn a slight variation of the story. Roy told me that when she left London she gave him such of my books as she had. Marie-Alice, on the other hand, remarked to me: 'Roy gave me some of your books, but he was horrid when we had to go back to France, saying they were first editions and I must give them back to him.' I can't remember whether Roy gave her other ones, or paperbacks, to take the place of the first editions. Michael Howard, sometimes a shade gloomy, was in good form. He is leaving Oxford for a year or two at Yale. I asked Roy if as Chancellor he had rooms of any kind allotted to him by the University. He said not, a nice room in the Clarendon Building, with Empire furniture, was appropriated by the Vice-Chancellor. Roy has no accommodation. Although nothing at all demanding at this particular party, I am always fascinated at the manner Roy fits naturally into the *beau monde* atmosphere. Utterly different from, say, Waugh, Connolly, always mesmerized by *beau monde* mystique, both in their different ways fundamentally ill at ease there, unless in a position to perform his own individual act, put on a turn in fact. Roy is intensely interested in details of social behaviour, rites, etc., at same time is quite unselfconsciously so. One wonders how Jennifer feels about all that side of their life. She keeps her end up perfectly well, at the same time one suspects she really prefers her public activities, like the National Trust. Egg-and-prawn cocktail, leg of mutton, cheese, fruit; magnums Château Léoville Poyferré '75, really first-rate. Drank more claret than I usually do nowadays at luncheon, having refused champagne as aperitif.

Wednesday, 7 June

Mr Mervyn Lewis and Mr McCortney, members of the Fishing Syndicate, to see me about 7.30 p.m., bringing bill for work done on the lake (mole built out by waterfall, etc.), turned out £495.56, quite enough, at same time certainly worth it.

I reread Paul Scott's *Staying On*, which I liked, even after having previously broken down on *The Raj Quartet*. I have changed my mind about these, now regarding *The Raj Quartet*, at worst, as a remarkable *tour de force*, while *Staying On* is certainly well done, at same time slightly different in tone, less 'serious' than the more massive structure on to which it aims to fit. This shows how uncertain a writer's own judgements can be.

When I finished *Dance* there were temptations (encouraged by several fans) to develop some aspects of the narrative in later books. I felt sure I should be unable to keep up precisely the same tone when pressure of knowing one had to write twelve volumes in sequence was relaxed. *Staying On* is a perfect illustration of this difficulty for a novelist, while at same time one admires its good points. I have been corresponding with Hilary Spurling about Scott's books. She emphasized how skilful he is on women (Barbie, etc.), with which on the whole I agree. He does not seem at his happiest with humour, sometimes forced, also when sexually explicit (not an easy vein in which to excel), while I still demur at some of the technique and some pedestrian phrases.

Saturday, 10 June

In consequence of letters exchanged, a distant American cousin, Edward Powell Willms, with his wife Wilma, looked in for tea on the way to a genealogical tour of the Welsh Marches. He is descended through his Powell mother (recently died aged ninety-five), not from Thomas Joseph Powell (arrived Baltimore 1819, then moved to Ohio), but the latter's nephew, John Powell, who went straight to Ohio in the

1830s, so EPW is scarcely a closer relation to the late Pauline Skinner (who revealed the American Powells to me) than to myself. Indeed it became clear after a certain amount of conversation that I knew a good deal more about the American Powells by now than EPW did.

The Willms family was from Hanover (arrived US *c.* 1850). EPW looked completely German, with odd touches (V and I both agreed) of the Widow Lloyd, which I suppose registered something of the Welsh Border. Wilma Willms (clever of him to have found wife with such an alliterative name, née Palmer, also with German blood), typical trim elderly American matron. EPW's father moved from Idaho to Auburn, State of Washington, for health reasons, a milder climate, where he ran successfully a general store. This EPW finally joined, after being an engineer, apparently employed by the Government, anyway during war. Also successful, now retired, late sixties. His son is in the Navy, about to become Captain on the Reserve. He assured me I was image of his Powell grandfather. I poured out a mass of genealogical material. They were staying the night at the George, Nunney, before proceeding to ancestral monuments in the Marches. An odd encounter.

Sunday, 11 June

Bob Conquest rang. He and Liddie on way to Russia on Monday – Leningrad, Moscow, Tbilisi (Tiflis). Bob is now well looked on in Soviet Union, something one little expected ever to hear. The tour should be interesting. Bob said a super-smart black girl working in the White House told him her great-grandfather was a Confederate colonel. Kingsley Amis and Tony Hartley lunched with Bob at The Travellers'. Kingsley only became normal self after couple of stiff whiskies. One is familiar with this development in heavy drinkers, needing a drink or two before getting into their normal stride. Roland Gant rang. He and Nadia are taking the ferry from Portsmouth on Tuesday, and will look in about tea-time.

I reread *Richard III*. An enjoyable play, which keeps it up all the time, if on rather same note. The language always good. One feels touch of personal Shakespeare in the Stage Direction: 'Enter Gloucester and Buckingham in rotten armour, marvellous ill-favoured.'

Tuesday, 13 June

Roland Gant rang about 3 p.m. saying they were late getting away, would not arrive before 6 p.m. Eventually they turned up at 7.15, saying traffic awful, including a reported serious accident on the road. V had to attend Church Council (finances). This went on for over two hours, weather so warm that much took place on the terrace of The Stables, therefore attended by Snook. Meanwhile the Gants, both of whom looked well, stayed on until 8. As they were supposed to embark by 9.30 at latest, Roland did not know the Portsmouth Road, booking for this ferry done three months ahead, that seemed running it rather fine. I suffered a good deal of vicarious train fever, only hoping they arrived in time. Roland is writing book about Provence, not a guidebook. Their combined great work, which takes so much research, seems broadly speaking to be about Napoleon, with whom one of Nadia's ancestors was fairly closely connected.

Thursday, 15 June

V and I voted (for Mrs Daly) in European Parliament Election. Went on to inspect replacement for collapsing wall at Bullen Mead. This is well done, in fact the fence probably looks better, anyway more rural, than expensive concrete blocks would have done.

Saturday, 17 June

Birthday Honours: Hugh Lloyd-Jones knighted; Robert Fellowes (who undertook administration of my CH, tho' we did not meet), KCVO.

Alison Lurie sent her short story 'The Highboy' (in this country 'tallboy'), about a haunted piece of furniture.

Monday, 19 June

In the afternoon V and I watched on (live) TV installation of King Juan Carlos of Spain as Knight of the Garter in St George's Chapel, Windsor. The weather was stewingly hot, perhaps accounting for Juan Carlos looking rather grumpy. I should have been sorry to have had to mill about in heavy Garter robes on such a day, but Frank [Longford], who was present, nearly my twin, as spry as could be.

Wednesday, 21 June

An American, Michael Shelden (hitherto not known), who wrote a recent book about *Horizon* and Cyril Connolly, rang to ask two specific questions about George Orwell, on whom he is also writing: (1) Did he ever talk about Burma; (2) Did he ever talk about the time when he was 'down and out'. So far as I can remember, George did neither, beyond saying 'In Burma one always used to have drinks at . . .' or things like that; Paris was never really mentioned at all, I think, again except saying

'As you know, when one's on the Metro . . .' Shelden made a good impression. He said he had collected some excellent photographs of George and Cyril. I asked about the adopted son, Richard Orwell. He is apparently doing pretty well, a fair amount of money coming in from royalties, to some extent invested in 'holiday homes' in Scotland. He seems to have a good business sense. This sounds much better than most adopted children one hears of, not without its funny side *vis-à-vis* George's feelings about money-making.

Talking all this over with V later she said George described to us how all the Burma Police officers had Burmese mistresses (whether or not he did himself unstated), but the real emotional life was between the officers themselves, who were like a lot of schoolgirls, not homosexual, but things like who played tennis with whom. All that would have made a good point in *The Raj Quartet*, Merrick, so far from being odd man out, the centre of that kind of chatter. 'Why is Ronald always changing his syce, etc.?'

Friday, 23 June

Helen Fraser, of Heinemann, came to luncheon to discuss Collected Occasional Writings, at present without title. She agreed it should be not less than 200,000 words, while at same time making the vol. too long would send up price. Some problems about photocopying, the *Telegraph* contributions going back thirty years. *DT* (John Coldstream) most co-operative. Helen Fraser is easy to deal with, and progress made, if somewhat exhausted myself after going into varied aspects of the project. Some will mean a lot of donkey work. Melon, Breton smoked cold chicken, salad, strawberries and cream, patisserie. Helen Fraser does not drink in middle of day. Mr Joyce rang in connexion with the small tumbledown cowshed, to which the Bullen Mead wall has called attention. This too will have to go. I arranged that with Mildav (£470+VAT).

Sunday, 25 June

Tristram, Virginia, Archie, at The Stables, also Andrew and Tammy Murray-Threipland, with children, Madoc, Charlotte, staying. Archie is recently back from New Zealand, which he greatly enjoyed. Everyone came up for drinks in the morning. Charlotte Murray-Threipland had a great time with Snook, who does not seem to mind children. Andrew produced a sample of his new reddish cheese (at present nameless), which he has originated, not bad, if rather mild. Tammy now teaches Law in London. V brilliantly arranged with Tessa Davies that Tessa (very kindly) will make copies of my *Punch* pieces on Butler & Tanner copying-machine, which solves one Collected Journalism problem. Terrapin (fresh water turtle) have appeared in lake. They eat fish.

Tuesday, 27 June

Helen Fraser rang. The *DT* will do copies of the reviews (about 700). There are about 46 *Punch* contributions in all, including parodies.

Wednesday, 28 June

Nicholas Shakespeare rang about my next book for *DT*. He said he dined with Helen Fraser last night (I presume she paid), who mentioned photocopying *DT* reviews, which of course he knew about. I was amused this subject had come up. I took our collection of bound *Punches* to Whatley House, where V and I had tea with Tess and Joff Davies. In the paper this morning there is a report of the late Arthur Duckworth's executor being fined for allowing 'listed' fixtures to be removed from Orchardleigh during the sale. Tessa was the magistrate who imposed the fine.

Thursday, 29 June

I wrote to newly appointed Editor of *Punch*, saying it had always been understood that my pieces written when Literary Editor should be available for collecting in book, all the same I thought it better manners to clear that with him right away. He is called David Thomas, an Etonian, age thirty. He rang today saying publication would be perfectly all right, adding he was a great fan of *Dance*, completely identifying himself with the Narrator, assuming that he had now reached about the *Lady Molly* stage in his own life. We talked of *Punch* problems. It seems that all humour these days must be based on TV. He said solely *Spectator* public would immediately cause a collapse of *Punch*. I put in plea for return of old Doyle cover. Thomas appears to be an agreeable young man. Interesting to see how he copes with a pretty hard nut.

Freddie (A. J.) Ayer obit. I always found him friendly, if immensely conceited, especially in his last vol. of Memoirs, which publishers sent me, but David Holloway refused to have reviewed he thought them so awful in their vanity. Talking with Freddie once before a British Academy dinner (to which for some inexplicable reason I had been invited), I asked him, purely as a matter of interest, to hear his answer, how he refuted Dostoevsky's proposition: 'If there is no God, everything is permissible.' Freddie at once became rather irritable in manner, replied: 'The matter is not conditional.' I was about to urge that Dostoevsky, after all by no means a fool, clearly thought it *was* conditional, even if one might feel the reverse oneself.

Dosteovsky could not be just dismissed like that, however agnostic. At that moment dinner announced, so I never heard the Ayer solution.

Freddie did, however, introduce me to the very pretty girl I was sitting next to, saying: 'This is Miss So-and-so [name I fear forgotten], who is a philosopher. Anthony Powell thinks philosophy nonsense.' Her mouth immediately went down, as well it might. I have no recollection of how dinner subsequently proceeded. I think I made my peace with her, tho' what Freddie said was not far from the truth. Nor do I recall who sat on my other side. Cyril Connolly said Ayer to be thought of best as one of those knowing little French intellectuals. One of Cyril's excellent comments.

Friday, 30 June

Bruce Hunter has arranged that the son of his partner Jacqueline Korn (who deals with journalism, serials, at Higham), called Roland Glasser, just leaving school, should do the *DT* copying for £100, paid by me in return for having an advance, 15%, rather than 10%, royalty for Collected Journalism, tentatively entitled *Miscellaneous Verdicts* (latter term suggested by V). Satisfactory.

Saturday, 1 July

Georgia to stay for the night. She shares a house next term (Morrell Avenue at the foot of Headington Hill, ought to be Lady Ottoline Morrell Avenue), with two young men, Oliver Lane-Fox, Dominic Hazelhurst. Tessa Davies brought back *Punch* photocopies admirably done. V will arrange to give Tessa an orchid plant (as it turned out, stephanotis) as small return. Mr Paul Lewis is said to have caught poacher putting out night-lines in lake, altercation took place, during which poacher allegedly thrown into lake, had to swim to far side, as Mr Lewis would not allow him to climb ashore on one of the landing-stages. A good story anyway.

Sunday, 2 July

Bob Conquest rang. Apparently they had great time in Russia, even if loos in Tbilisi (Tiflis) were gruesome beyond all description at even Russian standards. They will lunch here on Thursday. A comic incident to record. Not long ago a novelist, TV script-writer, called Frederic Raphael, probably now approaching sixty, never met nor his works read by me, reviewed a book on Somerset Maugham, in which he mentions that John Bayley, writing about Maugham, had invoked occasion at a *Punch* luncheon when Maugham spoke no more to me after my saying eldest sons were still occasionally called by their title in the family (which I suggested in the most inoffensive manner). Bayley quoted this as an instance of Maugham's extreme sensitivity in such matters. Raphael in the review said he supposed I had told Bayley the story, adding, quite gratuitously, that my Memoirs were not worth reading.

This elicited a letter to the *TLS* from Roy Fuller, saying that, in spite of giving his opinions, evidently Raphael had not read my Memoirs, because the story about Maugham was in fact there. I sent Roy a card of thanks, laughing about this. He replied by showing me what can only be described as a rigmarole sent him by Raphael, several pages of vituperation, beginning by complaining that (ages ago apparently) Raphael had adapted a novel of Roy's for TV, and Roy had never expressed appreciation of the way that was done. Raphael added that only the toadying of the *TLS* caused Roy's letter of accusation to be put in the paper. Really most bizarre. Roy, in his letter to me, said he replied 'mildly', receiving yet further pages from Raphael. I remember Janet Adam Smith, who never says an ill word about anyone, letting drop years ago how little she had enjoyed doing a radio programme with Raphael owing to his touchiness.

Tuesday, 4 July

Journalist Marcus Scriven, also works on the Peterborough column in *DT* (superior gossip), rang asking if I had been a member of The Grid (a rather stuffy undergraduate club at Oxford). I have an idea I was once put up, but matters never proceeded further, as the club was full of the least amusing Etonians, Wykehamists, etc. The Grid now seems to be without home. We talked of Oxford clubs of that period. All this took place while I was cooking a curry.

Thursday, 6 July

Bob and Liddie Conquest to curry luncheon. They hired a car to come down, which was very nice of them. Russia had been as uncomfortable as ever regarding food, accommodation, but gave a great welcome to Bob, regarded as the spearhead in attack on Stalinism. Among other things, he was asked to address the Writers' Union, which he did in rusty Russian (he said) full of Bulgarian words. This (or some other public occasion he attended) was alleged to take place in the room where Prince Andrei danced with Natasha in *War and Peace*. Bob thought more likely that it was where Prince Andrei had drinks before the party. Apparently people take windscreen wipers off their cars when parked, otherwise they get stolen. There is strong national feeling in Georgia, a race Bob didn't much take to, like Neapolitans he said, although fair in colouring. He saw where Stalin was born, went to school, the family's former middle-class house, his school an important-looking establishment.

Almost all currency transactions are now made by way of cartons (must have red line) of Marlboro cigarettes. Had a quarter of an hour with Mrs Thatcher on return. He and Liddie were going to the *Spectator* party that evening. Bob looked well, if a trifle tired, not surprisingly. Liddie in excellent form. Bob drank bottle of white wine (a quarter bottle of South African as aperitif, then a bottle of Orvieto less my own quarter, Liddie and V a bottle of Valpolicella between them).

Virginia gardening at The Stables managed to run gardening fork into her heel. V took her to the surgery. Later she dined with us and did not seem too bad. There was a tremendous thunderstorm that night, like that in *Confessions of a Justified Sinner*, when the devils were fighting above the house for the hero's soul. The noisiest storm since afternoon when the Conquests were here a year or two ago. It looks as if the devils got their calculations about Bob slightly wrong this time.

Monday, 10 July

Virginia had taken the train to London after her accident, so Tristram came down to collect her car. She is now improved except for antibiotic depression. Tristram and Georgia attended the *Spectator* party at Doughty Street, where Georgia is now working as receptionist. Hot and crowded. Frank and Liz [Longford] present. Frank said he could have played tennis at Wimbledon had he chosen. He is writing two books, one on Suffering, the other on Forgiveness. Liz was on two sticks.

Saturday, 15 July

Yesterday John brought down photocopies of the *DT* reviews left at Higham by Roland Glasser. Sorting them will be to say the least a Herculean task. Thomas Pakenham, with his daughter Eliza, to luncheon on way to the Boyd ball to celebrate Alice's year as High Sheriff. Thomas, who brought two bottles of Muscadet, much mellowed from what he used to be like, tho' rattles on ceaselessly about his relations in manner that apparently drives his wife and children off their heads.

Eliza is a nice girl, most inelegantly dressed in very short shorts under some black upper garment. She is up at Corpus, now waiting for result of her Schools (English). Not a trace of Pakenham in her appearance, some touch of her mother's Scandinavian strain observable. Thomas (one of those incredible coincidences in the light of my suggestion that Henry Mee should paint General Kitson) is to stay with the General (whom he has never met) for the ball. Roast beef, gâteau, bottle of rosé V won in local raffle (not too bad, in fact).

Tuesday, 18 July

Lees and Mary Mayall to luncheon, just returned from car trip to France, Spain. Mary a bit shaky, Lees with stick, but both in good form. Their daughter Alex now has a cottage on property of Cressida Connolly's husband at Pershore, Worcestershire. He is called Hudson, RC, rich. Lees, who pays the rent, has never set eyes on him, but received letter 'Dear Lees, how nice to hear from you . . .' Chilli con carne, meringues with our own raspberries, red and white currants, Crozes Hermitage '86 (bottle and a half).

IEC Wine Society no longer stock Italian White Vermouth, because they say it has gone off so much, tho' one can get it in shops. This we did. Wine Society, as one might expect, is perfectly right. I just tasted a drop (not mad about it as a drink), distinct deterioration.

I reread *Hamlet*, always enjoyable. Eliot's objection that Hamlet was making a fuss about nothing seems to me absurd. Interesting point: why was Hamlet himself so popular with the common people? One would think him not a popular type. Perhaps it was just from dislike of Claudius whom one might have supposed as popular. Perhaps Claudius was recognized as a great *faux bonhomme*.

Friday, 21 July

John brought down the remaining *DT* photocopies. Bruce Hunter thought Roland Glasser spent a good deal of time doing these, so might be paid rather more than originally stipulated. I told Bruce to decide sum. He thinks *Miscllaneous Verdicts* a good title. I plan to do a section called 'These Islands', 'Proustian Themes' (to include items with Proustian affiliations like Amiel, Svevo, etc.), 'Transatlantic', 'A Contemporary Mob', tho' no doubt adjustments will have to be made when sorting has taken place.

Saturday, 29 July

We attended the wedding of Lucinda Davies and John Sunnucks at Mells Church (where we again, with the Oxfords' permission, parked in their drive). Lucinda looked very pretty. Pages in Life Guards uniform, well behaved, tho' one (very) small bridesmaid a trifle difficult. V, John and I arrived fairly early when choir were still rehearsing what they were going to sing while register was being signed. Music seemed familiar. For some reason carried me back to Berlin in the 1930s with great vividness, the time when I was there with the Heygates. It did so again when the same tune came to be sung during wedding; then I saw from Service Paper it was by Andrew Lloyd Webber and recalled a likeness to song sung by Lilian Harvey in *Congress Dances*, 'Just once for all time', some such name ('*Das gibt's nur einmal, es kommt nicht wieder'*). John [Powell] said afterwards this was the theme song in Andrew Lloyd Webber's last show, only tune that was really any good. This sort of rehashing of tunes is apparently all the go now. Certainly there was a strong whiff of the *Congress Dances* tune in German, perhaps more apt than in English translation.

A 'small but reputable' Italian publisher, Lucani, wants to translate *Afternoon Men*, satisfactory after what is now approaching sixty years from publication.

Monday, 31 July

I received a request from Mark Holloway (son of David Holloway) to do an interview for London Weekend Television (*South Bank Show*) for *Writers in the War*. In principle I agreed to this.

Sunday, 6 August

Joff and Tessa Davies to drinks in morning, also Tristram, Virginia, Georgia, Archie. The Davieses are recovering from their two weddings. Pages *are* dressed in miniature uniforms supplied by the Regiment in question. Tessa went to Knightsbridge Barracks to arrange this. She told me old Knightsbridge Barracks (a place of great romance to me as a child, dismounted Life Guard Sentry to be seen through the arch, representing comparatively far Eastern walk in the Park) was built by Wyatt, which I had not known. Spanish copies of *El Rey Pescador* (Versal, Barcelona) arrived.

Tuesday, 15 August

Tristram and Virginia at The Stables, Georgia is in France, Archie in Italy. We dined there on Saturday, excellent dinner. They recently had Grey Gowrie and Frances Partridge to dinner, Frances approaching ninety, is still driving about London. Neiti (who apparently keeps Grey in some order) was not present. The Gowries recently had the Thatchers to dinner, more or less self-invited. V remarked that people like the Thatchers really have no private life, understandable that they should like to get out with friends occasionally, Lord and Lady Shelburne (Tristram said Shelburne had some reputation for good looks at Eton), Jacob Rothschild and wife, Harriet Crawley (met at Evangeline Bruce's), Mrs Thatcher's indispensable henchman Charles Powell. Mrs T. scarcely addressed a word to Neiti throughout the evening, talked all the time of getting rid of Geoffrey Howe, for whom she seemed to feel some animus. When she wrote a thank-you letter, called Neiti 'Dear Adel', Neiti's real name in German being Adelheid (Adelaide). Mrs T. presumably looked this up, and couldn't remember diminutive.

Finished *Miscellaneous Verdicts*. All being well John will deliver the typescript (or rather photocopies) to Bruce Hunter on Monday.

Sunday, 20 August

Jim Lees-Milne to luncheon. Jim invited himself, suggesting curry, as Alvilde was away. An excellent idea, especially as I had just finished a reread of all Jim's *Diaries*, in counterpoint with Rupert Hart-Davis's Letters to George Lyttelton. Rupert and Jim are about the same age, both at Eton, Brigade of Guards (Jim very briefly, invalided), friends, quite talented in their different ways. The contrast interesting. Rupert, not liking casual affairs, ended by marrying four times. Jim, a bit shaky, I thought, during luncheon, tho' V pointed out he always had a rather withdrawn side, coupled with extremely good knowledge of architectural matters. He has less of Rupert's practical grasp of how people react in relation to the arts, books, or journalism, although often acute in the *Diaries* about individuals' social behaviour, with which he came in much amusing contact among owners of more-or-less stately homes.

In fact curious thing is that Jim's *Diaries* are much more down-to-earth (not least in matters regarding sex), than the *Hart-Davis/Lyttelton Letters*, which are full of mutual admiration and romantic feelings about sport.

I like both of them, but quite misjudged Jim's reaction to my having reread (I think for third time) and enjoyed, all his *Diaries*. I supposed he would be greatly interested in small points in them I brought up, but he scarcely noticed these, only saying something like: 'Oh, how could you wade through all that?'

No doubt a matter of age, tho' Jim a year or two younger than me. On the other hand he was most appreciative of the curry (vegetable one), which I thought I put too much beetroot into (as we had a lot) making the whole rather too sweet. Jim no longer drinks wine at all. Alvilde was in Tangier, staying with David Herbert, accordingly went to the party, much written of in the papers, of billionaire called Forbes (not Ali), for 800 guests. Forbes apparently possesses 100,000 toy soldiers. Mr M. Lewis, of the Syndicate, arrived in middle of lunch, to leave letter he had received from Abstractions Licence Officer of Wessex Water. Jim brought bottle of '78 claret presented by Alvilde.

Monday, 21 August

John took MS of *Miscellaneous Verdicts* to deliver to Bruce Hunter. I had a longish telephone conversation with another Mr Hunter, of Wessex Water. He was agreeable, gave clear explanations. I explained that droughts and overflows had been normal since we came to the property in 1952. Neither of them had shown any sign of getting seriously out of hand. He explained that the grille built up in a manner to cause a somewhat violent outlet of water, rather than comparatively slow flow. Of course this has always been the case, certainly as long as we have been here, probably since turn of the century when Lost World came into being. The flow is now much affected by the arrangements at the Quarry. The two outlets, waterfall, North Sluice, normal in lakes.

Wednesday, 23 August

Selina Hastings wrote to say she has identified the woman living in Milton Abbas who sent passionate letter to Evelyn Waugh (about 1938, by which time he was married), referring to their previous adultery. It appears she was called Joyce Gill and died last year, twice married, dancer, when younger in a musical called *The Dancing Years*. Her son, Dominic Gill, ex-music critic for *Financial Times*, now editing kind of *Exchange & Mart* paper. This all emerged via sister-in-law of Grey Gowrie's brother Malise, sister-in-law's mother knowing Milton Abbas. Evelyn said to have met this woman when he was an undergraduate. If so, I should have thought it extremely probable that he did so through his brother Alec. I do not want to build fantasies on this information, but vividly remember a woman dressed in man's clothes being brought one night to The Hypocrites' club, said to be 'mistress of Alec Waugh' and 'daughter of a Dame at Eton'. I also suspect she was called Joyce.

Alec Waugh himself was not, I think, present. I can't remember who brought her. Evelyn certainly wasn't there. Although the occasion remains clearly in my mind, the details are dim, all the same perhaps worth recording. The lady in male attire (whom I don't think I talked to) was small, dark. She may well have been as described, yet not Joyce Gill. I recommended Selina to consult Billy Chappell, who knows a great deal about stage life, especially dancers. He might be able to recommend an aged thespian who knew her. This is all most amusing, brilliant research on Selina's part.

An American fan (Michael Henle, Oberlin College, grandson of publisher of *Mr Zouch: Superman*) sent me pack of Tarot cards called *The Aleister Crowley Tarot Cards*, with little book about them, introduced by 'Lady Frieda Harris' (Frieda, Lady Harris, wife of a Liberal MP), one of Crowley's patrons.

Tuesday, 29 August

Mr Joyce, of Cooper & Tanner, called. We examined the trees in Paddock Field thought to be stripped by Adrian Andrews's goat. On inspection these turned out to be about seven ashes, rather than three, obviously too badly ringed to be work of goat, probably deer. Annoying as all trees are almost certainly killed.

Wednesday, 30 August

In the afternoon Heidi Best, Editor of glossy magazine *Somerset & Avon Life*, with photographer Ian Newcombe, came for interview. Big blonde, perhaps thirty. I asked why she was called Heidi (possibly after Byron heroine Haidee), she said her father German. Instead of asking usual futile questions about myself simply enquired who, living or dead, I would like to invite to a luncheon party; what century I would live in, if not this one. I said Shakespeare, John Aubrey, Byron, Wilde, Kipling, Aubrey Beardsley, giving reasons I preferred this century, with all its failings, otherwise Victorian times ending with Edwardian. Much easier to talk about this sort of rubbish than answer 'profound' questions such as 'why do you write?', dear to certain type of interviewer. Amazing how these magazines flourish. This one has a circulation of about 8500, on lines of *Homes & Gardens*.

Friday, 1 September

A letter from Selina Hastings saying the Milton Abbas adulteress Joyce Gill was indeed daughter of an Eton Dame, so looks as if she certainly was transvestite lady who visited The Hypocrites when I was present 1923–4. So far as remembered, dividing women up into very rough physical types, she was not altogether unlike Evelyn Gardner, tho' not so pretty.

Saturday, 2 September–Monday, 4 September

V staying at Whitfield. John cooked here with great efficiency. Tristram and Virginia to drinks on Sunday morning. Andrew and Tammy Murray-Threipland are staying at The Stables to start Madoc off at Bryanston, where, oddly, he has to arrive on Sunday morning. Archie has now reached Greece; Georgia in Portugal, where it is raining. V returned on Monday having had enjoyable time. Fellow guests: Laurence and Linda Kelly, Hugh (Duke of) Grafton, the latter on a National Portrait Gallery Board with me, amiable, never knew him well. V reported favourably. Sunday morning, about 12.45 midday much black smoke arose just beyond the quarry, as if they were burning oil.

Tuesday, 5 September

Mark Holloway arrived with a camera crew (punctual) at about 11 a.m. for London Weekend TV (*South Bank Show*) programme *Writers in the War* : subjects apparently: Roy Fuller, Alan Ross, Stephen Spender, Julian Symons, self. Mark, son of David Holloway, late Literary Editor of *DT*, fortyish, does not greatly resemble his father in appearance, very tall, specs, not unlike less forceful version of Max Hastings, quite agreeable, bit neurotic. Crew nice, unnoisy: Ian Stanley, cameraman; Rima Neave, producer's assistant (V and I much amused by this first name, with overtones of W. H. Hudson, Kensington Gardens, Epstein rows of long ago), Rosie Alison (pretty, intelligent, brought two books to sign), Alan Philips, electrician. Struck, on thinking it over after, what strong effect producer's personality has on behaviour of crew. I wore a fairly sombre suit, Welch Regiment tie, as suitable dress for a veteran. V said I looked a perfect retired Major of Infantry. They finished soon after one o'clock, when we all repaired to the dining-room for a drink, hospitality for which they seemed surprised, grateful.

Mark Holloway sent the questions he was going to ask, which were unusually sensible ones: Vigny's views on a soldier's life as indicated in *Grandeurs et Servitudes Militaires*, did I agree that the more sordid side of army life gave a greater insight into the army than the more glamorous side; was it common in blitz to see house apparently all right outside, badly damaged within; could this principle be applied to individuals (I suggested ghastly look passing over ex-Japanese PoW's face, then instant return to normality). I always find difficulty in remembering all the things I intended to say after being shifted about in various chairs and having the light shining in one's face. Programme to be shown on 12 November (Remembrance Sunday), when I look forward to seeing not only myself but the others.

I reread Shakespeare's *Sonnets*, edited by Martin Seymour-Smith. It seems to me quite clear 'The Mortall Moon hath her eclipse indur'd' refers to half-moon shape of the Spanish fleet at defeat of Armada (1588), of which Leslie Hotson gives at least half-dozen instances. Seymour-Smith objects: 'It is difficult, however, to accept "indur'd" as meaning anything but "passed through successfully", and "mortall" in this interpretation has to mean "deadly".' But surely that is what it does mean, 'endured', i.e. 'suffered' an eclipse, was defeated; and why should 'mortall' not mean 'deadly', as in, say, mortal wound? It might mean 'mortal moon', as opposed to 'heavenly moon', I suppose. Usually Seymour-Smith's ideas are good, intelligent, but this seems merely obtuse, possibly because he wants to push one of the other interpretations.

Sonnet 145, 'Breath'd forth the sound that said I hate', in Hotson's eyes applies, not only to Anne Hathaway, but also to William Hatcliffe (Hotson's candidate for Mr W. H.). But the line 'I *hate*, from hate *away* she threw' obviously seems to mean Hathaway. The following is 'And saved my *life*, saying not you'. Hotson ignores 'away', suggesting 'hate . . . life' echoes Hatcliffe or Hatliffe. Could it combine both Hathaway and Hatcliffe? The feminine is used throughout, and after all Hatcliffe, 'Prince of Purpool', was a kind of Miss Inns-of-Court, who might well have been Shakespeare's Young Man, even if by no means proved. The bringing together of the two names would have been typically Elizabethan. I remember being made to learn 'Shall I compare thee to a summer's day?' at school. Did the beak know it was a man? I can't remember who set it. Possibly Tom Cattley (in whose house Lees Mayall was once kissed by Cattley, he said), or The Ram (A. B. Ramsay).

Saturday, 9 September

Letter from Helen Fraser saying she is delighted with *Miscellaneous Verdicts*, raising a few minor points which I hope to discuss with her on Monday. Archie at The Stables with some friends.

Sunday, 10 September

Archie brought his friends to drinks in morning: Daniel Barraclough and sister Gaby, nice intelligent girl; Daniel has been here before, going to Warwick University with Archie in October. Milly Jenkins (daughter of the political journalist Peter Jenkins and Polly Toynbee), Sophy Hutchinson. I was not feeling much like receiving them all, but in the end enjoyed it.

Monday, 18 September

I finished *The Odyssey* (tr. E. V. Rieu), never, I think, read before from cover to cover. One is staggered by the sheer drama of the narrative, characterization, conciseness of story, really the first novel. It is difficult to feel that the same writer was responsible for *The Iliad*, so utterly different in style, tho' he may have learnt, as writers do, from his own earlier work. Interesting phrase 'the glorious fellowship of the Dead'. The sequence of the killing of the suitors is thoroughly exciting; the fascinating flatness of Odysseus's final reunion with his wife Penelope is masterly. The epic ends with the negotiations required in dealing with the deceased suitors' relations, also skilful in its flatness.

Thursday, 21 September

V and I lunched with Robert and Mary Boscawen at Ivythorne Manor, near Street, a run of about three-quarters of an hour. Bob, our Tory MP for a number of years, is now retiring, as perhaps getting a bit elderly, tho' only in middle sixties. He has been a nice MP of the old-fashioned sort, aristocratic, good war record, by no means a fool, the sort of solid backbencher as needed. Mary Boscawen had grown rather plump since last seen (V said her plate at luncheon none the less piled high with food), née Codrington, directly descended from the Admiral Codrington of Navarino, also General Codrington, who took over from Lord Raglan in the Crimea when Raglan died. The house is full of relics of these two especially, and other historical odds and ends. Guests: Captain Colin Macgregor, a sailor about to move from Fleet Air Command at Yeovilton. I had wrongly imagined that an RAF Station. He is going to London to deal with naval recruiting. Agreeable, typical of one sort of quiet sailor, wife pretty, easy to talk with about general matters: Brigadier Francis Henn (11th Hussar), Anglo-Irish, commanding in Cyprus at time of Turkish/Greek troubles, when Bob Boscawen went out as political observer: his wife Monica perhaps a shade sticky, but V thought unwell.

A very fine silver bowl was on the centre of the table apparently 1650, associated with some Boscawen ancestor, Cavalier Captain of Horse. Any silver of up to that date is rare, as usually melted down for the King. Bob, until recently one of the trustees managing Widmerpool property in Nottinghamshire, evidently having vague memories of my Widmerpool being named after a Roundhead Captain of Horse (Hutchinson's Memoirs), as the men were leaving the dining-room, said: 'Widmerpool might have known the owner of that.' He then turned to the others, pointed at me, added: 'He was the creator of the awful Widmerpool.' Obviously neither the soldier nor the sailor had faintest idea what he was talking about. They both looked wildly round, wondering what they would do if he got violent.

V thought the Macgregors and Henns regarded Bob as being too obsessed about his and Mary's ancestors, not sharing the interests of such old genealogical hands as ourselves. The house is one of those moderate-sized manor houses which look as if they might have been built in 1911, the porch, in fact, dating from 1290, when the house had already been going for some time. No doubt fairly heavily restored, is still much of it old. The approach through thick trees down a most romantic winding lane. This is Monmouth country, Sedgemoor just visible on horizon.

During the Westland Affair, Bob had a meeting with some Cabinet Minister in what was formerly Judge Jeffreys's courtroom. A certain relish to this visit was given by report in the press some days ago that police, looking for poachers, came across a Black Magic ceremony in progress on a hill near Street about a mile away. Shades of Scorpio Murtlock. V discovered that Bob had not read *Hearing Secret Harmonies*, and urged he should do so. Bob spoke of rumours in the neighbourhood that the Black Magicians had left a number of sinister symbols of the Black Arts on trees, after performance of evil rites. Bob said these were, in fact, old CND signs chalked up by former nuclear disarmament folk. Rather exhausting party, if not without its funny moments.

Sunday, 24 September

Tristram, Virginia, Georgia, Christina Noble, her daughter Tara (age twelve), to drinks in morning. Virginia's birthday celebrated, which is really tomorrow.

Tuesday, 26 September

Charles Trueheart, *Washington Post*, arrived about 2 p.m. for an interview, leaving 5.30, this length of time unavoidable owing to the train service. He seemed rather awkward at first, we thought, in the end not too bad at all, indeed reasonably intelligent. His father is in the State Department, he himself was born in Washington, a rare place to be born. He said he lived in London as child when father was *en poste* in US Embassy. He said my name had been on the paper's books for an interview for a long time, so perhaps nothing to do with rivalry with *Washington Times*, as I supposed possible, after my writing for the latter. V took him down to lake at one point in afternoon. His questions were on the whole fairly sensible, which always makes one fear one has said something unwise in course of longish interview. Trueheart's family were originally Southerners, his wife Economic Correspondent of the *Washington Post*, now with him in London. She is expecting a baby in December. Trueheart was astonished to hear BBC went as far as approving four episodes of *Dance*, then ran out.

Wednesday, 27 September

Seymour Krim, journalist, author of *Views of a Nearsighted Cannoneer*, etc., obit. He did himself in, age sixty-seven. An odd fish who came down here once, a kind of post-Beat figure, of that curiously stranded Jewish-American type, latterly some form of academic, I think. He had a certain gift for self-expression, marred by uncontrolled egotism, that somehow never got him anywhere. Henry Mee rang in afternoon. He wants to do another portrait, so looking in next week. He said two Assistant-Directors at National Portrait Gallery were Malcolm Rogers and Robin Gibson, former in favour of Mee, the latter against him.

The American Express is now going to sponsor Mee's 'Distinguished People' show, but doesn't yet know where. Probably take place in May next year, which would, as it happens, also be a good moment, on account of the appearance of *Miscellaneous Verdicts*. He asked if I could revise my 'long caption' about Lord Forte, whose leg I had rather pulled, suggesting he looked like typical Italian Soho restaurateur, which he certainly does. The American Express did not want to offend him. Henry himself had mentioned his own personal lack of enthusiasm for Forte food, which had to some extent caused me to write this. I have said I will attempt a revise (by no means Henry's own wish), which can be checked when Henry comes here on Thursday.

Thursday, 28 September

The photographer Grant Lynch arrived at 8.45 a.m. while we were still at breakfast, to photograph Snook for 'Animal Passions' feature of *Sunday Telegraph Magazine*. Snook, in typically cat manner, knowing this was going to take place, just to keep us on our toes, left the house yesterday at 4 p.m. and did not return until 9.55 p.m. Lynch had a Greek profile, an ear-ring in one ear, but did not give impression of queerness. He brought enormous amount of photographic ironmongery, including a large hoop covered with gold material for reflections, which at one moment Snook showed signs of jumping through, as in a circus.

Lynch remained photographing hard until 10.25 a.m. doing this in dining-room. Snook was quite well behaved generally speaking, in fact put up with a good deal, tho' naturally became a bit restive at moments. Lynch was a nice young man, but maddeningly slow. I cannot imagine why animal photographers don't learn to get a move on. You cannot persuade animals like cats to hold the pose indefinitely. None of them ever seems to have learnt that. They go on talking of a shadow being in the wrong place, but as they take dozens of exposures one would have thought they could risk that to get something really good, even if some are useless.

Alison Nadel, who was to write the piece and due at 10.30, but lost her way and did not arrive until after 11. However, left at midday. She was quite a jolly girl, blonde, with floppy hair, not unattractive. Snook had remained in library after his exhausting photographic session, so she was able to see him stretched out asleep by the window. I poured out a lot of stuff about cats, which I hope will not sound too fatuous when retailed. She said she usually does this feature and has some odd experiences with different types and their pets.

Wednesday, 4 October

Gerry de Winton rang from Maesllwch. He was rather rambling, the gist of his talk being that he had been reading the *Somerville and Ross Letters* (which V's book about them mentioned), and that Edith Somerville hunted with the Quorn (possibly the Cottesmore) at the same time as Gerry's father. The latter kept a Diary in which at one point he writes: 'Had wonderful twenty minutes run, killed in waiting-room of Widmerpool.'

Thursday, 5 October

Henry Mee, planning to do another portrait, arrived about 3.30 p.m. to take a further look, as his sittings are all quite informal. He is one of those people who take a certain amount of winding up on arrival and first sat silently for some time, then, among other things, produced a fascinating story of his house in Jamaica Road, Bermondsey, being haunted. His more general information included the item that Lord Carrington had been responsible for appointing the woman called something like Esteve-Coll as Director of the Victoria & Albert, who is now the subject of some controversy.

The story of Henry's haunted house began by him saying that in his early days in Leeds he used to do odd jobs like painting signs for two builders (very traditional for a young painter). When he became more affluent, he bought small house in Camberwell and the two builders came down to do it up for him. Henry gave an amusing account of the shift in their social relations, the builders formerly giving him orders, he now arranging what they should do in his house (with which they were much impressed). The gap, which grew wider, became slightly resented when Henry moved to still larger residence, the house in Jamaica Road, built for a sea captain about 1735. Since the captain's day the house seems to have gone steadily downhill, became a one-room lodging house, and latterly headquarters of small minicab service. The house was full of indescribable filth when Henry took over, every day for weeks a skip appearing in which rubbish was piled up. When clearing had at last taken place, the two Leeds builders appeared again to do Henry's decorating. The builders actually lived in the house while they did this.

After a bit they said they couldn't work there any more on account of ghosts, unless Henry Mee slept there too. This Henry agreed to do, so used to work there with them. Henry gave an amusing account of this. They (and he) would work from 8 a.m. to 8 p.m., then drink in a pub. The pub had to be the lowest, most squalid, they could find. They would sometimes drive a comparatively long way to discover a really down-at-heel drinking establishment. Henry said he found all that dreadfully tiring. In this story of concentrated work, then fairly sordid debauch, I was reminded of play called *The Summer of the Seventeenth Doll*, in which Australian cane-cutters would work unremittingly for months, then spend several months carousing in a town.

Anyway, Henry used to sleep in same room as the two builders, on which they insisted. One of the builders suffered from awful nervous pressures, so that (Henry said) you really felt he might murder you or someone else, when he was in a bad stew. This builder woke in the middle of the night, shook Henry awake, saying (of which Henry gave a most convincing imitation): 'Why do you fucking well wake me in the night and frighten me.' Henry pointed out that he had done nothing of the sort. It must have been the other builder, who was in fact fast asleep. Henry himself could hear somebody 'in hobnail boots' walking about above them. Thinking house had been broken into, they searched it, but no one could be found. This happened several times on other occasions. When builders left, Henry used to sleep there with his girlfriend. They were there one night when again it sounded exactly like burglars. Henry armed himself with an iron bar, but no sign of anybody again.

Then, when sleeping there alone, he woke up one night to find a heavy piece of furniture (apparently a stand on which you hang suits, not far from his bed) was rocking this way and that. He thought he had knocked it with an elbow when asleep, tried to steady it, but it was too far away from the bed. He half climbed out of bed, took hold of it. It rocked too strongly for him to be able to stop the shaking. This sort of disturbance takes place from time to time, particularly if furniture is shifted, carpets are changed. Henry says he is quite used to all this now and rather enjoys it than otherwise. He left about 6.30 p.m., V gave him bag of apples.

I reread *Martin Chuzzlewit*, with not more than reasonable skipping. I did not remember story at all. Most of the book is incredible nonsense, though Mr Pecksniff (on occasions not wholly unlike Malcolm Muggeridge, as Dickens cannot prevent him having a certain wit) has his moments, also Mrs Gamp is often funny, as when she says her late husband, where drink was concerned, showed himself 'weak as flesh, if not weaker'. I read (I think for first time) *Eugene Onegin*. I could not lay my hand on our *Selected Pushkin*, so got through a lot of the poem in Charles Johnston's translation, which he gave me. Charlie Johnston claims his version is nearer the Russian than any other. It was given excellent reviews, but is not very pliable, I thought. Then at last I found the other one by Babette Deutsch. The latter goes much more easily; while not seeming all that different in sense. All the same there is no doubt that Pushkin is all but untranslatable, as *Eugene Onegin* is generally said to be his masterpiece, and (anyway for me) difficult to see any more than Byron without the humour, indeed more like Praed at his fairly serious, which is usually not Praed's best.

Friday, 13 October

I reread *Confessions of Zeno*. Did not enjoy this so much as formerly, the giving up smoking theme is always a shade silly, and found myself a trifle bored by the story itself. At the same time one must admire Svevo's determined naturalism, and sticking to provincial life in Trieste, without the least improbability or exaggeration. This he does exceedingly well. Perhaps his rather Chekhovian bitter-sweet approach, to some extent a period thing, palls after a bit, as I always find it does with Chekhov himself.

Saturday, 14 October

Adrian Andrews wanted to talk about fencing, so we did this in Paddock Field, where he will remove the broken iron rails running towards the Church and replace with posts, which should be considerable improvement. He will also cut bushes growing along the ha-ha to the south, opposite the house. Andrews is a nice chap. His wife and daughter (on a pony) were also present. They are a marvellously good-looking family, like a Gainsborough, I thought, then I remembered that

Gainsborough painted a Mr and Mrs Andrews, which perhaps made some sort of unrealized connexion in the mind.

The Stockwells are at The Stables. Tristram has installed a video machine there, so we watched Judith Medlicott's video of herself winning the New Zealand Mastermind with her knowledge of *Dance*. This was immensely funny. She is rather good-looking and vast, with tremendous assurance. I certainly could not have answered a lot of the *Dance* questions myself, still less the General Knowledge, which followed. The other items in the Mastermind programme (three) were also very funny, notably a sad little man, who hardly scored at all in his subject, 'Knowledge of French Cooking'. As this was a Semi-Final he must have had a very easy run in the early heats. He looked as if he'd never had a sumptuous meal himself in his life.

Thursday, 26 October

Adrian Andrews sometimes tethers his goat in the Paddock Field, where it bleats for notice when one goes past it on way to the post. I was talking to the goat and found myself roughly pushed aside by Snook. The goat and Snook greatly interested in each other, eventually touched noses in recognition of friendship.

Tuesday, 31 October

I reread *Antony and Cleopatra*, a favourite. 'Black vesper's pageants'; 'It's past the size of dreaming'.

Saturday, 4 November

V, John and I dined at The Stables with Tristram and Virginia. Excellent dinner: hors d'oeuvres, stew rather like *Boeuf Bourguignon* (apparently not that), Lebanese red wine called Musar, which I remember when we were there at time of anti-tourist riots at Baalbec, tho' saw nothing worse than overturned bus.

Tuesday, 7 November

Mr Moss, who repairs the drive from time to time, arrived on the doorstep. Mr Moss looks like an Edwardian comedian (V says Charley Chan perhaps better comparison). I said he could have £100, do what he could for that, not a penny more. After some haggling he agreed to this, result seemed all right. He was an immense time coming to be paid. I went to post letters, also hoping to give him his cheque, found him still pottering about. He explained he had been 'taken short', forced to retire to the hedge in Stoney Lane for a long time. I told him I had to replace all the house's gutters, so was not in mood to spend money. He replied: 'Never a dull moment.'

Ali Forbes (from London), rang complaining I had not sent a line to Georgina Ward [Tritton], after he told me some months ago she was having trouble with her hip. In fact I wasn't sure of her address in Mexico (apparently unchanged) after her card advertising 'Exclusive Jewellery'. In any case she never answers anything one sends. I didn't take in how unpleasant things were from Ali's account. However, I dispatched a postcard after Ali hung up. All he really wanted to do (which went on for hours) was to discuss Barbara Skelton's Vol. II Memoirs *Weep No More*, which I have for review. Not as lively as the first vol., tho' contains some amusing stuff. Both vols need to be read together, as there are things one wants to look back to from time to time. As with so many female writers with a touch of talent, she will not take sufficient trouble. Latterly she lived on and off for thirteen years with a French journalist called Bernard Frank.

We lunched at Sturford with Lees and Mary Mayall. Their exterior was so autumnal with fallen leaves that we almost missed entrance from the road, in fact whole place looked rather like the Sleeping Beauty's palace with shrubs growing all over the drive. Lees producing his Memoirs [*Fireflies in Amber*] (published on commission), showed us the illustrations.

We heard details of the story touched on in a recent book about Edith Olivier, where Evelyn Waugh is referred to with much dislike in her Diary, owing to some party where he got tight. Apparently Mary [Ormsby Gore], then staying with David and Rachel Cecil at Rockbourne, was taken to a party of Edith Olivier's at Wilton when aged about sixteen or seventeen. Evelyn, whom Mary did not know, came up to her, said: 'Why are you dressed like a little whore all in bows?' One suspects this was Evelyn's idea of making a mild pass, but David Cecil was, perhaps rightly, absolutely furious that his niece should be thus addressed, and swept out, taking Rachel and Mary with him. David always disliked Evelyn. This was evidently one of the incidents to cause that. Crab pâté, casserole, cherry tart (first and last course from Marks & Spencer, Mary said). I had one glass of white burgundy; V that, plus some red. Both of us excessively tired when we got home.

Remembrance Sunday, 12 November

The *South Bank Show* 9.30, *Writers and the War*, was an awful mess. It began with stuff about Spanish War, which had no earthly bearing on the subject, then a lot of material about Soho pubs, from a not very good book by Andrew Sinclair, which I recently reviewed. Sinclair himself, although only ten when war ended, took a considerable part in the film, all of little or no interest, except that he did emphasize that it was a great relief to those not in Auden's racket when Auden and Isherwood buggered off to the USA. Auden was shown answering someone heckling him as to why he scuttled, or rather not answering them. Auden looked extremely rattled on this occasion. Difficult to feel he is not in many ways a deplorable figure.

Stephen Spender did his usual waffle, given role of explaining what writers felt about the war, defined by Roy Fuller (perhaps not at his usual TV best) as being proletarianized. Julian Symons cut his material to the bone, read a poem, but nothing about the boil that got him invalided out of the army, a goodish story. From time to time Sinclair would reappear saying no one hated the Germans. Far from the case. This is absolute balls. If he had been grown-up during the war he would have known people felt very strongly about the Germans. My own appearance perfect example of the dictum that documentaries are simply plays written by the producer, those who appear in them actors who speak the lines, which are cut, if not what producer wants. In this case the usual BBC Leftishness, half-baked clichés. There was perhaps a thirtieth part of what I talked about to Mark Holloway, who wanted to know, for instance, about Vigny's *Grandeurs et Servitudes Militaires*, in relation to army experiences. I suspect this was not so much Mark Holloway as Melvyn Bragg, or an awful little bearded creep called Valentine Cunningham, who appeared from time to time, known by name as a most unsympathetic reviewer but seen in the flesh for the first time. Looked unattractive and talked of the Spanish War, example of left-wing legend which cannot be dispersed to prevent it being generally accepted that, if the Communists had won in Spain, they would have joined up with the Nazis. Alan Ross was good, having of course something more definite to recall in his naval service action as opposed to everyone else. Montage, especially Fitzrovian scenes, was overdone, confusing. Maclaren-Ross deservedly given quite good showing (from Tristram's early film on this subject), also poet John Heath-Stubbs (blind, toothless, slightly horrifying), however I was interested to see him. Jocelyn Brooke, Evelyn Waugh, not mentioned as war writers.

Tuesday, 14 November

V to London, where she lunched with Rosie Goldsmid. After luncheon a friend of Rosie's, Kitchie Levita, looked in. The latter was married to a cousin of Arthur Levita (dcd), husband of Shelagh Levita, née Ross-Skinner, who was Cyril Connolly's last attachment. Shelagh Levita plays a considerable part in Barbara Skelton's account of Cyril's final days, in Barbara's second vol. of Memoirs. Kitchie Levita said Shelagh Levita was a terrible bore, now married to an Italian who was even more of a bore than herself. They live in Venice. V recalled that Cyril had remarked of Shelagh Levita to Sonia Orwell: 'People say she is dull, but she is interested in Yours Truly, which is what Yours Truly wants.' Kitchie Levita alleged that when Shelagh Levita was about to marry (1963), Cyril sent her a telegram: 'Will you marry me? Cannot live without you.' The story should perhaps be taken with fair amount of salt. Rosie was less critical of Barbara's book than V expected, commenting (with truth) that Babs had a great deal of guts, among other things going alone to Cuba.

V moved on to Emma (Cavendish) Tennant's picture show (flowers), held in Alice and Simon Boyd's house in Warwick Square. Chloe Teacher turned up there, looking a bit frail, but superb considering she was scarcely recovered from frightful hunting accident. A large gathering, including Andrew and Debo Devonshire. Andrew at once said: 'Tony was marvellous in that programme about the War.' I was pleased at this, Duke or no Duke, regarding Andrew as most desirable member of the non-professional public to have liked my own appearance in a programme with which I felt decidedly fed up, after such savage cutting, plus reams of extraneous stuff. However, I was surprised by quite a large crop of press cuttings, with syndicated photographs, on the subject this morning.

I reread Kenneth Baker's *Anthology of English History*. I liked this less on second round and feel I may have overpraised it in review, as vol. contains a lot of second-rate stuff, distinct streak of vulgarity in what was chosen. I am suffering from upset inside which should perhaps be taken into consideration in relation to these critical comments.

Friday, 17 November

My inside still upset. I saw Dr Rawlins, who recommended twenty-four hours' starvation.

Sunday, 19 November

The starvation treatment worked. Evangeline Bruce rang from Washingon, saying she had just been reading John Russell's piece on the Powells in his collected essays, and thought it so good she must call us up. She asked if I had yet seen new Skelton volume, which she herself had ordered. Evangeline had not heard story (perhaps apocryphal) of Barbara pouring boiling water over casts of teeth made by dentist for whom she worked and with whom she was also in love. I dreamt about Sachie Sitwell. He and I were in an office, then restaurant, Sachie wearing grey flannel suit with rather marked white line in it.

Tuesday, 21 November

Mary Duckworth, widow of Arthur Duckworth, of Orchardleigh, dcd. Nice woman. Had great bad luck in suffering a stroke after marrying Arthur Duckworth (following her previous unsatisfactory marriage to a civil air pilot). She generally pulled Orchardleigh life together. The place will now become one or more hotels apparently and/or a golf course.

Friday, 24 November

John is godfather of Gerry Bowden's younger daughter Kate, whose confirmation took place today at Sherborne Abbey. John attended this, Gerry, elder daughter Emma, Kate herself (much urchin charm), dropped in on way back to London. Gerry happened to be in centre stage on the recent televising of the House of Commons. He said a hitherto utterly deserted wash-room was crowded with MPs cleaning themselves up just before the filming. He himself is against TV there on principle, but agreed that in a few months it will excite little interest. He said the Lords put on a much better show than the Commons. *Financial Times* recently compared the Tory MP Ian Gow to Widmerpool. Gerry knows Gow well, and said he would question him on this point.

I reread Andrew Sinclair's *Anthology of the 1940s*, reviewed the other day. Not adequate, a poor selection in both prose and verse, even the better people. It is mostly third-rate poets, tho' these are perhaps of some interest to collecting the whole lot together. Gerald Kersh, for instance, is omitted. Kersh certainly should have been in as prose writer, while the story about Kersh's poem appearing in Wavell's Anthology is attributed to an unknown poet who left it in the trenches, Kersh should certainly have found a place here too. Various persons claimed the poem, Kersh pointed out it had already appeared under his own name in the (?) *News Chronicle*. Jocelyn Brooke is included only with a somewhat Kiplingesque poem. None of Brooke's first-rate accounts of life in the ranks of the RAMC.

I reread *Macbeth*. The play goes with tremendous swing, almost like reading a thriller. Great chunks are by now proverbial sayings, but, unlike so much of Shakespeare, one does not feel, as in many if not most of the plays, that individuals known to Shakespeare himself appear, anyway characters to some extent modelled on 'real' people.

Saturday, 25 November

V, John, and I dined at the Stables.

I broke down trying to read (possibly reread, as I think I once got through it) *The Aeneid* (tr. Delabere-May). I told Georgia, who was rather shocked at this failure. She said she thought it must be a bad translation. Nice dinner, smoked salmon, spaghetti, I drank white Alsatian. The Stables party came to drinks on Sunday morning. Tristram is working on film near Bradford.

Monday, 27 November

Henry Mee rang, very pleased that American Express sponsorship of his show is now fixed to take place on 21–22 May 1990. It will then move to the Hop Exchange picture gallery in the City. A big Impressionist show is taking place at Sotheby's at same moment, which should bring people in. American Express is laying on dinner for 91 at Claridge's (the maximum apparently for their dinner party capacity), to which all sitters for Mee VIP collection will be invited. He wanted me to be driven both ways, with a night at Claridge's thrown in, but I did not feel up to such a party, which would no doubt be quite funny in its particular terms of reference.

Henry painted Neil MacGregor, Director of National Gallery, Robert Runcie, Archbishop of Canterbury. MacGregor in his early forties, very Scotch. His main problem will be overseeing construction of the new wing of National Gallery, which Henry says now really worse than the 'carbuncle' objected to by the Prince of Wales. The building has ended up with odds and ends of pillars and curlicues. I entirely agree with Henry that, if a wing has to be added to the present building, it should be built in the style of the present building (which has happened in the case of many country houses). No one in Great Britain seems to understand this, when a public building is in question.

Henry said the Archbishop was charming, amusing, easy, while being painted, yet Henry suddenly felt him like one of those Space creatures called Daleks, whose only limbs are a kind of claw (like the levers with which you scrape in sweets in slot machines on the pier), and an arm which fires a gun, reducing enemies to ashes. He said Runcie also looked as if he'd been under water for three hundred years. Attributed that appearance in the Archbishop to overwhelming wish to give satisfaction to everyone.

Wednesday, 29 November

In a piece in a recent *Sunday Times* on subject of freedom in language, Julian Symons said sexual explicitness was much overdone on the whole after the Chatterley Trial, mentioning *Dance* as example of sensible use of additional licence in freedom of expression. I sent him a line expressing appreciation of this bouquet, adding the hope that in the *Writers in War* programme he wasn't cut as savagely as I was. Julian replied he was 'not so much cut as obliterated'. The jacket for *Miscellaneous Verdicts* arrived, rather fussy perhaps, but stands out reasonably well when placed against other book jackets. I dreamt I was at curious party of about twenty people, Kingsley

Amis present, Barbara Cartland was pouring out tea from a kind of urn. She handed me a cup, put a piece of cake flat on the palm of my hand, as with a child. I said: 'We have never met, but I was in Duckworth's when they published your first book.' She put her arm round my shoulder, kissed me warmly.

Thursday, 30 November

Michael Shelden (Indiana University, Bloomington), who wrote a book on Cyril Connolly and *Horizon*, was informed by Nicholas Shakespeare that I remembered something to offer him of George Orwell, about whom Shelden is writing a book. He rang from Bloomington. I told Shelden that George spoke of the Burma police officers having native mistresses, but said their emotional life really centred on each other, not in a directly homosexual way, but commenting about who played tennis with whom, 'You said you were doing something else that afternoon . . .', like a lot of schoolgirls; in that respect probably, in fact, not very different from any other community of men cut off from their own women.

Shelden said he had interviewed several surviving Burma policemen, who had told him much the same thing. He asked if Orwell mentioned a Burmese mistress. That, so far as I can remember, George had not done. Shelden also asked if I knew anything of Orwell's friend Kopf, who was in the Left militia with Orwell in the Spanish War. I told him no, but that I corresponded with F. Frankford, who was talking with Orwell at a stand-to in the trenches when George was shot in the throat, George at that moment relating something about when he worked in a Paris brothel. I have no recollection of George talking about employment in a brothel (a somewhat opaque incident, one might add, did it ever happen?) and I suspect this was one of his undoubted fantasies.

V and I celebrated the anniversary of our wedding (in fact tomorrow) at dinner with smoked salmon, Bollinger '83 (presented by James Sandilands at my last birthday). Enjoyable.

Saturday, 2 December

V attended Silvy Thynne's wedding to Iain McQuiston at Longbridge Deverill, later reception at Longleat. I would have gone to church if feasible, but could not face standing for hours in a queue at the reception. V lunched with the Mayalls, therefore dropped me at our gates on the way, so I sat it out here with John. Silvy is thirty-two, McQuiston, a builder now graded as an interior decorator, about twenty-eight. V found Michael and Isobel Briggs at Sturford, also Robert Mayall with his latest girlfriend Margaret Johnson (early forties), who works in the British Library and is an authority on early Spanish literature. She looks not so very different from Robert's previous lady, dressed all in leather. All three of Silvy's small bridesmaids were illegitimate: one belonging to the bridegroom's earlier days; one his mother's 'slip-up' in later life; one Georgia Tennant's, who shows no sign of marrying the child's father. Everything seems to have gone quite well. V said Virginia Bath's reading of 'My true love hath my heart, and I have his' threatened embarrassment but she did it with great professionalism. On the whole she enjoyed herself if it was all a shade gruelling.

Tuesday, 5 December

Henry Mee rang about 7 p.m. just as I was about to have my bath. He said a paper called *Modern Painters* (which I have heard of as being reasonably lively) had asked him to do piece on Painters and Sitters. Henry felt he could not take that on, and would I do it? They are going to send me a copy of the next issue, so I will consider, as this would give boost to Henry's show.

Saturday, 9 December

I dreamt I was walking through a large building, half-museum, half-government office, characteristic scene for me in dreams. Chairs, desks, on one of which lay pile of papers. I saw these were notes on Matthew Arnold, so sat down to examine them. While doing this Frank [Longford] passed. 'Hullo, Charles,' he said. Frank is almost capable of that, if not quite. I looked at him in some surprise. 'Oh, sorry,' he said, 'I thought you were someone else.' He had a pile of high curly slightly Afro coffee-coloured hair of reddish tone, instead of baldness surrounded by a few wild grey curls as in real life.

We were to have lunched with the Roy Jenkinses today, but V's cold was very heavy, also the weather rather misty for driving, and car lights out of order, also with some doubts about getting them back in time, so cancelled with many apologies. Roy said if it had just been car lights we could have come by train to Didcot from Bath. Pamela, Lady Harlech (who lives at Hinton Charterhouse) could then have driven us back. V said later she could not imagine a journey less in my line, nor does one know how Pamela Harlech (whom we have not met) would have reacted, as Hinton Charterhouse not all that close.

Thursday, 14 December

The luncheon party (rearranged several times with Tessa and Joff Davies) took place. This was to meet Major Gerry Charrington, father of Richard Charrington, who recently married Mary Anne Davies. Major Charrington, formerly in his son's regiment, 9th/12th Lancers, is apparently a great fan of *Dance*, so wanted to meet. I was interested that this was not long-standing love of *Dance*, but quite recent. I gave both Davies girls American paperback sets for additional wedding presents, as both known to be readers of the novel. Major Charrington read Mary Anne's set. This is a striking example of the old publishing principle that a review copy is always worth while, if it sells one copy of the book; in this case whole set of British paperbacks. We thought Major Charrington looked less like retired cavalry officer than imaginable.

If not actually a Church Commissioner, he is that sort of thing, indeed one of the points of the occasion was that Mary Anne had never been confirmed. This was brought about by the Bishop of Truro the day before on Charrington family wishes. These ecclesiastical interests had obviously swamped any military air. Slight touch of Wyndham Ketton-Cremer, also Constantine FitzGibbon (who Osbert Lancaster said looked like an unfrocked clergyman). He was a shade deaf (as I am myself) and kept insisting he had been at Eton with Widmerpool (boy whom I could not find in OEA list). He was indeed tremendous professional Old Etonian. It turned out that the Charringtons knew Adrian Daintrey, the Major having bought one of Adrian's pictures at a show. Adrian then stayed with them, painted their daughter, a picture that turned out a frost.

Richard Charrington, a nice young man, is going as instructor to Sandhurst which usually indicates a successful career. I thought he looked younger since marriage. Mary Anne is a sweet girl. Mrs Charrington (Susan), a typical better-type army wife, agreeable, easy. Her husband went on and on about Widmerpool, who is an extraordinary instance of transcending his creator. I never supposed for a moment people would become so obsessed with him. V and I both rather exhausted afterwards, but gave them good run for their money. Roast beef (perhaps not quite so good as usual in Davies house, where meat first-rate), apple pie excellent, lively Stilton (I had only a sliver). I drank a glass of sherry before, rather than fizz, glass of Italian wine diagnosed by me as Montepulciano Nobile.

I received this morning postcard of Dostoevsky (Perov's portrait) written in Russian from Ludmila and Pentti Viikki (3 Sovetskaja, Dóm 7, kv. 16, 19636 Leningrad). I was told this was roughly Christmas or New Year Greetings. The man's name suggests Finnish origins, if Ludmila Russian. I sent back a postcard of Byron in Albanian dress. Will get Bob Conquest to translate.

I reread the *Merchant of Venice*. This play usually has a baddish press, but there are wonderful bits. Jessica is one of Shakespeare's most attractive girls (complete answer to any charge of anti-Semitism in the play). I find it hard to explain quite why Jessica is attractive. The repeated emphasis on music to be noted. One can just stand the caskets, but the ring business at end is exceedingly tiresome. A poor look-out for her husband with Portia behaving like that. 'Hard food for Midas' good title for book, perhaps about the City.

Thursday, 21 December

My eighty-fourth birthday. I don't feel too bad, rather stiff in right leg, which has recurred after two years or more freedom from all that. V gave me a blue-striped shirt, chosen by John, also a dark grey jumper, both admirable. John sent parodies of Simon Barnes, highbrow sports writer for *The Times*, which include *Dance*, also Dante, Proust, D. H. Lawrence, the last perhaps best. The Congressman sent an embroidered Welch Regiment crest, which V will probably work into a cushion design. I pottered about during morning doing usual odds and ends. *The Standard* (Londoner's Diary) rang to ask how I was spending my birthday. Said we might drink bottle of fizz at dinner, with spot of caviar. The journalist turned out to be Sebastian Shakespeare, brother of Nicholas. I said: 'You are a very talented family.' He replied: 'We don't think so.' Virginia, Georgia, Archie, rang.

In the evening the telephone went, slightly hoarse voice said something I could not catch, turned out to be: 'Will you give your father a kiss from me.' I replied rather stiffly that they seemed to have the wrong number, this was Nunney 314. Voice then said: 'Isn't it the Powells?' In short turned out to be Evangeline Bruce, who flatteringly thought I sounded so young it must be John. Some amusement about this surprising injunction. Sweet of Evangeline to ring from the US (not, I think, Washington).

Funny letter from Hilary Spurling describing adventures staying at Drummond of Hawthornden's castle in Scotland, now a resort for writers, supported by Mrs Drue Heinz, widow of Jack Heinz of the 57 Varieties. Hilary said Paul Scott is rather like Hogg's Justified Sinner. Talking of Simon Barnes reminds me that I recently read Julian Barnes's *History of the World in 10½ Chapters*. This seemed to be beyond my understanding. I simply could not see the point, a mystery why it should get good reviews, which it did, anyway in moderation. I think that Barnes is probably quite an intelligent, fairly conceited chap, without enough creative fantasy to be a continuing novelist. V said this book rather like a Digest, therefore appealing to what are no doubt many Digest readers, which may well be true. On the other hand, it may simply be that we are out of date for new stuff. We drank James Sandilands's Bollinger '83 at dinner.

Friday, 22 December

My lower plate came loose a day or two ago, characteristic of life this should happen just before Christmas. However, Mr Lister fitted in an appointment today in the afternoon, to which John drove me. There was a notice on front door of the Dental Mansion in Willow Grove which read: 'Please Do Not Let Boots In' with picture of Boots (a black cat with white boots) beneath. There was a Christmas tree in the waiting-room, where a man, like me of mature age, wearing a deerstalker was sitting. While the two of us waited one of the girls at the receipt of custom brought in two glasses on a tray, which she offered. 'What is it?' 'Well, I think it's red wine, whisky, and something else.' I refused on grounds of age no longer allowing me to mix drinks. The man in the deerstalker risked a glass, describing it as 'warming'.

Lister told me later the concoction was red cooking-wine, brandy, lots of sugar, stewed up by him and his wife the previous day. Just as well I was discreet about drinking it. Boots apparently lives next door, went away for a week or two, to find his owners had moved house. Accordingly he joined in with the dentists. He is not popular with Lister's partner, who lives on upper floors, because he jumps on people, sometimes anaesthetized, in the dentist's chair, and occasionally gives them a nip if they wake in the wrong direction, but Lister protects him. Boots gets on well with Henry, the exotic cock who lives in the small yard. The stud had broken in the plate, which Lister fixed.

Christmas Eve, Sunday, 24 December

Tristram and Virginia, Ferdie and Julia Mount, to luncheon; cold turkey, salads, mince pies, meringues, peaches, Stilton. We drank the magnum Ferdie gave me last year, Château Nenin (Pomerol) '77, medium year but not at all bad. Ferdie struck us as a bit tired. He said Andrew Sinclair (who recently produced that far from dazzling book about writers in London during the War) was at the top of College when Ferdie arrived; he was very trying, far from popular with everyone.

Christmas Day

V, John and I lunched at The Stables, Georgia, Archie, present; Ferdie, Julia, William, Harry, Mary Mount are staying. A classical Christmas Dinner. Tristram always produces brilliant crackers. V gave me a shirt with green stripes chosen by John. Tristram gave me a bottle of Nuits St Georges '85; Archie, Moulins Gressier Grand Poujeaux (Medoc) '79. Ferdie a magnum Santenay Les Gravières, 1 er Cru, '83. Enjoyable party.

Boxing Day, Tuesday, 26 December

The Stables Party (known as The Chantry and West) in the evening. I fixed myself up on sofa in the window, where I remained. From there I talked to various people, including Fram Dinshaw (who came with Candia and their small child). Fram has an extremely subtle intelligence. There were a fair number of people I didn't know at party, including Virginia's cousins Lord and Lady Chewton, the latter, rather attractive, I did not meet. Six Davieses. I feel a bit disorientated at parties these days. It is curious how often one adjusts one's views on a book when one reads it twice.

Wednesday, 27 December

A young man, Robert Shylon (Westmore Farm, Ditchett), assistant to David Brabon when cutting trees by Manor Farm, called to ask if I wanted to sell timber not worth Lang Brown's people taking away. I rang Lang Brown, Peter Munford suggested asking £45, as this was all right, which Shylon accepted. He will call one day again to do job. Samuel Beckett obit. Tristram filmed some of Beckett's later plays, obscure in the extreme, and liked him to work with. I can never feel deep interest, tho' I mildly enjoyed *Godot, Endgame, Krapp's Last Tape*. They are all too impersonal for my own taste, tho' moments of good dialogue are certainly to be admitted.

Friday, 29 December

I saw Dr Rawlins about the stiffness in the lower part of my right leg, which seemed circulatory rather than arthritic, as I am chiefly aware of it when lying full length. Rawlins said there was nothing wrong with the main artery, and one must just hope for the best and remember not to cross legs.

I reread (in bed) Francis Spufford's Anthology of Lists. I did not enjoy this so much as when running through it for review on reading more carefully, but some good items. A great many of second-rate writers are included. Reading in bed is a severe test for books.

Saturday, 30 December

New Year Honours, Vidia Naipaul knighted. Excellent. Vidia probably writes too much sense in brisk manner to get the Nobel, tho' certainly a suitable candidate. Also being British, even via Trinidad, is likely to be an obstruction. Some days after we failed to attend the Roy Jenkins luncheon party, Roy rang, saying Pamela, Lady Harlech was disappointed that we had not been there, but suggested Roy should bring us over to lunch with her. She lives near Hinton Charterhouse, about half an hour's drive. Selina Hastings would be staying there, who could drive us both ways. This took place today, Selina arriving about midday. Pamela Harlech, widow of David Harlech (Mary Mayall's brother), former Ambassador in Washington. His first wife, Cecy, was killed in car accident, as he was himself some years later. Pamela Harlech is American, tho' has lived over here a great deal, editing glossy papers, etc. Hinton Field, Lady Harlech's house bought some years ago, is a

Somerset farmhouse now being spectacularly transformed in a *Vogue* manner, bathrooms, glass pagodas, etc. She herself quite attractive, rather like a young witch by Goya, dead-white face, Afro hair-do, miniskirt, essence of Long Island American-Jewish chic, agreeable if shade overpowering, looking curiously like her late husband, whom I never knew, but just saw somewhere for a moment.

Also staying in house as well as Selina: Pandora Ormsby Gore, the Harlechs' daughter, and her friend Kate Benson (both about sixteen or seventeen) and two young men (one called Nugent identified by V as Westmeath family), Noel Davies, bearded actor-producer, evidently *habitué de la maison*. Luncheon guests, Roy and Jennifer Jenkins, V and I. I sat on Pamela Harlech's right. She told me when she became châtelaine of their Merioneth house (Glyn, Talsarnau) she sent for the local builder and said she was putting in bathroom for every bedroom, must have water system in which, if nine people wanted bath at 7 p.m., that would be possible. The builder asked: 'But why ever should nine people want a bath at 7 p.m.?' (One likes to think of this said in a very North Walesian accent.)

I like Jennifer Jenkins, I think in a way rather a simple soul, tho' obviously very good at her National Trust job and such things. She told me Roy is writing his autobiography, and found difficulty in unbuttoning about himself and parents. I asked what happened to him in the army beyond being a Gunner, ADC (I thought) to some General. Jennifer said: 'Oh, yes, he was, I believe, for four or five weeks. Then he went to decoding at Bletchley. Nothing at all glamorous, like fighting all the way up Italy, or anything like that.' Good wifely comment. Incidentally, you didn't go to Bletchley unless you were pretty skilful at that sort of thing, which after all in the last resort won the war.

Jennifer talked of Denis Healey's Memoirs recently appeared, said they were full of chestnuts, tho' some good stuff too. I said I had heard about the chestnuts from Ian Bancroft (who wrote a line or two on his Christmas card). Jennifer seemed staggered that I knew Lord Bancroft, whom I suppose she thought of purely as Head of the Civil Service, archetypal civil servant. Roy said: 'I see Naipaul has got a knighthood.' He didn't sound exactly disapproving but surprised. Perhaps, having met Vidia with us, he thought he ought to have been consulted. Lady Harlech, writing on cooking, does the cooking herself; rather run-of-the-mill mutton, vegetables, excellent pudding made of ginger-nuts, cream, brandy, great deal of both latter, far from thinning. Léoville-Barton '70, smooth, perhaps shade in decline. Enjoyable party, if slightly dazing.

Sunday, 31 December

Driven by John, we lunched with Rachel and Kevin Billington at Poyntington. Guests: Ruth, formerly married to Kevin Pakenham, with second husband, Guy

East (films, commercial side), both tolerable, hordes of children of varying ages from about four to university types. Considerable din throughout luncheon. Kevin is recently back from Russia on a film promotional scheme of some sort. He revealed the second bestselling novelist there, after Dickens, is now Melvyn Bragg. I was glad to find myself totally immune to any hard feelings. I drank a glass of white Macon.

Hilary Spurling rang in evening and talked of her stay at Hawthornden. Even in Drummond of Hawthornden's day, when he was visited by Ben Jonson, the mediaeval castle had been gutted, and a house built within walls. This sounds just like Stapleton Castle near Presteigne, where various Radnorshire Powell wives' families lived, the house within the ramparts was built by Harley family in seventeenth century. Hilary said that the last Drummond died about 1976, when the place was sold to developers who stripped the panelling, cut down trees; Robert Bruce's sword and other relics were sold. The place was then rescued by Drue Heinz for the present purpose. Mrs Heinz herself was present, separated from the literary elements, Hilary said, but friendly all the same, but difficult to know what she was like except through the servants. It was a fifteen-minute bus-ride to Edinburgh. Three or four other writers were there, all perfectly tolerable, if rather amateurish. They were apparently all Americans, who are used to such institutions. In fact Drue Heinz appears to find difficulty in getting British writers to fill the place.

Hilary mainly rang to say she would like a proof of Humphrey Carpenter's rather indifferent book *The Brideshead Generation,* in which I have marked at least a few of the innumerable mistakes. She said she also had copy of Lucille Iremonger's book on the Ghosts at Versailles, lent her by Joan Evans, who died before she could return it. It seems that, when Hilary was writing her first Compton-Burnett volume, she applied to Joan Evans, who knew Jourdain family well. Joan Evans replied that she hated Ivy Compton-Burnett so much that she would give no help, but later changed her mind when Hilary's book appeared and wrote to say she would see Hilary to prevent mistakes in the second volume. Hilary arrived, snow falling, at a house in a Cotswold bottom. The door was opened by infinitely ancient retainer, who showed her into the sitting-room of Joan Evans – half-sister of Sir Arthur (Knossos) Evans. Joan Evans did not rise, but indicated footstool beside her. She then told Hilary all about the Jourdains. Thus closes the Old Year.

Index